More Storytime Action!

2000+ More Ideas for Making 500+ Picture Books Interactive

Jennifer Bromann

Neal-Schuman Publishers, Inc.

New York · London

Published by Neal-Schuman Publishers, Inc.
100 William St., Suite 2004
New York, NY 10038

Printed and bound in the United States of America.

The paper used in this publication meets the minimum requirements of American
National Standard for Information Sciences—Permanence of Paper for Printed Library
Materials, ANSI Z39.48-1992.

Library of Congress Cataloging-in-Publication Data

Bromann, Jennifer.
  More storytime action! : 2,000+ more ideas for making 500+ picture books
interactive / Jennifer Bromann.
      p. cm.
  Includes bibliographical references and indexes.
  ISBN 978-1-55570-675-3 (alk. paper)
  1. Children's libraries—Activity programs—United States. 2. School libraries—
Activity programs—United States. 3. Storytelling—United States. 4. Picture books for
children—United States—Bibliography. I. Title.

Z718.2.U6B757 2009
027.62'51—dc22
                                                                      2009031724

Contents

Preface

In my graduate school program in library science, no classes were offered that taught anything about storytimes. My first experience with storytimes since attending as a child was during my summer internship in a public library. There, the librarian followed the traditional format of introduction, story, song or finger play, book, song or finger play, book, song or finger play, and craft. Because this was also the way professional books at the time recommended we structure programs, I followed this style for several years, but I gradually grew frustrated with having to pick not-so-stellar picture books just to fit in with the theme.

I was also frustrated with lack of good information about how to deal with children who would act up during storytime. Many just could not sit still. In such situations, according to information gained from professional workshops and books, the storyteller should inform the parents or guardians that their child was not ready for storytime and that they should try again next year. That conversation would never have taken place in *my* library! I felt like this was the child's first school, and it was my responsibility to adjust my "class" for them.

I quickly discovered that children who had difficulty focusing would often pay attention better when they were involved in the stories. They would be waiting for a turn or to repeat something. Because this worked for a few books, I wondered if it would work for all books. Gradually I tried to make all of the books in my program interactive. Because the children already moved around so much with the books, the activities between the stories were gradually eliminated and an all-book and all-interactive program was created. It worked! I didn't have children zoning out or running around. They heard stories while having fun.

Even the best readers and storytellers can have a difficult time holding the attention of a child when the story is long and the child has not yet learned to focus. For these reasons, I've shared my interactivity ideas in my first book, *Storytime Action!*, and now I have more to share in *More Storytime Action!*

While writing *Storytime Action!*, I was working at a public library. It was easy to have access to many books new and old to show that any book could be interactive. Smaller libraries or school libraries with little funding may very well have had the older titles on their shelves. Even though I am now working in a high school, I love doing storytimes, so I still do them in public libraries and also demonstrate the elements of an interactive storytime to the childcare class at the high school where I work and at workshops. Last year I began telling stories once a week at the daycare center located in my high school.

More Storytime Action! picks up where *Storytime Action!* left off—most of the books included in this volume have been published since 2003. The book follows a format similar to the first volume, but, in addition to including 520 new books for interactive storytime, the initial chapters cover updated material for selecting and making picture books interactive.

Chapter 1, "Interactive Storytime," begins with the Top Ten Interactive Elements as introduced in *Storytime Action!* For those who have not read *Storytime Action!*, Chapter 1 includes a summary of the ten types of interaction. Readers can consult the earlier volume for a more detailed description. The interactive elements are not original ideas. Librarians and teachers have been using storytelling and flannel board stories for ages. However, we often get stuck using the same traditional stories or patterns. These books are meant to expand the number of books available to use in many different ways with children. The chapter concludes with research about storytime, including reading aloud, attention span, and multiple intelligences; the research included here is intended to help explain why children react better to stories that involve action or participation.

Chapter 2 covers storytelling. Because storytelling is one of the methods of making picture books interactive, it was sure to be mentioned in this book. Storytelling is often an easy way to get stories started anywhere you go even without a book in hand. Included is basic information about selecting and preparing stories for storytime and suggestions for selecting stories and how to remember and tell them. This chapter also describes Kamishibai, a form of Japanese storytelling. When a student brought her Kamishibai stage and video to one of my classes, I was hooked. I bought the stage, sticks, and stories and use them with children as well as in my classes. In case you have not heard of this form of Japanese storytelling, told with cards and a stage, more information for you to get started and create more stories in this format is provided in this chapter. The chapter concludes with suggestions for roles that volunteers can play in storytimes.

Chapter 3, "Book Selection for Interactive Storytime," discusses the process of selecting books from book review sources such as *School Library Journal* and gives you clues to look for in review sources to locate books with participation. Also discussed in this chapter is multicultural awareness—something that every storyteller should take into account in selecting a book to use for storytime.

Twenty theme-based storytime plans are provided in Chapter 4. These plans can be starting points for using the information and books in *More Storytime Action!* to create your own plans, or they can be used with your own book choices.

Chapter 5 contains 520 new books, which were chosen for the same reason as those in *Storytime Action!*—to illustrate that literally any book can be made a dynamic experience. Without easy access to as many books to select new titles, I also read book reviews and obtained promising titles through interlibrary loan. Although catchy titles and quotes and descriptions from reviews clued me in on what books might work well with interactivity, I was never sure exactly what would arrive. In this way, I still attempted to select books that would adapt easily to interaction (see Chapter 3 for hints on choosing books that work for an interactive storytime).

The books in Chapter 5 were chosen because of their penchant for participation. From reading reviews, it was apparent that the books were the appropriate length and had the perfect content for interaction. For about 80 books, I went to the shelves of the Mokena Public Library in Illinois. I looked for books that appeared to be newer, checked the publication dates, and skimmed through them for possibilities for interactivity. Most of the titles selected were written since the last book was published in 2003. Therefore, *More Storytime Action!* may include more books that you recently purchased and have not yet weeded from your shelves. Each book entry includes a summary and an activity. In most cases, I have included multiple activities, thus providing over 2,000 possible activities in this book. Additionally, readers can draw on the 20 plans for interactive storytime to create even more activities.

If you find that your students or children are not always attentive or if you just want to liven up the storytime experience, consider using some of the ideas in *More Storytime Action!* Even if you don't want to break from the classic storytime mode, you can still use some of the ideas within your own format. But if you are a proponent of the traditional format, 20 themed storytimes using books mentioned here and in my first storytime book, as well as additional activities, are also included. Everyone has a different way of presenting storytimes. Try some of the ideas here and see what can work for you. Hopefully, just as I did, you will find your children moving more and having even more fun at storytime.

Acknowledgments

Thank you to the New Lenox Public Library for honoring all of my interlibrary loan requests and to the Mokena Public Library for allowing me to take many books from their shelves. Thanks also to my sister Natalie Bromann, young adult librarian at Glenside Public Library, for checking some information for the book and for creating the title index. I would also like to thank my husband Dale Bender, parents Barbara and Henry Bromann, my mother- and father-in-law Don and Judy Bender, and my sister Valerie Bromann for their support while I was writing this book and trying to do a million other things at the same time.

Chapter 1

Interactive Storytime

THE TOP TEN INTERACTIVE ELEMENTS

All interactive stories share familiar elements. No doubt you've used these building blocks outside of storytimes. The ten types of interaction are described in more detail in *Storytime Action!* (Bromann, 2003). Their summaries are repeated here, along with brainstorming questions, for easy accessibility.

1. Props
   - Can puppets or stuffed animals represent the characters in the story?
   - Are there a variety of different objects, people, or animals added or removed from the story?
   - Is dressing up or giving children something to hold an option?
2. Storytelling
   - Is the story easy to memorize?
   - Will parts of the story be a surprise if the story is told without pictures?
   - Would action be restricted with a book in hand?
   - Do situations reoccur with only slight changes in the story?
   - Are new people or objects added?
3. Movement
   - Do the characters travel from place to place?
   - Are actions already present in the story?
4. Questions
   - Are there already questions in the story?
   - Is there something new discovered on the next page?

1

- Is there something silly or unusual that the children might not expect?
- Are there no other interactive elements you can use?

5. Board Stories
   - Are there simple characters or objects that are repeated?
   - Is something being removed or added on?
6. Repetition
   - Is it a cumulative story?
   - Is there a phrase or word that is repeated over and over again?
7. Playacting
   - Are there simple roles for kids to act?
   - Are there many roles so everyone can have a part?
   - Are there a few characters that repeat something or don't involve much action or dialogue?
8. Music
   - Do you know of a song that goes with the story?
   - Can you think of a popular song that fits the lyrics?
   - Is there a simple rhythm that lends itself to tapping or playing a simple instrument?
   - Are instruments used in the story?
9. Art
   - Is drawing a part of the story?
   - Are colors used?
   - Is a person, animal, or object changing in appearance?
10. Games
    - Is there a game in the story?
    - Are there different objects to find?
    - Are objects repeated?
    - Are there colors, numbers, or letters?

RESEARCH ABOUT STORYTIME
Reading Aloud

Research shows that being read aloud to helps children learn vocabulary, develop a love for books, and practice social interactions and that it is most effective when an interactive experience is involved (Yaden, Smolkin, and Conlon, 1989; Sipe, 2000; Martinez and Teale, 1989; Morrow and Smith, 1990; Bellon and Ogletree, 2000; and Justice, Meier, and Walpole, 2005). The interaction is generally between a parent or teacher and the child or children (Morrow and Smith, 1990). "[C]hildren learn from the texts of storybook time" (Martinez and Teale, 1989: 126). "Reading research tells us that reading aloud is most effective when it is an interactive experience between the reader and the child" (Arnold and Colburn, 2004). Most studies do focus on smaller group readings or on one-on-one readings, but the principles can apply to a storytime atmosphere. Also, the importance of storybook reading to large groups is noted by some. "[W]hole-class story readings can lead to higher achievement in vocabulary, comprehension, and decoding" (Morrow and Smith, 1990: 216). Most studies would define interaction as a teacher or parent's questioning of a child or the retelling of a story. According to Kim and Hall (2002: 333), the features of interactive reading programs or shared readings are that the children are active listeners, the adults engage the children in the text, and "the participating children usually have opportunities to engage in play activity centered on the reading."

In *More Storytime Action!*, interaction is defined as active participation with a story. This could and often does include questioning and repetition for vocabulary, but the purpose is to strengthen the child's attention and retention abilities. More research needs to be conducted on the effects of participation in group storybook readings on comprehension and attention specifically in library settings.

Attention Span

Although not much research has been conducted about the attention spans of children in relation to storytime or storybook readings, much research has been conducted relating to television viewing and attention. "Frequent TV viewers in early childhood were most likely to score in the highest 10% for concentration problems, impulsiveness and restlessness" (Elias, 2004). Researchers do argue that either we have to pay more attention to how media affects children or we need to change the ways in which we teach to accommodate the "new brain" of children today (Elias, 2004). Interactive storytimes take the second approach where we may need to make some books more lively and interactive in order to reach these children.

Multiple Intelligences

Participation in storytimes is a perfect way to support multiple intelligences, as identified by Howard Gardner (2006), and other learning styles, in a storytime session with even the youngest of children. We know that children learn in different ways, and this is why some of our students can stay focused while others wander and drift off during our storybook readings. Gardner's intelligences, followed by a description of how they relate to participation with children and books, are listed on the next page. You can see that an interactive storytime allows for all of these at some point in the sessions of books shared. There are tests to identify in which intelligence you or your students may be placed.

GARDNER'S MULTIPLE INTELLIGENCES AND INTERACTIVE STORYTIME

1. **Musical intelligence:** Music has always been a huge part of storytime. Often we begin and end a storytime session with music. In *More Storytime Action!*, music is one of the ten forms of interaction. Some books have a song to accompany them, other books can be sung, and still others can involve instruments or chanting in repetition.

2. **Bodily–kinesthetic intelligence:** Many of the books shared here involve movement. This perfectly relates to those children who need to be more hands on and active in movement while learning. Many of the books involve children getting up to walk around or move their bodies. This does not need to be one's primary intelligence to find it useful.

3. **Logical–mathematical intelligence:** Although some books shared in *More Storytime Action!* involve math, this intelligence also involves problem solving and logical thinking. You will see this in books where you may ask children to make predictions or inferences or even when they categorize or classify information or concepts from the stories.

4. **Linguistic intelligence:** All books involve linguistics, but those with repetition especially enhance the vocabulary and use of language.

5. **Spatial intelligence:** Spatial intelligence is about visualization. Even though we may make a picture book interactive, most of the time we are still sharing the illustrations from which children gather meaning. Some children need these images to construct meaning, while others adapt to oral storytelling. Many activities also involve the children or reader in creating art or a visual experience.

6. **Interpersonal intelligence:** Interaction with one another is also a piece of storytime. Children will be holding hands or passing objects or asking each other questions or acting a story out together during a storytime session. Students whose primary intelligence in interpersonal need this time to work together and share ideas. Even many games fit into this category.

7. **Intrapersonal intelligence:** Reflecting on oneself is a part of intrapersonal intelligence. This can be a reminder that children may need to make these connections. An interactive storytime may be too busy for some, and quieter stories or time to sit and think about a story may be needed. Children will often consider how the lessons from stories connect to their own lives.

8. **Naturalist intelligence:** Sensitivity to nature is a component of naturalist intelligence. Many of the books we share do involve nature either in the activities we create or within the stories themselves. We should be aware to incorporate this more into our storytime sessions for those whose central intelligence is naturalist.

REFERENCES

Armstrong, Thomas. 2000. *Multiple Intelligences in the Classroom.* Alexandria: Association for Supervision and Curriculum Development.

Arnold, Renea, and Nell Colburn. 2004. "Children of the Cloth: Flannelboards Are a Great Tool to Help Kids Learn Early Literacy Skills." *School Library Journal* 12

(December 1). Available: www.schoollibraryjournal.com/article/CA482547. html?industryid=47190 (accessed July 1, 2009).

Bellon, M.L. and B.T. Ogletree. 2000. "Repeated Storybook Reading as an Instructional Method." *Intervention in School and Clinic* 36, no. 2: 75–81. Available: FirstSearch (accessed February 19, 2009).

Bromann, Jennifer. 2003. *Storytime Action! 2000+ Ways for Making 500 Picture Books Interactive.* New York: Neal-Schuman.

Elias, M. "Short Attention Span Linked to TV." *USA Today,* April 5, 2004. Available: www.usatoday.com/news/nation/2004-04-05-tv-bottomstrip_x.htm (accessed June 17, 2009).

Gardner, Howard. 2006. *Multiple Intelligences.* New York: Basic Books.

Justice, L.M., J. Meier, and S. Walpole. 2005. "Learning New Words from Storybooks: An Efficacy Study with At-Risk Kindergartners." *Language, Speech, and Hearing Services in Schools* 36: 17–32. Available: JSTOR (accessed February 19, 2009).

Kim, Daejin, and Joan K. Hall. 2002. "The Role of an Interactive Book Reading Program in the Development of Second Language Pragmatic Competence." *The Modern Language Journal* 86 (Autumn): 332–348.

Martinez, M.G. and W.H. Teale. 1989. "Classroom Storybook Reading: The Creation of Texts and Learning Opportunities." *Theory into Practice* 28, no. 2: 126–135. Available: JSTOR (accessed February 19, 2009).

Morrow, L.M. and J.K. Smith. 1990. "The Effects of Group Size on Interactive Storybook Reading." *Reading Research Quarterly* 25, no. 3: 213–231. Available: JSTOR (accessed February 19, 2009).

Sipe, L.R. 2000. "The Construction of Literary Understanding by First and Second Graders in Oral Response to Picture Storybook Read-Alouds." *Reading Research Quarterly* 35, no. 2: 252–275. Available: JSTOR (accessed February 19, 2009).

Yaden, D.B. Jr., L.B. Smolkin, and A. Conlon. 1989. "Preschoolers' Questions about Pictures, Print Conventions, and Story Text during Reading Aloud at Home." *Reading Research Quarterly* 24, no. 2: 188–214. Available: JSTOR (accessed February 19, 2009).

Chapter 2

Storytelling: Selecting and Preparing Stories

Because storytelling is one of the ten types of interaction, I want to share some easy ways for nonstorytellers to select and prepare stories. Remember that traditional storytelling does not involve memorization, but instead it is a fluid retelling of a story by the storyteller alone and usually without props. More ideas for successful storytelling follow. For some great examples of professional storytellers, check out videos from the National Storytelling Festival in Jonesborough, Tennessee. There are many ways to tell stories. *Shake It Up Tales!* by Margaret Read MacDonald (2000) shares many of the different techniques such as drumming and riddle stories. Just as with presenting storytimes, everyone has their own style. Many of the ideas discussed here were adapted from the book *Storytelling: Art and Technique* by Ellin Greene (1996). The chapter ends with some basic ideas for using volunteers during storytime.

STORYTELLING IS . . .

- *Not recitation.* It should not be or sound memorized.
- *Not acting.* Although you can play several characters, you are telling a story and not presenting a play.
- *Sharing.* You should be sharing a story that you want to share or that you want people to know about.
- *Rapport.* There should be a connection with the audience.
- *Visualization.* The audience should be able to visualize your story without the book or pictures.

- *Listening.* Storytelling is all about listening. Your audience can see your gestures and expressions, but it is the words and the sound of your voice that will hold their attention.
- *Introducing new books.*
- *Education.* Teach your audience about different places, cultures, or simply a new experience.
- *Meeting new characters.* This is your opportunity to introduce the unlikely characters to children of all ages.
- *Keeping alive cultural history.* Many stories can represent a teller's own history or bring to light stories that have been lost, especially stories not represented in picture books children read.

SELECTING STORIES

- *Repetition:* Books with repetition tend to be easier to remember and retell. Choose a story that repeats the same elements yet still has pieces of the story that change. For example, in "The Three Little Pigs," you have the same actions occurring, but to different pigs and with different houses. Many stories, not just fairy tales or folktales, have something repeated over and over again with only minor changes. These stories are best for storytelling.
- *Folktales, fairy tales, and fables:* These stories often have three elements repeated, although with slight differences. Storytellers are also usually familiar with them.
- *Picture books:* You can reread a book and retell it. Just remember to be careful of copyright if you are getting paid to perform the story outside of your library.
- *Prewritten tales:* Some storytellers have published books with stories that are good for telling and that often have tips for how to tell them.
- *Adaptable to audience participation:* If you can get your audience to participate, you can better hold their attention and make the experience more enjoyable.
- *Easy to remember:* When selecting stories it is important to select ones that are familiar or that you have a personal connection with. Picture books, books with prewritten tales, and folktales work best. Try not to select a book that is too complicated with many subplots. The best tips in selecting stories are to choose a story that is easy to remember and to reread it several times. Storytelling is not meant to be time-consuming unless it is your career.
- *Meaning, enjoyment, and enthusiasm:* It will be easier to remember and tell a story if it has meaning to you. You can even turn a childhood anecdote into a story for children.
- *Trial and error:* You may select a book that does not work. You just can't remember it or it bores your students. Try again.

- *Read:* Read many books, and read them over and over to find the right tales and to get the best flow.
- *Shorter story:* Don't try to retell a lengthy book. Choose shorter ones, especially at first. They will be easier to remember, and you are less likely to get discouraged.
- *Single theme:* Stories with subplots get too complicated for the teller and listener and are more difficult to remember.
- *Well-developed plot:* A story with little plot will also not interest your audience. So choose wisely. Select a short story, yet one with some meaning behind it.
- *Characterization:* Your characters should also be interesting and appealing to children. Your audience should care what happens to them by the end of your telling.
- *Style:* You may develop your own personal style with regard to the stories you select, your voice inflections, or the way you share your stories.
- *Personal:* Stories that are personal, such as ones you heard as a child, are not only easier to remember but will demonstrate your connection to the story and your audience in a more meaningful way.
- *Familiar:* In the same way, stories that are familiar to you and your audience will also make a more comfortable experience for everyone.

HOW TO REMEMBER A STORY

- *Read it over and over.* I guarantee you that if you select a book that is not too long and not too short and has a strong plot, along with some repetition, even just by reading it three times, you will be able to retell most of the story. You may need to read it more times before you are ready to present the story to an audience. Reading a book again and again will allow you to become familiar enough with the story to tell it without the aid of a book.
- *Time it.* You don't want the story to go too long or too short, so try timing it. It may get longer or shorter the more you practice—longer if you remember more each time or shorter if your retelling becomes more fluid.
- *Read it out loud.* Practice as if you have an audience or in front of a mirror. Maybe a friend, family member, coworker, or child in your school or library will be your practice audience.
- *Put the story in pictures.* If you can visualize the stages of a story you will be better able to remember its sequence.
- *Practice the sounds of words.* Different words require different inflections or lengths of pauses. What is the most effective way to get the meaning of individual words across?
- *Choose something familiar or repetitive.* This tip was mentioned previously and will only help you remember a story better.

TELLING STORIES

- *Gestures:* Because it will likely be you with no prop or no book, your hand gestures can help tell the story.
- *Facial expressions:* In the same way, your eyes and expressions can also convey your emotions.
- *Movement:* Move around the stage and into your audience to keep their attention.
- *Pauses:* Pause for laughter or thoughtful consideration.
- *Emphasize words:* What words need to stand out? Make sure they do by emphasizing them with the tone and sound of your voice.
- *Poetic—speak slowly:* If your story is more poetic, try speaking slowly.
- *Action—speak rapidly:* If you have a scary story or an adventure or one with action, speak rapidly as the story progresses.
- *Make it your own:* You can change things around for your story by adding or subtracting details. What is easy for you to remember about this story, and what will help it appeal to children?
- *Caution with dialect:* If you are not comfortable with a culture or a country's dialect, then be cautious about using that story. Your adaptation may offend.
- *Music:* Although background music may be frowned upon by traditional storytellers, you might want to sing or hum part of your story if it is appropriate.

KAMISHIBAI

Kamishibai seems to have made a resurgence in popularity with Allen Say's (2005) *Kamishibai Man*, the Web site Kamishibai.com, and the book *Kamishibai Story Theater: The Art of Picture Telling* by Dianne de Las Casas (2006) as well as several articles. Kamishibai is a form of Japanese storytelling whereby the story is told with cards. Typically there would be a small tabletop stage or a creative alternative to a stage that could fit on a bicycle. The cards would be in order behind the stage. The wording is written on the back of the last card shown. When you are finished reading that card and when the audience has viewed the last card displayed, you move the front card to the back and read the next lines. These words were on the back of the last card you showed, which are now at the back of the stage for you to view. The Japanese storyteller traditionally mounts the stage to a bicycle and travels to tell stories while also selling a variety of sweet and savory treats.

From Kamishibai.com you can order a stage, sticks to announce the story, and one story for about $300. You can also often find discounted Kamishibai stories from Amazon.com or eBay. If this is still too much for your budget, you can create your own stage from a cereal box, picture frame, or handmade wooden box. You don't need a bicycle. You don't even really need the stage. You can create your own stories from drawing your own pictures or cutting up old books or magazine pictures. This could even be a project for which older children can participate. Even younger children can draw the pictures you request to add to the story. Children of any age can create their own stories. Students can recreate a story they have memorized by drawing pictures to illustrate it.

Add Kamishibai to storytimes as a change of format once in a while, or have a whole session devoted to it. I have my graduate school students create their own stories. Additional ideas and resources can be found at Kamishibai.com. Any book discussed here or found on your library shelves can be adapted to the Kamishibai format.

USING VOLUNTEERS

If you have a volunteer program at your library or school or if you have a teen summer volunteer program, you can use these people as part of your storytimes. Here are some tasks that your volunteers can perform:

1. Hold the book for you while you are retelling the story so children can see the book as you use props or other storytelling methods
2. Assist craft set up
3. Assist children having difficulties following along
4. Distribute and collect supplies during stories
5. Act out roles of the stories
6. Place objects on the board for board stories
7. Participate with children as a model for behavior, songs, and movements
8. Read the story while you act it out
9. Take part in a tandem story
10. Teach songs or play music

REFERENCES

De Las Casas, Dianne. 2006. *Kamishibai Story Theater: The Art of Picture Telling.* Westport, CT: Libraries Unlimited.

Greene, Ellin. 1996. *Storytelling: Art and Technique.* New Providence, NJ: R.R. Bowker.

MacDonald, Margaret Read. 2000. *Shake It Up Tales! Stories to Sing, Dance, Drum, and Act Out.* Little Rock: August House.

Say, Allen. 2005. *Kamishibai Man.* New York: Houghton Mifflin.

Chapter 3

Book Selection for Interactive Storytime

You probably already make excellent choices for books to line your library or class-room shelves. Most can easily be adapted for an interactive storytime. But after you start reading reviews with a storytime purpose in mind, you will find that you have even more options for books that lend well to this model. An important part of book selection is multicultural awareness, which is discussed at the end of this chapter.

EXAMPLES FROM *SCHOOL LIBRARY JOURNAL*

To illustrate how you can determine books that lend themselves to participation by reading reviews, I selected one issue of *School Library Journal* (February 2008) from which I read reviews and made decisions on what books to order or what books could be used interactively. Not all selections work out as planned, but it is easy to recognize clues that offer possibilities. These are just some of the ideas gleaned from the reviews. Of course more would be discovered after reading the entire book, and only after reading it can a true decision of how to approach each book be determined. Still, reviews are great ways to get ideas of books that will help you to create more interactive storytimes.

For *Stuck in the Mud* by Jane Clarke (Walker Books for Young Readers, 2008), the story of a chick stuck in the mud and the animals who try to help him, the review reads, "One by one, the rescuers also become mired in mud." The words "one by one" were an instant clue for participation, especially playacting, where children can take the roles of multiple characters.

In *The Tear Thief,* Carol Ann Duffy (Barefoot Books, 2007) says of the tear thief: "She slips into the homes of crying children during the time between supper and bed to steal their tears." From this description, I thought that I might be able to approach each child in the room and pretend to steal their tears.

In *Oliver Has Something to Say!,* by Pamela Edwards (Lobster Press, 2007), "Every time someone asks Oliver a question, a member of his family answers for him before the youngest can open his mouth." For this story, I imagined that I might have a child pretend to be Oliver or I could use a puppet as Oliver and have him pretend to open his mouth but also have the family jump in before he could speak.

The words "waking up with a talking feline on your head" were all I needed to read to know that the book *A Very Improbable Story: A Math Adventure* by Edward Einhorn (Charlesbridge, 2008) would involve a prop of a cat on my head.

On the Farm by David Elliott (Candlewick, 2008) is described as having "motion in the illustrations of the strutting, crowing rooster; the kicking hind legs of the pony; and the head-butting rams." This automatically indicates the possibility of using movement with the children.

"A forgotten pink mitten and a lone blue sock meet on a city sidewalk in this picture book about friendship and adventure," called *Smitten* by David Gordon (Atheneum, 2007). A lost mitten is an indication that children can find a match on a board, on the wall, from a pile, or from a classmate.

In *Night of the Veggie Monster* by George McClements (Bloomsbury USA Children's Books, 2008), when a boy has to eat veggies, his "fingers become all wiggly, his eyes start to water, and he squirms in his seat." These are clues for movement. Children can act out how he reacts.

Any counting book, such as *One Tractor: A Counting Book* by Alexandra Siy (Holiday House, 2008), can involve children counting objects on the page or identifying the pictures that are counted. I thought this might be the case for *One Tractor* as well. The review starts with a tractor and then adds two airplanes, which falls into this storytime pattern.

The title alone of *The Duck Who Played the Kazoo* by Amy Sklansky (Clarion Books, 2008) indicates the activity right away. Immediately my mind was drawn to the bags of cheap kazoos I have purchased in the past or the toy sound makers I have had children make out of toilet paper rolls and tissue or wax paper. Without even reading the review, I knew I could have fun with music and this book.

In the review of *Truck Stuck* by Sallie Wolf (Charlesbridge, 2008), a traffic jam is identified as the theme of this story. Children can pretend to be part of the traffic jam, or a board story could be created with all the vehicles stuck in this jam.

WHAT TO LOOK FOR IN REVIEWS THAT PROMOTE PARTICIPATION IN CHILDREN'S STORIES

The following features are just some of the many things to look for in reviews that give you clues about how you can use the books with participation.

1. *Sound:* Children find most sounds intriguing—animal sounds, city sounds, transportation sounds, etc.
2. *Multiple characters:* Characters can usually be added or removed to act out a mini play, and everyone can participate.
3. *Music:* Children's songs turned into books or books with a repetitive verse lend themselves to sound. Instruments might also be mentioned in the reviews.
4. *Something missing:* When something is missing, children can always actively search for it.
5. *Various locations:* If a story takes place in different places, children can walk around the room with you, pretending to be in each place.
6. *Repetition:* When words are repeated, you know you can either have children repeat them or play a game where children react when the words are mentioned in the story.
7. *Short sentences:* If a review mentions that the book is brief or has short text, then this also is a clue that it can be used with participation. Longer stories need more work to paraphrase.
8. *Counting books:* For most you can have children count the objects in the story or identify the pictures being counted. Children can also role play the items counted, or the items can be replicated on a board story.
9. *Statements:* Any book with statements that explain something or suggest something can be turned into questions. The sillier the better.
10. *Questions:* Some books ask questions or characters ask questions of other people or animals. These are inherently set up for interaction.
11. *Cumulative tales:* Any time the words "cumulative tale" show up in a review, you can easily make a board story by adding things from the story to it.
12. *Shapes:* Anything with shapes can turn into an art lesson of children creating their own pictures with shapes.
13. *Folktales:* Most folktales lend themselves easily to storytelling, because most have something similar repeated several times.
14. *Clothing or hats:* Whenever the word "hat" appears in a review you can be sure that a board story with pictures of hats or props for you or your children to wear will be effective. Anything with clothing can also be added to a board story or worn by a child or the presenter.
15. *Bedtime:* Most bedtime stories or good night stories can usually be adapted for a bedtime storytime. Often these can involve children pretending to fall asleep or taking turns falling asleep.

16. *Transportation:* Board stories can be used to illustrate transportation, or children can pretend to operate the vehicles.

17. *Letters:* If a book shares letters or is a journal, children can take turns presenting the letters.

18. *Poetry:* Poetry can be used in many ways depending on the theme. For more comprehensive poetry books, children can take turns selecting the poems to be read.

19. *Dancing:* Any book with dancing in the title or in the summary or review description will most likely allow for interaction in the way of dancing.

20. *Opposites or similarities:* These books can be used with pictures or children as partners or by locating mismatched or similar items. Children just have to match up the similar or opposite pictures on a board or find them in the room somewhere.

21. *Art or drawing:* Any book that mentions art or drawing of any kind can usually be accompanied by the children participating in an art activity no matter how primitive their work may be.

22. *States or large quantities:* For any book that includes a concept such as the states in the United States or nouns or something else that exists in a large quantity, children can take turns by standing up or putting them on a board or presenting them to the librarian or teacher when their state or object is mentioned. Even though you may provide a nametag or picture, younger children should be told what their word is.

23. *Food:* Often with books about food, children can pretend to cook or eat or use pictures of food as part of a board story.

24. *Hugs and obvious titles:* Books with titles with words like "hugs" in them lend themselves to obvious uses. Hugs, for example, will involve children hugging one another. Books about mail can be used for children to pretend to send or write mail.

25. *Movement:* Some books and reviews will mention movements such as jumping, skipping, and hopping. These books are inherently set up for interaction.

26. *Hair:* Books about hair give you the opportunity to pretend to cut and style the hair on a hand-created paper doll or on a real doll or wig. Children can be given safety scissors to cut the hair on a paper doll as well.

MULTICULTURAL AWARENESS

When *Storytime Action!* was published, I was taking a multicultural children's literature class at Northern Illinois University. I was embarrassed to learn that one of the books I had included in mine had been criticized for its stereotypical content. That book was *Tikki Tikki Tembo* by Arlene Mosel (Henry Holt, 1968). I never even liked the book, but since so many teachers and librarians had used it and loved it, I thought it should be included. As taught in that course and as stated in *Teaching Multicultural Literature in Grades K Thru 8th* by Violet Harris (Christopher-Gordon, 1993), *Tikki Tikki Tembo* actually pokes fun at Asian names that may be long or unpronounceable. This may go unnoticed by children who just find the story fun but could have consequences if used with an audience with some Asian-American children. Imagine students turning to a Chinese child and comparing his name to Tikki Tikki Tembo's. It may seem harmless, but in certain situations the books we choose to represent other cultures can be harmful or can unknowingly portray the wrong image to children. For this reason, more multi-cultural books with positive reviews from inside the cultures from which the books are written are included in the present book. Keep in mind that people within a culture may still disagree about a book depending on their background and experiences. Many issues regarding multiculturalism are still debated.

Now when I select multicultural books for children, I try to stick with the books by well-known authors and illustrators; choose books reviewed in journals such as *Multicultural Review*, which are reviewed by members of the culture the books represent; look for insiders of the cultures; and consider the guidelines that follow. All of the books I include here have met many of the following guidelines. When I use the word "multicultural," I am referring to a group of books represent-ing various cultures. A book about Japanese children would be a Japanese or Japanese-American children's book and not a multicultural book on its own unless considered with a group of books on various cultures. When known, it is best to refer to the characters of a book by their country of origin or culture rather than an umbrella term such as Asian American.

Consider these guidelines when selecting multicultural books for children:

- **Insider or Outsider?**
  Is the author or illustrator an insider or outsider? The definition of an insider can be debated. Who is an insider? Typically an insider is a member of a spe-cific culture. So if a book about Hopi Indians is written by a Hopi Indian, then the book would be considered authentic and written by an insider. If I wrote a book about any Native American tribe or nation, it would be written by an outsider, that is, by someone with a perspective outside of the culture. However, is someone who has lived in a particular country for 20 years or someone who was adopted into a culture more of an insider than someone who was born into a family or looks like someone from a certain culture? These are questions that can be difficult to answer, as even the best authors and illustrators of multicultural stories can make errors in their writing or illustrations. Still, this is the first thing to consider when selecting multicul-tural books and a good indication that the book is authentic. Consider the

background of an author and illustrator when deciding to use books representing other cultures. What you may think is cute or a good lesson may be offensive to someone else.

- **Names**

  Don't judge a book by its author's name. Just because Ann Gonzalez has a last name that sounds Latino does not mean she is a Latina. Ann may have married Mr. Gonzalez. Ann may have been born to Alice Czarnecki and Mr. Gonzalez. Ann may have never been to a Latin American country and may have lived in a predominately white community. So, although names can be a first indication, you should still investigate the background of the author.

- **Book Jacket and Other Author Information**

  The first step is obviously to review the book's jacket. A picture of the author can also be misleading, because a person may have been born into a culture yet never followed any of the traditions or never immersed himself or herself into the community. Just because a person looks Asian doesn't mean that he or she has ever been to Asia or has participated in any Asian traditions. Still, look for information provided about book authors. Where do they live? Go to school? What did they study in school? What other books did they write? What is the focus of their art? What do they promote or stand for? Where have they lived or spent much time? If the book jacket is vague, the Internet provides plenty of Web sites by the authors or illustrators or by the publishers. If all else fails, go to sources like electronic databases or book series such as *Something about the Author* (published by Gale) to further investigate.

- **Stereotypes**

  Although we do not see stereotypes in current literature as frequently as in the past, it still happens. Some more easily noticeable stereotypes might be food or characters with similar appearances. Although stereotypic characteristics may be true for all or many of the people belonging to a certain culture, they are still stereotypes if we use them to represent all of a culture. Although it is an older title, *The Snowy Day* by Ezra Jack Keats (Viking, 1962) continues to be used in classrooms and libraries today. Still, it shows a slightly larger African-American woman in a dress with an appearance close to the mammy stereotype. To see more African-American stereotypes of the past, visit the Jim Crow Museum of Racist Memorabilia's Web site (www.ferris.edu/jim-crow).

- **Inaccuracies**

  Does it matter if a Japanese character is wearing Chinese clothing? Does it matter if illustrations are from India but should be from Pakistan? It might if the book was about America and clothing was from a different time period or country, or if the illustrations represented New York but the book was about Chicago. It might if someone you read the book to is from these countries. Such inaccuracies should be considered for every book we share. Therefore, it is important to consider factual flaws in text and illustrations even if we think the children will not notice or understand.

- **Omissions**

  Is a group of people left out of history? For example, are Native Americans left out in a story about the California Gold Rush? This will mostly occur in history books, biographies, and historical fiction. See the Oyate's Web site (www.oyate.org) for books that tell the whole story about Native Americans in history.

- **Language**

  Are Spanish words sprinkled in with English in a natural or forced way? Is stereotypical language like "Ugh" used for Native Americans?

- **Sources**

  Does a book list sources known to be inaccurate? Are no sources listed? Are general sources listed? Who are the authors of these sources? Did the authors write books on various subjects and cultures or countries?

- **Diversity**

  Does the book include a various array of people? Does a book about families include gay parents? Does the story show the diversity within a culture or a country? Are the books you share diverse? The most important thing to remember is that not everyone from the same country is the same. There is diversity within cultures.

- **Effects on a Child's Self-Image**

  Even though derogatory terms may have been used at different times, does sharing literature containing these words with young children have a harmful effect? Will the content draw attention to some children in the room? Are multicultural books included in the classroom or storytime room to show children that they are included in the stories? Can children see themselves in the stories? Are children being exposed to other cultures in the stories? Consider your children and your purpose when choosing stories to share.

Chapter 4

20 Theme-Based Plans for Interactive Storytime

This book is written with a loose format and little discussion of specific themes and additional activities, because it is meant to promote using the best books and activities while giving yourself the freedom to avoid being married to a topic. However, if you prefer to work with a theme, the 20 theme-based plans provided in this chapter can be starting points or formulas for using the rest of the information in this book to create your own.

The participation activities for each book listed are described in Chapter 5. Additional activities to use with these books are also included in each plan in this chapter. Use the theme index to find alternate titles that you may have in your library. Use iTunes to find songs that you may be able to download or use as replacements for the songs suggested here. Although it would be best to indicate the craft supplies needed for the books as well, they are not included for some because some books have several possibilities for interaction. You can fill in the details with what you actually plan to use or use the blank form provided to create your own. Several times I will ask you to search for your own rhyme or poem. I do this because many of the Web sites I would suggest might have changed by the time you use them. It is easy to search for a finger play on a certain topic using the keywords of "fingerplay" or "finger play." If you are creative, you might write your own. I am not a personal fan of finger plays, but I include them as possibilities because people do like to use them, and children do love them. There are only a few I truly enjoy that are easy to remember and that I find livelier.

More craft ideas and descriptions can also be found in the original *Storytime Action!* Although I prefer to use Raffi's song "The More We Get Together" as a familiar song to open each storytime session with, you may choose another song that works better for you. With this information in mind, what follows are 20 themes that can be used with books from *More Storytime Action!* or as ideas for additional activities accompanying your own book choices. Complete citations for the selected books in this chapter are given in Chapter 5, where the books are listed alphabetically by author.

STORYTIME PLAN 1		
	Date:	Ages: 3–5
Theme: **Body/Clothes**	**Book or Activity**	**Supplies**
Activity	"Stand up if you are wearing red today. Stand up if you are wearing green today. . . ." "The More We Get Together" (song)	Raffi's Singable Songs Collection (CD)
Book 1	*Arthur's Nose* (Brown)	*Arthur's Nose* Noses for board story
Activity (song, finger play, book, board story, game, etc.)	"Head, Shoulders, Knees and Toes" (song), slow version	*It's Toddler Time* (CD)
Book 2	*Under My Hood I Have a Hat* (Kuskin)	*Under My Hood I Have a Hat* Clothing or board pieces
Activity	"Head, Shoulders, Knees and Toes" (song), fast version	*It's Toddler Time* (CD)
Book 3	*Head, Body, Legs* (Paye and Lippert)	*Head, Body, Legs* Black body pieces for kids or board
Activity	"Shake Your Sillies Out" (song)	Raffi CD
Additional activity or book	Find Your Shoes: Everyone takes off their shoes, places the shoes in a pile, and then runs to find their shoes and put them back on. Then they walk to the craft table—and/or find the missing socks. Give all children one paper sock or mitten, and they must find the matching one.	Sock or mitten patterns in different colors or designs
Conclusion	"Now that we have talked about bodies and clothes, we are going to dress a bear."	
Craft	Monster Feet or Dress the Bear	Patterns and crayons

\

STORYTIME PLAN 2		
	Date:	Ages: 3–5
Theme: Frogs	**Book or Activity**	**Supplies**
Introduction	Show frog puppet. Ask kids what it is and what they know about frogs. "The More We Get Together" (song)	Frog puppet Raffi's Singable Songs Collection CD
Book 1	*Jump Frog, Jump!* (Kalan)	*Jump Frog, Jump!*
Activity (song, finger play, book, board story, game, etc.)	"Five Green and Speckled Frogs" (song)	Raffi's Singable Songs Collection CD
Book 2	*Froggy Gets Dressed* (London)	*Froggy Gets Dressed* Board pieces
Activity	"Five Little Froggies" (rhyme)	
Book 3	*The Wide-Mouthed Frog* (Faulkner)	*The Wide-Mouthed Frog*
Activity	Find the Frogs: Place frog pictures around the room. Have children find the frogs while jumping around like frogs and put the pictures in the frog puppet's mouth.	Frog puppet and frog patterns
Additional activity or book	"Five Little Frogs" (song)	*It's Toddler Time* (CD)
Conclusion	Ask children what they like about frogs.	
Craft	Jumping Frog	Frog patterns and crayons

STORYTIME PLAN 3		
	Date:	Ages: 3–5
Theme: Alphabet/ABCs	**Book or Activity**	**Supplies**
Introduction	"The More We Get Together" (song) Ask the children if they know their ABCs. Sing the song with or without a CD.	Raffi's Singable Songs Collection CD "The Alphabet Song"
Book 1	*Superhero ABC* (McLeod)	*Superhero ABC*
Activity (song, finger play, book, board story, game, etc.)	Backwards Alphabet Children will repeat the alphabet backwards. Point to the letters on an alphabet chart.	Alphabet chart
Book 2	*A Is for Zebra* (Shulman)	*A Is for Zebra*
Activity	A Is for . . . : Go through the alphabet saying, "A is for . . . , B is for . . . ," etc., and have the children shout out words that begin with those letters. You may want to have pictures displayed to help the children.	
Book 3	*Zoopa* (Marino)	*Zoopa* Animal pictures, plate, bowl, or board
Activity	Alphabet Walk: Place alphabet cards or printed alphabet letters on the floor. Children can walk on the letters for a musical chairs type of game or they can just walk on the letters, and say their own letter as they reach it.	Letter cards and music
Additional activity or book	Children will find the letter for their name on the wall to use for their craft.	Cardboard alphabet letters for each child's name
Conclusion	Sing the alphabet without accompanying music.	
Craft	Each child will receive a cardboard letter that represents the first letter of his or her name to decorate and make into a magnet.	Glitter, beads, feathers, cut paper, etc. to decorate letters; and magnets

STORYTIME PLAN 4		
	Date:	Ages: 3–5
Theme: Dancing	**Book or Activity**	**Supplies**
Introduction	"The More We Get Together" (song) Ask children what dances they know. Have them demonstrate all at once or one at a time.	Raffi's Singable Songs Collection CD
Book 1	A Dictionary of Dance (Murphy)	A Dictionary of Dance
Activity (song, finger play, book, board story, game, etc.)	Dance Play dance music appropriate for children.	Dance music
Book 2	Hula Lullaby (Kono)	Hula Lullaby
Activity	Play hula music and teach children to hula	Hawaiian music, hula skirt
Book 3	The Numbers Dance (Nobisso)	The Numbers Dance
Activity	Dance Contest	Dance music
Additional activity or book	Teach a new dance from a video or a book. Even a dance shown on a children's cartoon video would work.	Video and music
Conclusion	Ask children to name all the different kinds of dances they can think of.	
Craft	Make hula skirt or leis or a musical instrument.	

STORYTIME PLAN 5		
	Date:	Ages: 3–5
Theme: Farms	**Book or Activity**	**Supplies**
Introduction	"The More We Get Together" (song) Ask children what animals are on farms. What do they grow on farms? Have they ever been to a farm?	Raffi's Singable Songs Collection CD
Book 1	*Down on the Farm* (Kutner)	*Down on the Farm*
Activity (song, finger play, book, board story, game, etc.)	"Old MacDonald Had a Farm" (song)	"Old MacDonald" song
Book 2	*Cock-a-Doodle Quack! Quack!* (Baddiel and Judd)	*Cock-a-Doodle Quack! Quack!*
Activity	Animal Sounds Have children make different animal sounds. They can choose their own, or give them each a different picture to make the sound for that animal.	Animal pictures
Book 3	*Stuck in the Mud* (Clarke)	*Stuck in the Mud*
Activity	Tell a version of the story "The Enormous Carrot" but use farm animals. Each child can take a part. See examples in *Storytime Action!*	
Additional activity or book	Select another version of "Old MacDonald Had a Farm" (song).	"Old MacDonald" song
Conclusion	After hearing these stories and singing these songs, can children think of any other farm animals? Who wants to visit a farm now?	
Craft	Animal Sound Maker: Cover a toilet paper tube with animal print on the sides and wax paper on one end. Children can moo into it or make other animal sounds.	Toilet paper rolls, animal print paper, and wax paper

STORYTIME PLAN 6		
	Date:	Ages: 3–5
Theme: Hats	**Book or Activity**	**Supplies**
Introduction	"The More We Get Together" (song) Show a variety of hats or pictures of hats, and ask the children who would wear each hat.	Raffi's Singable Songs Collection CD Hats or pictures of hats
Book 1	*Under My Hood I Have a Hat* (Kuskin)	*Under My Hood I Have a Hat*
Activity (song, finger play, book, board story, game, etc.)	Use "Hats Song" (available: http://step- bystepcc.com/hat.html; accessed May 22, 2009), sung to the tune of "Are You Sleeping," or write your own simple song.	
Book 2	*Stormy's Hat* (Kimmel)	*Stormy's Hat* Hats
Activity	Play "Hats" (song) by The Wiggles. Children can march around to this song.	Wiggles CD
Book 3	*Where's Mary's Hat?* (Barroux)	*Where's Mary's Hat?*
Activity	Where's the Hat?: Place pictures of hats around the room, or hide real hats, and have children find them.	Pictures of hats or real hats
Additional activity or book	Dress Up: Children can try on different hats and decide which they like best. Take instant pictures for them to take home.	Hats
Conclusion	Ask the children what kinds of hats different people wear.	
Craft	Make a hat! A visor or a strip of paper with a picture added would work.	Paper, pictures, tape, and glue

STORYTIME PLAN 7		
	Date:	Ages: 3–5
Theme: Music	**Book or Activity**	**Supplies**
Introduction	"The More We Get Together" (song) Ask children what their favorite songs are.	Raffi's Singable Songs Collection CD
Book 1	*The Duck Who Played the Kazoo* (Sklansky)	*The Duck Who Played the Kazoo*
Activity (song, finger play, book, board story, game, etc.)	Use the kazoos passed out during the reading of *The Duck Who Played the Kazoo* and have children hum different familiar songs such as "Mary Had a Little Lamb."	Kazoos
Book 2 (one from list)	*Puff the Magic Dragon* (Yarrow) *On Top of Spaghetti* (Johnson and Glazer) *William's Doll* (Zolotow) *Take Me Out to the Ballgame* (Norworth) *The Cat Came Back* (Penner) *If You're Happy and You Know It* (Cabrera) *Just the Two of Us* (Smith)	CD with the chosen song and copy of the chosen book
Activity	Follow with another one of the above mentioned books. Play the song to accompany turning the pages of the book.	CD with the chosen song and copy of the chosen book
Book 3	*Jazz Baby* (Wheeler)	*Jazz Baby*
Activity	Give the children instruments to play and march with around the library or room.	Instruments
Additional activity or book	Play any song and have the children dance and play instruments.	CD and instruments
Conclusion	Ask the children what instrument they would like to play.	
Craft	Make an instrument such as a noise maker with two cups taped together and something inside to shake.	

STORYTIME PLAN 8		
	Date:	Ages: 3–5
Theme: **Transportation**	**Book or Activity**	**Supplies**
Introduction	"The More We Get Together" (song) Ask children to name different forms of transportation.	Raffi's Singable Songs Collection CD
Book 1	*The Wheels on the Race Car* (Zane)	*The Wheels on the Race Car*
Activity (song, finger play, book, board story, game, etc.)	Play the song "The Wheels on the Bus"	"The Wheels on the Bus" on CD
Book 2	*A Train Goes Clickety-Clack* (London)	*A Train Goes Clickety-Clack*
Activity	Play the song "Beep Beep." Give the children something to beep, or have them pretend to beep and sing "Beep Beep" every time it is sung in the song.	"Beep Beep" by Broadway Studio
Book 3	*Truck Stuck* (Wolf)	*Truck Stuck*
Activity	Children can grab onto one another and say "Chugga chugga choo choo" as they pretend to be a train.	
Additional activity or book	Give children a paper plate either by itself or dressed up with a horn and cut to form a steering wheel shape. Children can pretend to drive around the room.	Paper plates; horns optional
Conclusion	Ask children what their favorite form of transportation is.	
Craft	Create the steering wheels mentioned above. Make a car or train magnet out of cardboard cut into shapes with a magnet attached.	

STORYTIME PLAN 9		
	Date:	Ages: 3–5
Theme: Animals	**Book or Activity**	**Supplies**
Introduction	"The More We Get Together" (song) Ask children what their favorite animal is.	Raffi's Singable Songs Collection CD
Book 1	*Simms Tabacks's Safari Animals* (Taback)	*Simms Tabacks's Safari Animals*
Activity (song, finger play, book, board story, game, etc.)	Play the song "Be Nice to Animals" by the Salteens. Children can repeat the lines "_____ are my friends" and sing along. This short song can be played several times.	"Be Nice to Animals" on MP3
Book 2	*On the Farm* (Elliott)	*On the Farm*
Activity	Use a finger rhyme, such as "Five Little Monkeys," with finger puppets	Finger puppets
Book 3	*Sleep, Black Bear, Sleep* (Yolen)	*Sleep, Black Bear, Sleep*
Activity	"Going to the Zoo" by Raffi Children can be taught and practice the chorus.	Raffi CD
Additional activity or book	Ask children to bring a stuffed animal. They can explain why they like this animal and have an animal parade.	Stuffed animals
Conclusion	Ask children what their favorite pet is.	
Craft	Make an animal picture frame by cutting a frame shape out of cardboard and gluing animal pictures around it.	Cardboard, animal pictures, and glue

STORYTIME PLAN 10		
	Date:	Ages: 3–5
Theme: **Dogs and Cats**	**Book or Activity**	**Supplies**
Introduction	"The More We Get Together" (song) Ask the children if they know or have any dogs or cats. What are their names? What sounds do they make?	Raffi's Singable Songs Collection CD
Book 1	*What Will Fat Cat Sit On?* (Thomas)	*What Will Fat Cat Sit On?*
Activity (song, finger play, book, board story, game, etc.)	Play a game similar to Red Light, Green Light or Simon Says, only have half of the children be cats and half be dogs and they will come when called.	
Book 2	*Look What the Cat Dragged In* (Hogg)	*Look What the Cat Dragged In*
Activity	Name different activities that cats and dogs do. Children can bark if it is something a dog would do or meow if it is something a cat would do.	
Book 3	*Wag a Tail* (Ehlert)	*Wag a Tail*
Activity	"Who Let the Dogs Out" (song) by the Baha Men or other version Kids can bark.	"Who Let the Dogs Out" on CD
Additional activity or book	*Dog's ABC* (Dodd) Add this or another additional book to make it even between dogs and cats.	*Dog's ABC*
Conclusion	Have children raise their hands to vote on whether they like cats or dogs better.	
Craft	Children can color a picture of a cat or dog, depending on their preference.	Crayons and dog and cat pictures to color

STORYTIME PLAN 11		
	Date:	Ages: 3–5
Theme: Fruits and Vegetables	**Book or Activity**	**Supplies**
Introduction	"The More We Get Together" (CD) Ask children what fruits and vegetables they like to eat.	Raffi's Singable Songs Collection CD
Book 1	*Orange Pear Apple Bear* (Gravett)	*Orange Pear Apple Bear*
Activity (song, finger play, book, board story, game, etc.)	Sing the song "Fruits and Veggies" by Lori, Lori What's the Story Children can repeat the refrain.	"Fruits and Veggies" on MP3
Book 2	*Carrot Soup* (Segal)	*Carrot Soup*
Activity	Make a veggie soup. Give children pictures of ingredients for a soup and have them sit in a circle, bringing their items to the center to stir and eat.	Pictures of soup ingredients
Book 3	*Night of the Veggie Monster* (McClements)	*Night of the Veggie Monster*
Activity	Name the fruits and vegetables. Bring in real produce or use pictures for students to identify.	Real fruits and vegetables or pictures of them
Additional activity or book	Search online or in a book for a poem or finger play or rhyme about fruits or vegetables.	Copy of a rhyme
Conclusion	Repeat a song or a rhyme.	
Craft	Make a planter out of baby food jars.	Baby food jars, dirt, seeds, decorations, and glue

STORYTIME PLAN 12		
	Date:	Ages: 3–5
Theme: Colors	**Book or Activity**	**Supplies**
Introduction	"The More We Get Together" (song) Create a color wheel for children to spin. They can then receive a square of the color they had spun and that will be their color for the day.	Raffi's Singable Songs Collection CD Color wheel and color squares
Book 1	*Green as a Bean* (Kuskin)	*Green as a Bean*
Activity (song, finger play, book, board story, game, etc.)	Select a color rhyme to repeat.	
Book 2	*Color Zoo* (Ehlert)	*Color Zoo*
Activity	Play the song "Colors" from *Blue's Clues* Since some of the colors in the song like aquamarine and magenta may be unfamiliar, tell the children who have similar colors that they selected from the spin, what other colors look like their color. Then they can stand up when their color is sung in the song.	"Colors" on CD
Book 3	*White Is for Blueberry* (Shannon)	*White Is for Blueberry*
Activity	Play a game like Twister by spreading out different colors and shapes asking children to find one and stand on it. They could also play a game like Hot Potato in which they pass their colors or other colors and, when the music stops, whatever color is called wins that round.	Colored shapes
Additional activity or book	Show different colors in different shades or different objects in different shades and have children identify the colors.	Colored objects or squares
Conclusion	Call the names of the colors children had spun and collect them.	
Craft	Finger paint or color with different colors. A collage of shapes could also be made.	Finger paint or coloring supplies and paper; or cut paper colors and white paper

STORYTIME PLAN 13		
	Date:	Ages: 3–5
Theme: Counting	Book or Activity	Supplies
Introduction	"The More We Get Together" (song) Ask children to count with you as high as they can count and to sit down when they have reached their highest number.	Raffi's Singable Songs Collection CD
Book 1	10 Little Rubber Ducks (Carle)	10 Little Rubber Ducks
Activity (song, finger play, book, board story, game, etc.)	Any counting finger play such as "Five Little Monkeys"	
Book 2	One Tractor (Siy)	One Tractor
Activity	Dance and count to "Numbers Rhumba" by the Wiggles.	Wiggles CD
Book 3	Ten Little Fish (Wood)	Ten Little Fish
Activity	Ask children to name things they can count in the room or library that add up to the numbers from one to five.	
Additional activity or book	Have groups of pictures or objects to count.	Pictures or objects
Conclusion	Have a backwards countdown from ten to announce craft time.	
Craft	Make necklaces with laminated numbers from one to ten. Children can attach the numbers to the yarn.	

STORYTIME PLAN 14		
	Date:	Ages: 3–5
Theme: Manners and Lessons	**Book or Activity**	**Supplies**
Introduction	"The More We Get Together" (song) Ask children to name some good manners and bad manners.	Raffi's Singable Songs Collection CD
Book 1	*The Nice Book* (Stein)	*The Nice Book*
Activity (song, finger play, book, board story, game, etc.)	Please and Thank You Game: Pass a wrapped gift around and have the children practice saying "please" and "thank you" in a circle.	Wrapped gift
Book 2	*The Wise Shoemaker of Studena* (Lieberman) or *The Secret Olivia Told Me* (Joy)	*The Wise Shoemaker of Studena* or *The Secret Olivia Told Me*
Activity	Set a table. Give children a placemat with a plate or circle on the middle or a paper plate. Give them plastic spoons and a napkin and practice table manners.	Plate, spoon, and napkin
Book 3	*Never Take a Shark to the Dentist* (Barrett)	*Never Take a Shark to the Dentist*
Activity	"I'm Gonna Wash Those Germs Right off of My Hands" by Judi the Manners Lady	*It's Fun to Have Good Manners* MP3
Additional activity or book	"Please and Thank You" song from Barney	Barney CD
Conclusion	Name some manners, and ask children if they do these things or if they are good or bad manners.	
Craft	Manners Book: Children can decorate a journal you have given them from folded paper with a cover to be their book to draw and record their manners and lessons they have learned. They can glue in phrases describing manners that you have provided.	Journals, crayons, and phrases

STORYTIME PLAN 15		
	Date:	Ages: 3–5
Theme: Animal Sounds	**Book or Activity**	**Supplies**
Introduction	"The More We Get Together" (song) Say some animal names and ask children to make the sounds they make.	Raffi's Singable Songs Collection CD
Book 1	*Mung-Mung* (Park)	*Mung-Mung*
Activity (song, finger play, book, board story, game, etc.)	"Animal Sounds" by Patricia Lamarca Kandel This song is a guessing game with pauses for children to say the animal that makes each sound.	"Animal Sounds" on CD
Book 2	*Baa for Beginners* (Fajerman)	*Baa for Beginners*
Activity	"Old MacDonald Had a Farm," any version	"Old MacDonald" on CD
Book 3	*Bird Songs* (Franco)	*Bird Songs*
Activity	Play bird songs from a bird songs CD. Ask children to identify the birds by pictures you provide. You will have to give them most answers.	Bird songs on CD
Additional activity or book	Give each child a picture of an animal and have them make the sounds at first taking turns and then in a group as if they were in a zoo. They can act out their animals as well.	Animal pictures
Conclusion	Ask children what their favorite animal sounds are. Make the sounds.	
Craft	Make an animal sound maker from toilet paper rolls, an animal pattern, and wax paper. Alternatively, make animal straws by cutting a picture of an animal with two slits, allowing children to color it, and then sliding the straw through.	Wax paper, animal paper, toilet paper rolls; or animal pictures and straws

STORYTIME PLAN 16		
	Date:	Ages: 3–5
Theme: Winter	**Book or Activity**	**Supplies**
Introduction	"The More We Get Together" (song) Ask children what they like to do in the winter.	Raffi's Singable Songs Collection CD
Book 1	*Snowball Fight!* (Fallon)	*Snowball Fight!*
Activity (song, finger play, book, board story, game, etc.)	Make snow balls out of crumpled paper and have a "snow ball fight."	Crumpled white paper
Book 2	*A Mountain of Mittens* (Plourde)	*A Mountain of Mittens*
Activity	Hide mittens around the room for children to find whether real or paper. Matching mittens would work best.	Real or paper mittens
Book 3	*One Winter's Day* (Butler)	*One Winter's Day*
Activity	Make a snowman. Give each child a different size of snowball for the snowman as well as a hat, scarf, eyes, nose etc. for the snowman. They can gather together to assemble it like a puzzle.	Paper pieces to build a snowman
Additional activity or book	Search for a snow or winter rhyme, poem, or finger play in books or online.	
Conclusion	Ask the children what their favorite season is.	
Craft	Make a snowman by gluing cotton balls to a snowman shape. You can also turn this into an ornament.	Cotton balls, yarn, and snowman shape

STORYTIME PLAN 17		
	Date:	Ages: 3–5
Theme: Monsters	**Book or Activity**	**Supplies**
Introduction	"The More We Get Together" (song) Ask children if they are afraid of monsters or if they have seen any monsters. Assure them that they are not real. Tell them that you are going to talk about friendly monsters today.	Raffi's Singable Songs Collection CD
Book 1	*Bye-Bye, Big Bad Bullybug!* (Emberley)	*Bye-Bye, Big Bad Bullybug!*
Activity (song, finger play, book, board story, game, etc.)	"Monster Mash" (song) Children can dance to the monster mash song	"Monster Mash" on CD
Book 2	*The Shy Creatures* (Mack)	*The Shy Creatures*
Activity	Follow the monster feet. Make big monster feet and have the children follow them until they find a hidden door where there is a friendly monster drawn on or cut from cardboard. Alternately or in conjunction with this activity, you could create one big monster foot out of cardboard and see if the children can all stand on the monster foot and use clues on and around the foot to determine what the monster is.	
Book 3	*Stinky* (Davis)	*Stinky*
Activity	Write sentences that start with, "What would you say if a monster _____?" and instruct the children to repeat, "Go away monster." Examples might be, "What would you say if a monster was on your lawn?" Children can also take turns asking questions.	
Additional activity or book	Create a monster rhyme or find a poem, rhyme, or finger play online or in a book.	
Conclusion	Ask children what monsters they like now that they have hard about more in storytime.	

STORYTIME PLAN 18		
	Date:	Ages: 3–5
Theme: Art	**Book or Activity**	**Supplies**
Introduction	"The More We Get Together" (song) Show students picture of famous paintings. Ask them if they know the artist, where they might see the painting, or what they think the painting is showing.	Raffi's Singable Songs Collection CD Paintings and reproductions
Book 1	*The Dot* (Reynolds)	*The Dot*
Activity (song, finger play, book, board story, game, etc.)	Have children tell a familiar story while you draw pictures on the board. Select a story you recently read or a fairy tale.	Large paper or poster board
Book 2	*Found Alphabet* (Shindler)	*Found Alphabet*
Activity	Find objects from which children can create their own sculptures. This could include boxes, feathers, leaves etc.	Found objects
Book 3	*I Ain't Gonna Paint No More* (Beaumont)	*I Ain't Gonna Paint No More*
Activity	Select a simple story. Give each child a piece of paper. Now have them draw pictures to the story that you read.	
Additional activity or book	Play the song "Drawing" by Barenaked Ladies. Kids can dance with a crayon and/or paper in hand.	*Snacktime* CD
Conclusion	Ask children if they like art. What is art?	
Craft	Have a variety of materials available for children to create their own art.	Variety of materials

STORYTIME PLAN 19		
	Date:	Ages: 3–5
Theme: Bedtime	**Book or Activity**	**Supplies**
Introduction	"The More We Get Together" (song Have children come in pajamas with a stuffed animal. Children should gather around close with pillow or animal in hand to hear bedtime stories.	Raffi's Singable Songs Collection CD
Book 1	*The Book of ZZZs* (Alda)	*The Book of ZZZs*
Activity (song, finger play, book, board story, game, etc.)	Have a snoring contest.	
Book 2	*Goodnight, Me* (Daddo)	*Goodnight, Me*
Activity	"Stretching" song or "Bedtime" song by the Figureheads	Either song on a Figureheads CD
Book 3	*Goodnight Kisses* (Saltzberg)	*Goodnight Kisses*
Activity	Find a bedtime rhyme, poem or fingerplay online, from a book, or create one yourself.	
Additional activity or book	Play a book on CD/tape/MP3 for children to listen to as they lie down and close their eyes.	Appropriate song
Conclusion	Walk around the room with a "magic wand" and pretend to put each child to sleep. Play a lullaby as you do so.	A lullaby on CD and a wand
Craft	Children can make their own wands.	Stick, streamers, ribbon, and other decorations

STORYTIME PLAN 20		
Date:		Ages: 3–5
Theme: **More Animals**	**Book or Activity**	**Supplies**
Introduction	"The More We Get Together" (song) Ask children to tell you their favorite animal.	Raffi's Singable Songs Collection CD
Book 1	*Animal Band* (Jennings)	*Animal Band*
Activity (song, finger play, book, board story, game, etc.)	Guess the animal. Show pictures of animals from which children can guess. You might do this on a PowerPoint with a projector.	Picture and projector
Book 2	*I Feel a Foot!* (Rinck)	*I Feel a Foot!*
Activity	Any animal finger play, rhyme, or poem	
Book 3	*A Good Day* (Henkes)	*A Good Day*
Activity	Follow a yellow brick road chanting "Lion and tigers and bears oh my!" as you pass these and other animals in the room following the yellow trail. You may have to introduce the story of *The Wizard of Oz* or show a film clip.	Yellow rectangles of construction paper
Additional activity or book	Play a song such as "Yodel-Moo" by HI-5 or "Gorilla Song" by Sandra Boynton. For the second song, children can pretend to be gorillas and hold a fake or real banana.	CD containing the chosen song
Conclusion	Ask children to tell you the names of their pets or their favorite animal books or their favorite animal from TV.	
Craft	Make an animal clock using a different animal picture for each number.	Cardstock circles, animal pictures, and fasteners

STORYTIME PLAN—CREATE YOUR OWN		
	Date:	Ages: 3–5
Theme:	**Book or Activity**	**Supplies**
Introduction		
Book 1		
Activity (song, finger play, book, board story, game, etc.)		
Book 2		
Activity		
Book 3		
Activity		
Additional activity or book		
Conclusion		
Craft		

Chapter 5

2,000+ Ideas for Making 520 Picture Books Interactive

Ada, Alma Flor. 2007. *Extra! Extra! Fairy-Tale News from Hidden Forest.* **New York: Atheneum. Illus., Leslie Tryon.**

Summary:

Newspaper stories express shocking happenings related to well-known fairy tales.

Activity:

This is best for older children, but preschoolers can also give it a try. Read pieces of some of the newspaper stories, and ask children to name the fairy tales from which the stories came. It may be helpful to share some of the tales with the children in advance in order to familiarize them with the tales. Most of the stories relate to Jack and the Beanstalk and Pinocchio, but there are hints of others such as the half-chicken and three little pigs. For example, one story begins, "Many Hidden Forest neighbors have expressed their desire to get rid of the strange plant that has mysteriously appeared in Hidden Meadow." Read as many paragraphs as necessary until the children uncover the fairy tale behind each story, but stop along the way to ask them if they know what fairy tale or character the story could be about.

Agee, Jon. 2007. *Nothing.* New York: Hyperion.

Summary:

A woman buys nothing from a store, which starts a frenzy in the town of buying nothing until people realize they need something.

Activity:

You need simply nothing for this story. Start by giving the children a handful of nothing. Then begin telling the story. Pass around the nothing as you tell the story.

Ahlberg, Allan. 2008. *The Pencil.* Cambridge, MA: Candlewick. Illus., Bruce Ingman.

Summary:

A pencil starts to draw a boy, a cat, and a dog that become more demanding, and so a paintbrush and eraser must appear.

Activity:

This is a long story, so it would be difficult to draw all of it. Use a pencil and white art paper to illustrate the story as you read, or use a teen or adult volunteer to read or draw for you. You could also start with the pencil illustrations and not continue with the color of the paintbrush or the eraser. Alternatively, give each child a pencil and paper and ask them to draw, color, and erase what they hear from the story.

Ahmed, Said Salah. 2007. *The Lion's Share.* Saint Paul: Minnesota Humanities Commission. Illus., Kelly Dupre.

Summary:

The tale explains how the phrase "the lion's share" came to be.

Activity:

As the lion asks the other animals how the meat should be shared, ask the children in your group to share their ideas. Which animals should get the meat, and how should it be divided? Let every child have a turn. You might want to share with them the animals that were present. In the end you discover that the lion's share is actually that the lion gets everything.

Alborough, Jez. 2005. *Tall.* Cambridge, MA: Candlewick.

Summary:

A monkey feels small or tall depending on whom he is standing on or next to.

Activity:

There are two possibilities for this story. The first is to step on and off a stool or chair to demonstrate being taller or smaller. In the story, when Bobo feels small, jump down and crouch; when he feels tall, stand up on the chair. Raise your hands when Bobo feels even taller, and get down lower when he feels even smaller. Show a picture of an animal on poster board to demonstrate the size. Kids can stand up and sit down as well. Alternatively, make this into a board story by cutting out the animals Bobo sees and ask three children if Bobo is small or tall compared to each animal. For example, Bobo is on top of a cat, but when the elephant comes he now seems small. Children would first guess tall and then small. The book comes with a height chart. If it is missing in your library copy, create your own and then measure each student. You might want to purchase inexpensive measuring tapes or charts or make your own for children to color and take home as their craft.

Alda, Arlene. 2005. *The Book of ZZZs*. Plattsburgh, NY: Tundra.

Summary:

The book shows different animals and people sleeping.

Activity:

For this quiet story, children act out the different ways people sleep. They can stand up for "Some stand up. . . ." And they can stretch their arms for "others s-t-r-e-t-c-h out." Other actions will be more difficult, such as sleeping on rocks.

Allen, Jonathan. 2005. "*I'm Not Cute!*" New York: Hyperion.

Summary:

An owl wants to be scary, but everyone tells him he is cute.

Activity:

The phrase, "I'm not cute!" is repeated several times in the story. When you tell children the name of the book, ask them to repeat the title. Then have them repeat the phrase again each time the owl says it in the story. Signal them with a hand gesture or say, "And what did the owl say?"

———. 2008. *The Little Rabbit Who Liked to Say Moo*. New York: Boxer.

Summary:

A rabbit gets other animals to make animal sounds other than their own.

Activity:

Children will make the animal sounds. For example, when the text reads, "Little Rabbit and Calf made the biggest 'baaa' they could," the next page shows the enlarged sound, "BAAA" in a bubble. Point to children, indicating when they should make this sound. Children can also be the characters in the book, such as the calf, rabbit, sheep, pig, donkey, and duck. The final sound is "WOOF!" even though no dog is shown.

Alvarez, Julia. 2005. *A Gift of Gracias.* **New York: Alfred A. Knopf. Illus., Beatriz Vidal.**

Summary:

A failing farm is rejuvenated with oranges as a gift from Our Lady of Altagracia.

Activity:

Most of the story describes a message and a tradition rather than relates a series of actions conducive to participation. However, children can pretend to plant orange seeds. Then, roll some oranges out to the children as they magically and quickly grow on the farm in the story. Children can each keep an orange.

Archer, Peggy. 2005. *Turkey Surprise.* **New York: Dial. Illus., Thor Wickstrom.**

Summary:

Two pilgrims try to find the hiding turkey to eat for dinner.

Activity:

Use this as a fun Thanksgiving story if you can ignore the stereotypical Pilgrim pictures. The turkey keeps finding new hiding places when the Pilgrim boys get closer. Tell this one as a story, and jump high or onto a chair when the turkey climbs a tree to hide. Crouch down when the turkey tries to hide in a gopher hole. Hold your nose and make underwater sounds or puff your cheeks when the turkey hides underwater. Hide behind a table and chair when the Pilgrim boy shows the turkey a pile of wood to hide behind so the boys can bring home a pumpkin for pie instead. Children can act out the motions with you. You can also turn this into a board story by creating a pond, hole, tree, and pile of wood for your picture of a turkey to hide behind. The back of the book shows the scene with the location of all the places the turkey hides (even in the Pilgrim brothers' house).

Arnosky, Jim. 2008. *Gobble It Up! A Fun Song about Eating.* **New York: Scholastic.**

Summary:

The story, accompanied by a song, tells you what you would eat if you were different animals.

Activity:

The story is full of repetition and music. Play the music from the accompanying CD, make up your own melody, or just read the text. If the song is played several times, children may be able to sing along.

Ashman, Linda. 2005. *To the Beach.* **New York: Harcourt. Illus., Nadine Bernard Westcott.**

Summary:

A family tries to get to the beach, but they keep returning home for things they forgot.

Activity:

This is a perfect story for a flannel board or finding game. Provide pictures of every object that the family forgets at home: a kite, umbrella, cooler, tote, ducky pail, dog, boat, fishing gear, and a ball and net. Place the pictures in a pile, and put the appropriate one on the board each time the family has to drive home for an item they forgot. A another fun activity is to tape the pictures around the room. When the family forgets something, ask different students to find the picture of the object and bring it back to the front of the room. Have a picture of a car or draw one on a board or cardboard, and have the children tape the object into the car.

————. 2008. *Stella, Unleashed: Notes from the Doghouse.* **New York: Sterling. Illus., Paul Meisel.**

Summary:

The book contains poems about dogs.

Activity:

Write the names of all the poems on a board or poster board. Draw little pictures beside them. Ask the children to select which poems they want you to read, because it would take too long to read them all. You can use this technique for any poetry book. Children won't remember all the names you read, so have them take turns pointing to the poems they want you to read.

Aston, Dianna Hutts. 2007. *A Seed Is Sleepy.* San Francisco: Chronicle. Illus., Sylvia Long.

Summary:

Words describe seeds followed by more factual notes.

Activity:

Ask the children what they think each phrase means and then follow with the factual descriptions given in the text. For example, a more poetic phrase might read, "A seed is fruitful." Ask the children what they think this means. Chances are they will say that a seed produces fruit. The text then elaborates. "Ninety percent of the plants on Earth are flowering plants. Flowering plants produce fruits. . . ."

Atwell, Debby. 2005. *The Warthog's Tail.* Boston: Houghton Mifflin.

Summary:

A young witch learns to use persuasion rather than magic.

Activity:

The twist in this story is that the girl's witch mother dresses as an old man to teach her daughter the lesson that she does not always need a spell, but that persuasion can work. In the story the young witch is trying to get a warthog to move from the gate so that she can get into her home and get ready for

Halloween. Libraries and schools where Halloween and witches are not a part of the lessons will probably want to avoid this book. To get rid of the warthog, the girl wants a match to burn a stick so the stick will hit the dog and the dog will bite the warthog. However, none of this happens until the old man helps. Turn this into a board story, and every time the dog or stick or warthog is mentioned place its image on the board or point to the image on the board.

Avi. 2003. *Silent Movie*. New York: Atheneum. Illus., C.B. Mordan.

Summary:

A young immigrant boy finds himself an actor in silent movies.

Activity:

Simply show the pictures of the story, and have the children describe what is happening in this silent movie. You could also read the sparse text, show the pictures, and have the children act them out. You could even follow up with a story of your own for the children to act out as they pretend they are in a silent movie. Provide props.

Aylesworth, Jim. 2007. *Little Bitty Mousie*. New York: Walker. Illus., Michael Hague.

Summary:

In this alphabet book, Mousie finds different items in a home.

Activity:

There are several activities for this book. Find a picture of each object for each letter of the alphabet. Tape the pictures around the room, and have children take turns finding them as you read the story. You could instead use these objects in a bingo card. You would need pictures of an apple, butter, carrot, dish, eggshell, fish, garbage, letters "happy" on a cake, icing, jelly, ketchup, lipstick, mirror, napkin, orange, pepper, quarter, rose, slipper, truck, umbrella, vacuum, wrapper, sugar "X" on a bun, yarn, and the Zzzzz snoring of a cat. The rhyme that appears on every other turned page could be repeated: "Tiptip tippy Went her little mousie toes. Sniff-sniff sniffy sniffy Went her little mousie nose."

———. 2009. *Our Abe Lincoln*. New York: Scholastic. Illus., Barbara McClintock.

Summary:

An old campaign song is the basis for this original rhyming story about Abe Lincoln.

Activity:

Sing the song to the children using your own melody or the melody of the original campaign song if you can locate it. There are many lines that repeat, so point to children when they would repeat a line. For example, "Smart Abe Lincoln read late by the firelight/Late by the firelight/Late by the firelight/ Smart Abe Lincoln read late by the firelight/Many dark nights ago."

Bachelet, Gilles. 2006. *My Cat, the Silliest Cat in the World*. New York: Abrams.
Summary:
> A man describes his cat, which is actually an elephant.

Activity:
> The book reads as if the narrator is talking about a cat; however, the cat is an elephant. "When my cat's asleep on the couch, I have to warn guests that he's not just another cushion." After phrases such as this, stare at the book quizzically and ask the children, "Is this really a cat? It doesn't look like one. What could it be? An elephant? No way! He says it is a cat." In the end, the owner gets a cat book but cannot find his cat's breed.

Baddiel, Ivor and Sophie Jubb. 2007. *Cock-a-Doodle Quack! Quack!* New York: Random House. Illus., Alie Busby.
Summary:
> A rooster asks farm animals what sound he should make to wake everyone up in the morning and gets a different response from each animal.

Activity:
> Children guess and make the animal sounds with you. First Baby Rooster asks the pigs what to say. Ask the children, "What sound do you think the pigs told the rooster to make?' They will probably answer, "Oink! Oink." So the next morning the rooster yells, "Cock-a-Doodle Oink! Oink!" You could pause before "Oink! Oink!" to see if the children can guess what is next. They should catch on for the other animals, and they will be adding "moo" and "quack" to the end of "Cock-a-Doodle." The rooster is still confused in the end and tries a few other sounds until he finally gets it right. Children should be able to guess what sound he really makes.

Baek, Matthew. 2008. *Be Gentle with the Dog, Dear!* New York: Dial.
Summary:
> A baby is not always so gentle with the family dog.

Activity:
> Act out the story by doing the things to a stuffed dog that the baby in the story does. Ask the children if these things are nice to do to the dog. Alternatively, have children bring a stuffed animal and have them copy the actions with their animals. Be sure to warn them that these are not nice things to do. Some of the things the baby does to the dog is pull his tail, squeeze him, and tackle him.

Bang, Molly. 2004. *My Light.* **New York: Blue Sky.**

Summary:

The story describes how the sun aides the planet.

Activity:

Instead of showing the page that mentions and includes a picture of the sun, continue to ask the children who the "my" in the story might be. This would be an interesting book to accompany a science or inference lesson.

Banks, Kate. 2005. *The Great Blue House.* **New York: Farrar, Straus and Giroux. Illus., Georg Hallensleben.**

Summary:

The book describes the noises in a house until a family arrives.

Activity:

This is a quiet book, but the children can make the sounds of the empty house. Crickets sing, clothes billow, children giggle, a pot bubbles, water gurgles, lights blink (children can scrunch and open their hands for this), a faucet drips, a cupboard swings, a mouse nibbles, etc. You can also just show the pictures and ask the children what sounds they think are occurring in the empty house.

Barkow, Henriette. 2004. *If Elephants Wore Pants. . . .* **New York: Sterling. Illus., Richard Johnson.**

Summary:

A boy can't sleep, so, instead of counting sheep, he counts elephants.

Activity:

Really he does not count the elephants but sees them wearing different pants in different patterns. Create pairs of pants in all the patterns mentioned in the story. Give each child one of these patterns or colors. When that pattern is mentioned in the story, the child who has it holds it up. Alternatively, place an elephant picture on a board at the front of the room. Children take turns bringing their pants pattern to place on the elephant picture as they are mentioned in the story. A final activity is to give each child his or her own elephant picture or pictures either to decorate according to the patterns mentioned in the story or to place their pants pictures on when the time comes in the story. The patterns or colors you will need for the elephant pants are pink, brown velvet, rainbow, pear green, stars, sunflower, sparkling red, and bright golden. Of course, you can adapt the pictures as necessary.

Barrett, Judi. 2007. *Never Take a Shark to the Dentist (And Other Things Not to Do).* **New York: Atheneum. Illus., John Nickle.**

Summary:

Illustrations help show why you should never allow animals to do such things as take a shark to the dentist.

Activity:

Change the statements to questions. Instead of, "Never sit next to a porcupine on the subway," ask, "Why shouldn't you sit next to a porcupine on the subway?" Children will see the porcupine's needles in the illustration and respond appropriately. Other things not to do are to shop with a centipede, take an ant to a picnic, bring a giraffe to the movies, and more. End by adding your own questions or by asking for suggestions from the children.

Barretta, Gene. 2006. *Now & Ben: The Modern Inventions of Benjamin Franklin.* New York: Henry Holt.

Summary:

The author compares modern conveniences with Benjamin Franklin's inventions.

Activity:

Make two signs to place on sticks to hold up. One will say "Now," and one will say "Ben" (or one could have a picture of a modern invention and the other a picture of Ben Franklin). Hold up the "Now" when you read the now section of the story, and hold up "Ben" when you read the parts about Franklin's inventions. You could also make one for each child and ask him or her to hold up the appropriate one as you read. Then when you are finished, have a list of other inventions that were Ben Franklin's, or change it to a past and present inventions exercise.

Barroux, Stephane. 2003. *Where's Mary's Hat?* New York: Viking.

Summary:

Mary the cow lost her hat and asks other creatures if they have seen it.

Activity:

Make this a board story by having a cow, stork, fish, elephant, beaver, chicken, pig, kangaroo, monkey, rabbit, toucan, penguin, bear, and, of course, a hat. Keep putting the animals' pictures on the board as Mary asks a different animal if he or she has seen her hat. In the end have a hat that looks like a kite to fly around the room over the children's hands. This can be done simply by tying a paper hat to a string. In the end children can make their own paper hat kites.

Bartoletti, Susan. 2005. *Nobody's Diggier Than a Dog.* New York: Hyperion. Illus., Beppe Giacobbe

Summary:

This book describes all the actions in which a dog participates.

Activity:

This is an excellent story for movement. Have children stand up and start acting like dogs. You could even provide dog ears or tails for them made out of construction paper or material to help them get into the game. The text of the story follows this pattern, "Nobody's diggier than a dog —a bury-the-bone dog, a shake-a-paw dog." For each page the word "diggier" is replaced with another doggy word followed by a description. So, for "diggier," children can pretend to dig on the ground or on their legs. For "piggier," pretend to stick their head down in water (the toilet) and shake their heads. For "mightier," stand tall. For "flightier," pretend to shiver. For "naggier," lick. For "waggier," shake their behinds to wag their tails. For "crazier," spin in circles. For "lazier," hold their hands to their heads to sleep. For "sorrier," turn their heads with guilt. For "starrier," stick their noses in the air. For "scratchier," scratch. For "catchier," pretend to catch a ball, or you can throw some out to them. For "happier," jump up and down. For "yappier," bark or whimper. For "muddier," roll on the ground. For "buddier," pound their chests with pride. For "leggier," lift their legs. For "beggier," pretend to beg by sticking out their hands or scratching. For "hairier," touch their heads. For "scarier," growl. For "puddlier," shake off their water. For "cuddlier," wrap their arms around themselves.

Base, Graeme. 2004. *Jungle Drums.* New York: Harry N. Abrams.

Summary:

A small warthog makes a wish that, to the dismay of the other animals in the jungle, changes them.

Activity:

One thing you can do is to have children pretend to play the drums when the warthog does in order to make his wish. However, this only occurs twice in the story. It is reminiscent of Dr. Seuss's book *The Sneeches.* Whereas the Sneeches change from star-bellied to plain, in this case the animals change from brightly colored and striped to plain and vice versa. So, as with the Sneeches, another activity is to give half the children a colorful necklace or hat to wear and give the other half something plain. Then, children switch objects after the warthog makes his switch. In the end, the author surprises you by saying that the animals did not all completely change. You have to carefully examine the pictures to find the small differences that have changed among all the animals. This part works best with smaller groups, but you can try some comparisons with a larger group.

Bateman, Teresa. 2004. *April Foolishness.* Morton Grove, IL: Albert Whitman. Illus., Nadine Bernard Westcott.

Summary:

Grandpa's grandkids try to fool him on April Fool's Day, but Grandma has the last laugh.

Activity:

Children may not always pick up on the fact that Grandpa is ignoring the children, knowing that it is April Fool's Day. Therefore, ask questions throughout the story, such as, "What should Grandpa do?" or "Do you think the chickens really got out?" or "Are the grandkids telling the truth?" or "What could the children be up to?" See if they guess it is an April Fool's joke because of the title. Follow with questions about any tricks the children may have played on April Fool's Day. They may likely just make some up.

————. 2008. *The Frog with the Big Mouth.* Morton Grove, IL: Albert Whitman & Co. Illus., Will Terry.

Summary:

A frog brags about being able to catch flies until he is almost caught.

Activity:

Have a frog puppet and snap his mouth at children when he approaches each animal in the story to ask who they are and what they eat. Because the animals are all unusual rainforest animals, (descriptions are provided in the back of the book), children will most likely not know what the animals eat. You can have children repeat the phrase, "Don't you wish you were me?" which is what the frog says after he finds out what each animal eats.

Bates, Ivan. 2006. *Five Little Ducks.* New York: Orchard.

Summary:

The book illustrates the words to the song "Five Little Ducks."

Activity:

Sing the song with the children, or play a version of it, such as one by Raffi, as you turn the pages. Have the children color and wear duck finger puppets, and take them off as the story continues and the ducks disappear. You can also do the same with bag puppets, but have five children hold the puppets and have one sit down each time a duck disappears. You can also do the same with pictures on a board.

Beaumont, Karen. 2005. *I Ain't Gonna Paint No More.* Orlando: Harcourt. Illus., David Catrow.

Summary:

A mother is upset that her son painted the floor, but he can't stop painting so he paints his body parts. The story is sung to the tune of "It Ain't Gonna Rain No More."

Activity:

First, teach the children the tune of the song "It Ain't Gonna Rain No More," and have them repeat the refrain, "I ain't gonna paint no more." While telling/singing the story, paint your own body parts, or draw on them with markers. Make sure to wear a long T-shirt you do not care about. You'll be "painting" your head, neck, chest, arm, hand, back, leg, and feet. Give the children magic or invisible paintbrushes, and they can pretend to paint these body parts as well. End with the song "Head, Shoulders, Knees and Toes" for even more music.

Bedford, Annie North (retold). 2006. *Frosty the Snowman*. A Backpack Book. New York: Dorling Kindersley. Illus., Corinne Malvern.

Summary:

The 1950s song "Frosty the Snowman" comes to life in this retro version.

Activity:

Have the song playing in the background as you tell this story. Dress in white, and pretend to be Frosty as you read. You can also have the children build a snowman by giving them each a piece to add to the snowman. The snowman will simply be several pieces of flat paper, poster board, or cardboard. Children can have his eyes, nose, buttons, scarf, mouth, hat, and pipe (if the connection to smoking is allowed).

Bee, William. 2005. *Whatever*. Cambridge, MA: Candlewick.

Summary:

Billy answers "whatever" whenever his dad tries to entertain him.

Activity:

Children can simply repeat the word "whatever" whenever it is time to reply. The dad continues to try to impress his son. "Show him something very small and he'll say "whatever." "Play him a tune on the world's curliest trumpet . . . and he'll say . . . 'whatever.' " In the end the dad shows him a hungry tiger that eats the child. When the boy tells the dad he is still inside the tiger, the dad replies, "whatever." For this reason, you may want to consider your audience when selecting this book.

Belle, Jennifer. 2005. *Animal Stackers*. New York: Hyperion. Illus., David McPhail.

Summary:

The book contains animal acrostic poems.

Activity:

Read some of the acrostic poems, and then put pictures of different animals on the board. Write out the letters of the animal's names vertically. Ask the children to help you come up with words or sentences for these animals. You can use the pictures in the book, and see if the children give responses different from the author's. Even the youngest can give it a try with some help.

"Fairy-tale prince. *Ribbit!* Only the lily pad gets annoyed" is just one example.

Bell-Rehwoldt, Sheri. 2007. *You Think It's Easy Being the Tooth Fairy?* San Francisco: Chronicle. Illus., David Slonin.

Summary:

A tooth fairy dispels myths about herself and her profession.

Activity:

Turn the statements into questions, and ask the children if they think the things mentioned are true about tooth fairies. For example, begin with, "Do you think tooth fairies wear pink flouncing skirts?" Then follow and read the text either by itself or with the assistance of a fairy doll or puppet in your other hand. The text would then read, "Let's get one thing straight, okay? I NEVER wear pink flouncing skirts or twinkling glass slippers!"

Berry, Lynne. 2005. *Duck Skates.* New York: Henry Holt. Illus., Hiroe Nakata.

Summary:

The fast-paced story describes what five ducks do.

Activity:

You only need to count to five for this story. Therefore, make or use five duck finger puppets for your hand. If you make them, have a set for each child. Coloring these can be the craft, and you can send the children home with a duck rhyme and the name of this story. Alternatively, make five ducks for a board story or use five rubber ducks. Toward the beginning of the story, it reads, "Two ducks run for the bright new boots, Race for the snow in their new snowsuits. The last three follow. All five tromp down to the pond for a duck-skate romp." So, first raise up two fingers, finger puppets, pictures on the board, or rubber ducks. Next put up five and then three. When the action becomes fast, it gets frantic to switch, especially if you are knocking ducks off and onto the table or board.

Bertrand, Diane Gonzales. 2003. *The Empanadas That Abuela Made.* Houston, TX: Piñata. Illus., Alex Pardo DeLange.

Summary:

A cumulative tale describes what happens while Abuela makes empanadas for the family.

Activity:

Turn this into a board story by continuously adding or having children add the images to make the empanada. Alternately, give pieces in an envelope to the children so they can create their own empanada at their seats. You would need abuela, happy faces, milk, a dog, grandchildren, a rolling pin, pumpkin, and dough.

Best, Cari. 2005. *Are You Going to Be Good?* New York: Farrar, Straus and Giroux. Illus., G. Brian Karas.

Summary:

A boy goes to his first big party, which is for his aunt, and everyone warns him to be good until his aunt appreciates his energy.

Activity:

Whenever Robert does something bad, before you respond with, "Don't do that," as stated in the book, ask the children if he should have done what he did. For example, "There is a lot of food to choose from. And Robert is very hungry. He tastes some things. And puts them back." You could say to the children, "Should Robert do that? Should you take food and put it back?" Wait for a response and say, "You are right. And his dad says, 'Don't do that.'" The children can also respond with the repeated phrase. In the end, have children dance crazily like Robert who is joined by his aunt.

Billingsley, Franny. 2008. *Big Bad Bunny.* New York: Atheneum. Illus., G. Brian Karas.

Summary:

A mouse pretends to be a big bad bunny.

Activity:

One side of each double-page spread shows the mouse dressed as the Big Bad Bunny. The opposite page shows a peaceful baby mouse family. Have a bunny puppet on your right hand, and make him look bad as you tell the story and read his part.

Bloch, Serge. 2008. *Butterflies in My Stomach and Other School Hazards.* New York: Sterling.

Summary:

The book illustrates figures of speech, such as, "in a pickle."

Activity:

Ask older children what the meaning of each figure of speech is. The book includes "zip his lip," "laughing his head off," "ants in his pants," "top banana," and much more. Find a book or a Web site of idioms to share more.

Bluemle, Elizabeth. 2006. *My Father the Dog.* Cambridge, MA: Candlewick. Illus., Randy Cecil.

Summary:

A child describes why her father might actually be a dog.

Activity:

This is a cute story, but if you don't want to say "toots" or "pit stop" you may need to avoid it. Simply ask children if they think the actions mentioned mean the dad is a dog. Read a statement from the book, such as, "He fetches the newspaper every morning." Then ask the kids, "Does this mean her dad is a dog?" Wait for responses. Read, "My father can lie around for hours." Then ask, "Does this mean he is a dog?" You may get some surprising responses.

Boswell, Addie. 2008. *The Rain Stomper*. New York: Marshall Cavendish. Illus., Eric Velasquez.

Summary:
A girl is worried that the rain will ruin the parade day.

Activity:
Children repeat all the sounds of stomping in the rain after you. There are many sounds to repeat, such as, "Slap clatter clatter slap! . . . Boom walla Boom Boom!" Say each sound first, and have the children repeat after you. Children can also pretend to stomp in the rain.

Bottner, Barbara and Gerald Kruglik. 2004. *Wallace's Lists*. New York: Harper-Collins. Illus., Olof Landström.

Summary:
Wallace cannot do anything without creating a list until his neighbor helps him become a little more adventurous.

Activity:
Give each child some notebook paper and a crayon and have them pretend to write a list as Wallace writes a list at different times in the story about what he will do that day, places with funny names, accidents that happened to him, and more. You can model this on a board as well.

Bowen, Anne. 2006. *What Do Teachers Do (after YOU Leave School)?* New York: Carolrhoda.

Summary:
The book describes what teachers do to have fun when all the kids are gone from school.

Activity:
A number of activities are suitable for this book. The story has a rhythm. For example, the text goes, "They play games of basketball down in the gym—high-fiving, slam-dunking it, over the rim." Have the children clap their hands to the beat as you read. You could also have the children raise their hands like they are in class, or stand up and sit down, every time a teacher's name is called. A final activity is to make bingo cards with pictures of objects that represent the activities the teachers do, and play bingo. The children would mark the objects on the cards when the activities are mentioned. Objects could be jeans, a slide, skates, basketball, pizza or other snack, red

toenails, Scrabble, socks, blocks, beakers, soup, bubbles, goggles, and clock. The bingo card can be small to accommodate all these words, or you can use other pictures represented in the text.

————. 2008. *I Know an Old Teacher.* **New York: Carolrhoda. Illus., Stephen Gammell.**

Summary:

Similar to the versions of *The Old Lady Who Swallowed a Fly*, in this story a teacher brings class pets home for the long weekend by swallowing them.

Activity:

Draw a teacher on two poster boards taped together with a slit for the mouth. You or the children slide pictures of the creatures inside the mouth of the old teacher. The creatures you need are a flea, spider, fish, rat, snake, and lizard. You may even have a picture of a child. When the teacher says she would never swallow a child, pull the child from the teacher's mouth. Alternatively, wear an apron that you can tuck the animals behind.

Brett, Jan. 2008. *Gingerbread Friends.* New York: G.P. Putnam's Sons.

Summary:

A Gingerbread Baby is lonely, so he goes into town to seek some friends.

Activity:

When the Gingerbread Baby seeks friends, he repeats a rhyme that has the same two last lines. Children can repeat this with you. The words go, "I'm the Gingerbread Baby, Peppy as can be, I'll be friends with you, If you'll be friends with me." You can keep the same two first lines the same each time rather than change them, or just have the children recite the last two lines. You might also give each child a real cookie or a picture of a different cookie you have created from construction paper, and have your Gingerbread Baby approach each child to find out if he or she will be a friend. In the end, the Gingerbread Baby gets scared away by a mouse.

Bright, Paul. 2008. *Fidgety Fish and Friends.* Wilton, CT: Tiger Tales. Illus., Ruth Galloway.

Summary:

Short poems represent different fish.

Activity:

Here are two activities for this book. One is to have children act out the motions of the fish when described. Some poems do not provide opportunities for much movement, but some do. For example, the poem "Jiggly Jellyfish" goes, "We wibble and we wobble, Like jelly in a dish. We bounce and bop and bobble, We're the jiggly jellyfish!" Kids can jiggle and wiggle.

Another activity is to hang pictures of each fish on the wall. When you read the poems the children take turns locating the correct sea creature on the wall. The water creatures you need are any fish, a shark, angelfish, crab, jelly-fish, starfish, snail, sea horse, puffer fish, and turtle.

Browne, Anthony. 2003. *The Shape Game*. New York: Farrar, Straus Giroux.
Summary:
A family visits an art museum where they discover the secrets to actual paintings.
Activity:
In the story, the parents try to get their children to think about the meaning of art. Augustus Egg's "Past and Present No. 1" has details of all the clues to show why the painting is about a man who has read a letter written to his wife by another man. Although younger children will not go into much detail, ask the children in your group what they think each painting means. See if they can determine what is different between each of the two deceptively similar women in the painting "The Chrolmondeley Ladies." Follow with pictures of paintings from other books for children to practice their interpretations. Then end with students creating their own artwork and frames and asking other students to determine the meanings.

Bruchac, Joseph and James Bruchac. 2001. *How Chipmunk Got His Stripes*. New York: Dial. Illus., Jose Aruego and Ariane Dewey.
Summary:
The story tells how the chipmunk got his stripes.
Activity:
This is a Native American retelling. When I read this story, I change my voice to a gruff voice for the bear and a meek voice for the chipmunk. This story is better suited for storytelling without reading from the book. The chipmunk once was a squirrel until he upset the bear and the bear's claws created the stripes on his back. There are several phrases throughout the story that chil-dren can repeat to make it more interactive, such as, "The sun will not come up." Ask the children to repeat these phrases again and again.

———. 2004. *Raccoon's Last Race: A Traditional Abenaki Story*. New York: Dial. Illus., Jose Aruego and Ariane Dewey.
Summary:
The story tells how the raccoon came to get his looks, size, and lack of speed.
Activity:
The raccoon gloats about his speed until a big rock flattens him. Use this as a board story, displaying pictures of a raccoon, rock, bear, fox, rabbit, and ant. On the board, show how the raccoon outruns the three animals and is not

helped by them in the end, how the rock flattens him, and how the aunts try to help him until he refuses their help and refuses to say thank you, which ends up being his demise.

Bruel, Nick. 2005. *Bad Kitty*. New Milford, CT: Roaring Brook.

Summary:

A family runs out of food so a kitty decides to be bad.

Activity:

This is an alphabet book. First the story presents foods Kitty doesn't like, something for every letter of the alphabet. Then, in turn, it presents the ways Kitty is good for every letter, then the good food Kitty gets for every letter, and then all the good things Kitty does for every letter. Because it would be too complicated to replicate or have props or pictures for all 104 items and things Kitty does, simply have a large cat puppet and make it emulate Kitty's expressions. Open its mouth for joy, close its mouth and look down for disgust, etc. Walk Kitty around the room with you as he talks about what he does and gets to eat to each of the children. Skip some of the letters if you think the activity will take too long for your group. You might also ask children what letter comes next and what food they think Kitty will get or what they think he will do next that starts with that letter; or, after the story is over, go through the alphabet asking what else Kitty could eat or do good or bad that starts with each letter of the alphabet.

Bryan, Sean. 2008. *The Juggling Pug*. New York: Arcade. Illus., Tom Murphy.

Summary:

A juggling pug annoys his family.

Activity:

Be aware that the word "poop" is mentioned twice. Use your juggling skills (or pretend to have them) and juggle while telling the story, or give children two soft balls or crumpled-up wads of paper to juggle as you tell the story. If you need to read the book, have a volunteer or child hold the book for you, or simply have a child or volunteer hold the book. You could even ask a parent or guardian to help.

Bunting, Eve. 2007. *Emma's Turtle*. Honesdale, PA: Boyds Mills. Illus., Marsha Winborn.

Summary:

A turtle gets away from his owner and finds adventure.

Activity:

Attach a toy turtle to a pole, stick, broom, or string and move it around as you tell the story, pulling it back when it is frightened. Alternately, use a turtle puppet as your prop.

Butler, John. 2006. *Ten in the Meadow.* **Atlanta: Peachtree.**

Summary:

Animals go round and round as they find one another hiding in a game of hide-and-seek.

Activity:

Play a game of Ring a Round the Rosie. Give each child a nametag with the name of one of the animals or a picture of one of the animals from the story. Have children hold hands in a circle. When an animal is mentioned in the story, the child with the corresponding nametag will come to the center of the circle. You could even start another ring in the center, which could change to the outer circle when it gets too large. You may have to add more than one child with the same animal so that everyone can participate. The rhyme goes, "Round and round the bluebells, The friends join in the race. Looking here . . . looking there . . . They've found a hiding place! 'Found you, Badger!' 'Found you, Fox!'" Alternatively, put pictures of the animals on the walls for children to find in your version of hide-and-seek. Count how many different animals you have in the end to equal ten. The animals for which you need pictures or nametags are bear, rabbit, porcupine, mole, badger, fox, squirrel, raccoon, beaver, and mouse.

Butler, M. Christina. 2004. *One Snowy Night.* **Intercourse, PA: Good Books. Illus., Tina Macnaughton.**

Summary:

Little Hedgehog receives the gift of a hat that is soon passed as a present from one animal to another.

Activity:

Bring a hat. Children pass the hat from one child to another after rewrapping it each time as the animals in the story each receive and then pass on the hat as a gift. The children will pretend to be a hedgehog, rabbit, badger, fox, and small hedgehog. It turns out to be Little Hedgehog that needs the hat's warmth most of all. You can add animals to the story to extend it for larger groups.

———. 2006. *One Winter's Day.* **Intercourse, PA: Good Books. Illus., Tina Macnaughton.**

Summary:

Little Hedgehog is blown away on a cold windy day and gives away his clothing to help others keep warm.

Activity:

Don a hat, scarf, and mittens. As you tell the, take the items off and give them to the children as the children pretend to be the mice, otter, and deer in the story. In the end, when the animals return the warm items to build a house for Little Hedgehog, have the children return the items to the front of the room. Children will like the feel of the velvety scarf, mittens, and hat.

Buzzeo, Toni. 2006. *Our Librarian Won't Tell Us Anything!* **Fort Atkinson, WI: Upstart. Illus., Sachiko Yoshikawa.**

Summary:

A librarian purposely holds back information so that children learn how to use the library themselves.

Activity:

Use this book when teaching children how to search for information. Read part of the book, and then stop to show the children how to use a library finding aide, such as the online catalog.

Cabrera, Jane. 2005. *If You're Happy and You Know It.* **New York: Holiday House.**

Summary:

Animals illustrate this classic song.

Activity:

Sing along! Have the children sing and act along. Some movements will be basic, such as, "If you're happy and you know it, CLAP your hands." Other movements will relate more to animals, such as, "If you're happy and you know it, ROAR out loud." Follow with another version of the song.

Calmenson, Stephanie. 2008. *Late for School!* **New York: Carolrhoda. Illus., Sachiko Yoshikawa.**

Summary:

A teacher may have to break his rule about never being late for school.

Activity:

Because the action in the book is rushed as the teacher tries different methods of transportation to get to school, just have the students move in place as if they were rushing to school. An example of the fast-paced story is, "I missed the train. I won't make a fuss. Down the street, I can catch the . . . bus!" In this case the bus is too crowded, and the teacher gets into an animal rescue van. With school tardiness counting for so much, the ending—the teacher changes his rule to, "Please try your best to be on time for school!"—might not be a message you want to share.

Campbell Kids Alphabet Soup. 2004. New York: Harry N. Abrams.

Summary:

Artwork from Campbell's Soup advertisements during the first half of the twentieth century illustrate the alphabet.

Activity:

Read the short paragraphs for each letter, such as, "W is for window and words we write, And water and weights, a wedding in white." Next, point out the Campbell's Soup children's pictures and ask the children to tell you what words that start with W are represented in each picture. If the pictures are too small for them to see, just ask them about the larger pictures. Alternatively, present this as a game. For older children, name each letter and ask them to write down or to name for you all the words they can think of that start with that letter. If their words are on the pages, they get points.

Carle, Eric. 2005. *10 Little Rubber Ducks.* New York: HarperCollins.

Summary:

Eric Carle based this book on the 1992 incidence of a shipment of ducks falling overboard from a ship. The story describes where ten ducks landed.

Activity:

Purchase at least ten rubber ducks. Sometimes the Cost Plus World Market store or baby stores have them. They can always be used for other activities. (You could also make ducks out of construction paper for children to have a memento and to save money.) A number of activities work well with this story. One is to place the ducks around the room. Give each child a number from one to ten, as in the book, and when that number is read, the child or children with that number has to pick up the ducks until they find the one with the correct number. You can also play this as a memory or matching game in which children find the ducks with their number. The children can work in pairs, and they have to sit down until it is their turn again to find the matching duck. Another activity is to have ten ducks that are used only by the librarian or teacher. After reading, "The 1st little rubber duck drifts west. A dolphin jumps over it," throw a rubber duck in the direction of west, and jump or throw a dolphin toy over it. After reading, "The 6th little rubber duck drifts to the right. A turtle glides past it," throw a duck to the right. You might want to have enough ducks for all the children to be able to grab one; instruct them to pick up only one duck. On the title page, there are 10 white ducks with numbers. When you are collecting ducks, children can return them to their numbered duck on this page. End with a tub or pool of water for children to pick a duck and win a prize that matches the corresponding number that you have written on the bottom of each duck. You might have small prizes in brown bags with that number so children would have to find their own. This is good practice for very young children to learn numbers. You might also tell the children about the true story on which the book was based.

Carter, David A. 2007. *Whooo? Whoo?* **New York: Simon & Schuster.**
Summary:
Cut-out pieces combine to form a different animal on each page.
Activity:
It took a second reading to realize that the cut-out shapes on each page formed animals. The book starts out with a question mark and some triangles, ovals, and a cloud shape. Have children guess what these cut-out shapes could make. For example, a lamb is shown that can be created by the pieces cut out on the following page. Demonstrate one example, and have the children guess the following pictures. This is a good activity for inference as well. You can follow with additional shapes you create, or give children shapes to piece together like a puzzle on their own. This could be done individually or as a board story.

Chin, Oliver. 2005. *The Adventures of Wonder Baby from A to Z.* **San Francisco: Immedium. Illus., Joe Chiodo.**
Summary:
This animal alphabet book contains words beginning with the same letters as the animals it describes.
Activity:
Children can identify the animals in this book. Begin the statements, but let the children finish them. For example, say, "Bites like a . . . " and show them the picture. They should say, "beaver," even though the picture looks like an exaggerated abstract beaver.

Christelow, Eileen. 2007. *Five Little Monkeys Go Shopping.* **New York: Clarion.**
Summary:
The five little monkeys return in this new book. They get lost and find new friends while shopping.
Activity:
This story can help children learn to add and subtract. For preschool children, have seven monkey pictures or finger puppets. The children can help count with you as monkeys wander off or if monkey friends join the family. Use as a board story or with finger puppets. Alternatively, have children stand in front of each other, pretend to be monkeys, and stand up and sit down as monkeys are added or subtracted. The message about children wandering off in the store will hopefully be ignored by children.

Church, Caroline Jayne. 2007. *Digby Takes Charge.* **New York: Margaret K. McElderry.**
Summary:
Digby the sheep dog is having no luck herding the sheep until he uses the magic word.

Activity:

Children pretend to be the sheep. You or another child can be Digby and try to round them up. Encourage the children to respond as the sheep do at different points in the story by shrugging and wandering, smiling and laughing.

————. 2008. *Ping Pong Pig.* **New York: Holiday House.**

Summary:

A pig wants to fly, so his friends make him a trampoline.

Activity:

Every time the pig bounces or tries to fly in the story, the children jump up and down.

Clarke, Jane. 2007. *Stuck in the Mud.* New York: Walker. Illus., Garry Parsons.

Summary:

A chick is stuck in the mud, and all the farm aimals help get it out.

Activity:

This is like the traditional stories of the gigantic turnip or enormous potato and other similar stories where a vegetable is too big to lift and other people and animals need to be called in to get it out. I tell these stories without the book in a storytelling format with assistance from the children. For this story, put a little chick picture or stuffed animal on top of a brown piece of cardboard or paper cut to look like mud. You be the rooster and try to get it out. Next ask the children to grab onto you or to the mud and help push and pull. The words "pushed" and "pulled" are repeated in the story, so, if you do not tell the story word for word, you can at least repeat these words. Next a cat, hen, dog, sheep, horse, and farmer try to help. Add more animals so that all children can patrticipate. In the end, the chick jumps out on her own, because she was just having fun in the mud after all.

Cleary, Brian P. 2006. *A Lime, a Mime, a Pool of Slime: More about Nouns.* Minneapolis: Millbrook. Illus., Brian Gable.

Summary:

This book gives examples of nouns.

Activity:

Have the children stand up and sit down every time they hear a noun, which will be at least three times per page. They will be constantly moving. You could try to trip them up in a Simon Says way by throwing some verbs in there. Because preschool children will not really be able to identify a noun, they will just be standing and sitting as you do throughout the story and maybe picking up a little knowledge about nouns.

Clements, Andrew. 2005. *Naptime for Slippers.* **New York: Dutton. Illus., Janie Bynum.**

Summary:

Like most dogs, Slippers is a sometimes bored, sometimes sleepy, and sometimes active dog.

Activity:

Children can pretend to be Slippers, or any dog, and dig, nap, scratch, growl, wag, push their nose, chew, eat, drink, yawn, curl up, close their eyes, sniff, bury, lick, and follow. Children can also bring or use a stuffed animal to replicate the actions in the story.

Colandro, Lucille. 2006. *There Was an Old Lady Who Swallowed a Bell!* **New York: Scholastic. Illus., Jared Lee.**

Summary:

A lady swallowed a bell and other Chirstmas and gift wrapping items to the format of "There Was an Old Lady Who Swallowed a Fly."

Activity:

Sing the song to the tune of "There Was an Old Lady Who Swallowed a Fly." Have all the objects she swallows in an apron pouch or a bag tied to you or hanging from you under a robe to represent what the woman has swallowed. You will need a bell, bows, gifts, sack, sleigh, and reindeer.

Collins, Ross. 2004. *Germs.* **New York: Bloomsbury.**

Summary:

A germ goes to school to learn how to infect others with germs, but a stubborn girl is his first target.

Activity:

Place a picture that you have found or drawn of basic anatomy or even just of a child on the wall or a board. Give each child a blobby creature you have cut out or drawn on colored paper. When the germs attack in the story, the children stick their germs onto the body picture. The germs should be pretaped. When the germs are rejected, the children remove their germs. You can add to the story to give children more opportunities to add and remove their germs. The children should be instructed to remember which germ is theirs and to take turns. Alternatively, the children can put the germs anywhere on a wall.

Cook, Sally. 2004. *Good Night Pillow Fight.* **New York: Joanna Cotler. Illus., Laura Cornell.**

Summary:

Brief words describe things that happen at bedtime.

Activity:

Although the pillow fight is mentioned only at the beginning of the book, children will love to pretend to have a pillow fight. They can make pillows by gluing the ends of two pieces of paper with scalloped edges together after putting some stuffing inside. Instruct them to hit only another child's pillow, not their bodies.

Cottin, Menena. 2008. *The Black Book of Colors.* Berkeley: Groundwood. Illus., Rosana Faría.

Summary:

Colors are described in words and raised images on black paper and are accompanied by a Braille translation.

Activity:

This book works best with small audiences. Children take turns feeling the pictures and guessing what they are and what the colors are before you read the text. For example, they would feel the raised image of feathers. Then you would read the text, which goes, "Thomas says that yellow tastes like mustard, but it is as soft as a baby chick's feathers."

Coward, Fiona. 2005. *Swing High Swing Low: A Book of Opposites.* Cambridge, MA: Barefoot Books. Illus., Giovanni Manna.

Summary:

A family demonstrates the concept of opposites.

Activity:

As for any book on opposites, children can act out the motions. For "Up the ladder, down the stairs," children pretend to climb up and climb down. Many of the opposites will also be predictable. Let children guess the opposite. "Red says stop, green says . . . what?" "Yes, go." "Swing low to the ground, then high in the . . . what?" "Yes, sky."

Cronin, Doreen. 2005. *Wiggle.* New York: Atheneum. Illus., Scott Menchin.

Summary:

A dog wiggles in many ways.

Activity:

Children can stand up and wiggle to each page. "Do you wake up with a wiggle? Do you wiggle out of bed? If you wiggle with your breakfast, it might wind up on your head." For this, touch your head and pretend to look at the food in your hand in disgust. For something like, "Can you wiggle with your toys?" toss a ball. Have the children make gorilla sounds for "When you wiggle with gorillas, do they make a wiggle noise?" Have children move their arms like fins and pucker their lips like fish lips for "Can you wiggle in the water? Wiggle one fin on each side." For the crocodile, move your arms like a croc's mouth. This is a fun one that gets kids moving. Consider making up a tune to turn this into a song.

————. 2008. *Thump, Quack, Moo: A Whacky Adventure.* New York: Atheneum. Illus., Betsy Lewin.

Summary:

The farmer needs help from the animals to get his corn maze ready.

Activity:

Give children a stick or some kind of instrument and have them pound with it when the text uses words like "thump" or "thwack," and have the children make the animal sounds when they are mentioned. You can repeat the sounds more than provided in the text as well. The sounds for the chickens are, "Cluck Whack!"; for the cows, "Moo Thwack!"; and for the ducks, "Thump Quack"—all repeated several times. They will also sometimes join together.

Crowther, Robert. 2005. *Opposites.* Cambridge, MA: Candlewick.

Summary:

A pull-the-tabs and lift-the-flap book of opposites.

Activity:

Simply show the words and pictures. Read the first word, "in," and point out the dog in the doghouse. Pull it out, and instruct the children to answer with the opposite. Their reply should obviously be "out." Continue with up and down, high and low, wet and dry, short and tall, thick and thin, empty and full, dark and light, one and many, new and old, off and on, little and big, open and shut, and above and below.

Crumpacker, Bunny. 2005. *Alexander's Pretending Day.* New York: Dutton. Illus., Dan Andreasen.

Summary:

A boy asks his mother what she would do if he were different creatures and objects.

Activity:

You will be Alexander, and tell the children that you are a mouse, lion, train, monster, river, dinosaur, and book. Ask the children what they would do if you were those creatures or objects. Then read the mother's answer. Change it to, "Well, the mother in this story said she would. . . ."

Curtis, Jamie Lee. 2008. *Big Words for Little People.* New York: Joanna Cotler. Illus., Laura Cornell.

Summary:

This book is about learning big words.

Activity:

Use this book with older children. After reading each word and scenario, ask the children to repeat the word and to explain what it means or give another example. For example, read, "When you are at school and you get into trouble for chewing your gum, then exploding a bubble, and you stay inside when your friends get to play, your CONSEQUENCE is no recess that day." Then follow with, "Can you repeat the word 'consequence'? Now tell me what it means."

Cutbill, Andy. 2008. *The Cow That Laid an Egg.* New York: HarperCollins. Illus., Russell Ayto.

Summary:

A cow is made to feel special by the chickens after they slip an egg under her.

Activity:

Give the children a picture of an egg covered in cow spots to sit on as you tell this story. Ask the children if they think a cow could lay an egg. Ask them what the chicken says after it is hatched? The answer is "Moooooooo!"

Cuyler, Margery. 2002. *Skeleton Hiccups.* New York: Scholastic. Illus., S.D. Schindler.

Summary:

A skeleton cannot get rid of his hiccups.

Activity:

After each remedy to cure the hiccups, children make a hiccupping sound. Alternatively, you make the hiccup sounds and ask the children if they think each cure will work. For example, the text reads, "Hold your breath." Ask the children, "Do you think holding your breath can cure the hiccups?" After they answer, continue to hiccup. You can also use a skeleton decoration from Halloween as your prop. Follow by asking children what other ways they think would cure the skeleton's hiccups.

Daddo, Andrew. 2007. *Goodnight, Me.* New York: Bloomsbury. Illus., Emma Quay.

Summary:

An orangutan says goodnight to all parts of his body to get them all to go to sleep.

Activity:

When body parts are mentioned in the story, ask children to point to those parts on their own bodies. They can also move those body parts. An example from the text is, "You can let go now, hands. We're all going to sleep. No need to hang on any longer, arms." Alternatively, have a picture of an orangutan on the board and ask the children to point out the parts on the picture. In the end, ask children to point out or name other body parts.

Daly, Niki. 2007. *Pretty Salma: A Little Red Riding Hood Story from Africa*. New York: Clarion.

Summary:

In this version of Little Red Riding Hood from Africa it is a dog that tricks the girl and her grandmother.

Activity:

Older children can read the traditional and this version and make comparisons. For younger children, there is a repeated song. It goes, "Oh, Salma, Pretty Salma, Come kiss Granny, your darling old Granny, who loves you soooooooo!" Because it is sung in the text, create a melody for it and have the children sing it when you give them the signal.

Davis, 2008. *Stinky*. New York: The Little Lit Library.

Summary:

A stinky monster loves stinky things and wants a boy out of his swamp so he tries to scare him away.

Activity:

Instruct the children to say the word "stinky" every time a smelly word is mentioned in the story. For example, the monster says, "Kids don't like gross stuff . . . and YOU are the grossest, smelliest toad in the swamp." The book is filled with smelly words.

Day, Alexandra. 2005. *Carl's Sleepy Afternoon*. New York: Farrar, Straus and Giroux.

Summary:

Everyone in town needs Carl the dog's help.

Activity:

Because this book is more about the beautiful pictures than the simple text, focus on the pictures. When Carl is left alone for his nap, he does anything but rest. Ask the children to name the activity in which Carl is participating. They can suggest, "carrying a plate," "delivering medicine," and "rescuing dogs from a fire." Make this a prediction activity by having children guess what might happen based on the picture. This book works best for smaller groups of children.

De Anda, Diane. 2004. *Kikiriki/Quiquiririqui*. Houston: Piñata. Illus., Daniel Lechón.

Summary:

Two children try to save a rooster that the family plans to eat.

Activity:

Have children make the rooster sound of "kikiriki" every time it is mentioned in the story or more frequently for added fun. They can also make the sound every time the rooster is mentioned in the story. Use with *Gracias the Thanksgiving Turkey* by Joe Cowley (Scholastic en Espanol, 1998).

De La Hoya, Oscar with Mark Shulman. 2006. *Super Oscar*. New York: Simon & Schuster. Illus., Lisa Kopelke.

Summary:

Oscar forgets to distribute the list of items needed for the picnic, and so he rushes around to do it all himself.

Activity:

The end note to parents suggests that children get at least 30 minutes of exercise a day. You could have children do the suggested activities, such as jumping rope, after the book is read. For the story, put a clock together with fasteners. While reading, move the clock hands until Oscar is out of time. He starts with 20 minutes to get the picnic together, then has 15, then 10, and then 5. Because the idea of the story is that children should exercise, you could have them stand and pretend to rush around as if they were helping Oscar go shopping and make the food such as guacamole.

De Séve, Randall. 2007. *Toy Boat*. New York: Philomel. Illus., Loren Long.

Summary:

To a boy's disappointment, his toy boat is lost at sea.

Activity:

Find an inexpensive toy boat or create one from construction paper, adding a pencil as the boy creates his own in the story. Move the boat around, or have the children pass it around with each page as you tell the story. You could also turn this into a board story by having a picture of the boy's toy boat and the other boats the toy boat meets along the way.

Deacon, Alexis. 2003. *Beegu*. New York: Farrar, Straus and Giroux.

Summary:

Beegu is an alien looking for his way back home.

Activity:

I use this book when teaching inferences in a college reading class and when teaching about the relationship between the text and illustrations of a book in my children's literature classes. It is a favorite of mine. First read the story without the pictures. Next ask the children or even teenagers who Beegu is. They will not likely guess that he is an alien, because there really is nothing until the end to indicate that he is one. Then read the last part that mentions he is an alien, and re-read the story showing the pictures to illustrate the point you are making. It can be just a guessing game for younger children.

Delaney, Mary. 2006. *Mabel O'Leary Put Peas in Her Ear-y*. New York: Little, Brown. Illus., Kathy Couri.

Summary:

Mabel hides her peas in her ears so that she doesn't have to eat them, but it causes trouble with her hearing.

Activity:

Stick green puffs of cotton balls or yarn or something else soft and green into your ear, but advise children not to do this at home. Then pretend you are Mabel and you cannot hear her mom's instructions. When the mom says something about Mabel's manners, she hears "hammers" and goes wild in the house. Pretend to do the same. Because the belief that Native American clothing should not be a play item, I do not like that the book mentions making a headdress. However, the illustrator wisely left out such pictures.

DePalma, Mary Newell. 2005. *A Grand Old Tree*. New York: Scholastic.

Summary:

A tree's life and death are described.

Activity:

Use this as a board story with a tree on the board. You show the roots, flowers, fruit, seeds, leaves, and animals that rest on the tree. When the tree gets old, show the snow and animals using its remains. Alternately, have children stand up and use their arms to represent the tree as it lives and dies.

Diakite, Penda. 2005. *I Lost My Tooth in Africa*. New York: Scholastic. Illus., Baba Wague Diakite.

Summary:

A girl gets a chicken for losing her tooth during a visit to Africa.

Activity:

Use chicken puppets to represent the chickens in the story. These can be puppets made out of construction paper and attached to a stick. Follow by asking the children about what the tooth fairy leaves for them or other gifts they may receive.

DiPucchio, Kelly. 2005. *Dinosnores*. New York: HarperCollins. Illus., Ponder Goembel.

Summary:

The rhyming text describes various dinosaurs snoring.

Activity:

This book is ripe with possibilities for action. Children won't be sitting down at all. First of all, every few pages show a double-page spread of different dinosaur snores, such as, "Bronto-booms, tricera-cries, raptor-rumbles, stego sighs. . . ." Read each type of snore and have children create the sound to accompany it. The other text also leaves room for action. "While dinos slept, winged lizards leapt, and mammals ran to hide." Children can fold their hands to their heads to pretend to sleep, jump up and down to leap, and run in place or find a small space to hide. You could also assign each student a different dinosaur by giving them a nametag and telling them what dinosaur or animal they will be. When their creature is mentioned in the story, they are to do what the animal or dinosaur does or make the snoring sound that dinosaur makes. In the end, have them invent their own dinosaur snores.

————. 2005. *What's the Magic Word?* New York: HarperCollins. Illus., Marsha Winborn.

Summary:

A little bird gets blown from his nest and asks various animals if he can enter their homes while trying to figure out the magic word that would allow him to be welcome in each dwelling.

Activity:

This book lends itself to a number of possibilities. The first is for children to pretend that they are the animals in the book. You would have a cow, bee, dog, owl, pig, and bird. You are the little bird and approach each child and ask if you can enter the home. The children would ask for the magic word, which is the sound that their animal makes. So, the cow's magic word is "moo-moo." Another option is to have all the children follow you around the room, approaching pictures or stuffed animals or puppets of the various animals. The third option is to turn it into a flannel board story. Place pictures of all the animals around the board, and move the bird picture around as he speaks to each animal.

————. 2008. *Grace for President.* New York: Hyperion. Illus., Le Uyen Pham.

Summary:

After realizing that there has never been a female class president, Grace runs for president against a boy.

Activity:

Preschoolers won't understand this story, so use it with older children, perhaps second grade and up. It is also suitable for an introductory lesson on elections for high school students. As in the story, give each child a name of a state along with the number of electoral votes that state has. Children then vote for Grace or Thomas, as in the story, or have them vote for two stuffed animals (that you bring in) or two popular television characters (whose pictures you show). In the end, tally the votes on a board as they do in the story. You can skip the electoral votes and simply go with one vote per person as well. The end of the book explains the electoral college.

Ditchfield, Christin. 2007. *Cowlick!* New York: Golden Book. Illus., Rosalind Beardshaw.

Summary:

A mysterious cow enters a child's room, giving him a lick and hence a cowlick.

Activity:

This is a very short and quick read. Make cowlicks out of curling the ends of paper pieces or cutting curly cues from construction paper to give to each child. Begin by having kids guess what the shadow is that is entering the boy's room, which is a cow. Walk around the room with a cow puppet or toy and put a cowlick on top of each child's head, pretending they have been licked by a cow and hence given a cowlick.

Dodd, Emma. 2002. *Dog's ABC: A Silly Story about the Alphabet.* New York: Dutton.

Summary:

A dog's activities are described in words that represent each letter of the alphabet.

Activity:

After each page of reading, ask the children which words started with the letter of the alphabet represented on that page. For example, "The bird flies back to her nest and sits on her eggs. That was a good adventure, thinks dog." Ask the children, "Now which word started with an E? An F?" The answers are "eggs" and "frog." You may have to re-read the page for the children. The last couple pages represent the words from the story. You might replicate this in some way to help children with their answers or turn it into an alphabet bingo game.

Dodds, Dayle Ann. 2007. *The Prince Won't Go to Bed!* New York: Farrar, Straus and Giroux. Illus., Krysten Brooker.

Summary:

A child prince will not go to bed, and everyone tries to find remedies for his insomnia until someone gives him a goodnight kiss.

Activity:

Have the children repeat the phrase, "Waa! Waa! Waa! I will not go to bed!' the teeny-tiny, itty-bitty, little Prince said," when cued. Either during or after the story. ask the children what might help him go to sleep. During the story, children might find clues within the illustrations, and after the story they can share their own remedies for falling asleep. You can also ask them if they think these cures will work.

Donafrio, Beverly. 2007. *Mary and the Mouse, the Mouse and Mary.* **New York: Schwartz & Wade. Illus., Barbara McClintock.**

Summary:

> A girl and a mouse share a house and common interests even when they both get older.

Activity:

> This is a lovely story that is not perfect for interaction. Have the children pretend to be the girl and mouse peeking at each other through the hole in the wall.

Donaldson, Julia. 2008. *Where's My Mom?* **New York: Dial. Illus., Axel Scheffler.**

Summary:

> A butterfly helps a monkey find his mom, but the monkey's descriptions lead them to different animals.

Activity:

> Children can help the monkey find his mom. For example, after the butterfly mistakenly takes the monkey to a snake after the monkey says his mom's tail coils, the monkey says that his mom has more legs. The butterfly then brings the monkey to a spider. Ask the children if they think the spider is the monkey's mom. You can also keep asking the children what they think the mom looks like.

Doughty, Rebecca. 2005. *Lost and Found.* **NY: G.P. Putnam's Sons.**

Summary:

> A girl continues to lose all her belongings.

Activity:

> Make pictures of or find objects to represent all the lost items in the story, such as shoe, sock, book, snack, homework, and dog. Pretend to look for the items. Ask children if the shoes they are wearing are the girl's shoes. Also ask them if they have seen the items anywhere. "Have you seen my homework? I'm sure I did it." Then either hide the items around the room or under something that looks like a bed or has been made to look like a bed. This is where the character finds her belongings in the end. Pull everything out at this time.

Downard, Barry. 2008. *The Race of the Century.* **New York: Simon & Schuster.**

Summary:

> The book tells the story of the tortoise and the hare.

Activity:

> Use this as a board story with the tortoise and hare racing, even though the photographs and illustrations are visually appealing. Ask two children to act out the race, with one moving slow and one moving fast and then resting.

Downs, Mike. 2005. *You See a Circus, I See* . . . . **Watertown, MA: Charlesbridge. Illus., Anik McGory.**

Summary:

   A boy describes how he sees the circus differently because it is his home.

Activity:

   Show the pictures and ask the children what they see. "What do you see?" For one picture, they should reply, "A lion tamer." You can then tell the children how he is a lion tamer in the circus but he is actually the teacher of the boy in the story and read the text that follows. Other pictures you will ask about are of a strong man, juggler, tattooed man, trapeze artist, and clown, all of whom are friends or family of the main character.

Duke, Shirley Smith. 2006. *No Bows.* **Atlanta: Peachtree. Illus., Jenny Mattheson.**

Summary:

   A girl shares her likes and dislikes.

Activity:

   At first I was confused and thought the girl was not getting the things she wanted but was happy with what she was given. However, after reading the front flap, I realized the first item shared is what she does not like and a turn of the page shares what she does like. Therefore, have children guess what she does like. For example, when the girl says, "no pink," ask the children what color they think she likes until they guess or you give them a hint. In this situation, her favorite color is purple. Others may take longer to guess. In other, examples, she prefers a lizard to a puppy and tutti frutti ice cream to vanilla. The guessing will keep the children's attention.

Dunn, Todd. 2007. *We Go Together!* **New York: Sterling. Illus., Miki Sakamoto.**

Summary:

   Each page describes two things that go together..

Activity:

   Turn this book into a song. I used the basic melody for the song "We Go Together" from the movie *Grease.* You can also point to the pictures and have children guess what goes together, such as "cow and moo" and "string and kite."

Durango, Julia. 2005. *Dream Hop.* **New York: Simon & Schuster. Illus., Jared D. Lee.**

Summary:

   A boy hops to a seemingly better dream each time the dream goes bad.

Activity:

   This has an obvious activity. On the corner of every other page is a graphic with the words "DREAM HOP!" underneath it. Instruct the children that when you point to them, they should yell, "Dream hop!" Sometimes this will be obvious in the story, such as, "You gather your goose bumps and yell out. . . ." Other times you will need to tell the children when to repeat the phrase. Because children are hopping to a new dream, you can also have them stand throughout the story and hop when they say, "Dream hop!," or they can jump up from their seats or from the floor each time. This is a fun story, which can also help children try to avoid their bad dreams. Use this for a bed-time stories storytime.

————. 2006. *Cha Cha Chimps*. 2006. New York: Simon & Schuster. Illus., Eleanor Taylor.

Summary:

Ten chimps go to a dance club to cha cha cha.

Activity:

This delightful story is perfect for moving around. Have ten children be the chimps and stand up to dance. The repeated phrase is, "ee-ee-oo-oo-ah-ah-ah! 10 little chimps do the cha-cha-cha." Then, as other animals enter the pic-ture, the number of chimps is reduced, although it is not clear why. I assume to make room or the new animals. If you have more than ten children, they can be the other animals, such as rhino, cobra, lion, cheetah, hippo, giraffe, meerkat, zebra, and ostrich, that make their way into the dance. You be the mama that calls them all to bed. Children can also pretend to dance in the way that the other animals do, such as slither and tango.

Durant, Alan. 2008. *Billy Monster's Daymare*. Wilton, CT: Tiger Tales. Illus., Ross Collins.

Summary:

A monster has daymares about children under his bed.

Activity:

Use a doll as a prop. Start by asking children if they think that the doll is scary. Show them a monster and ask if that is scary, or wait to reveal the doll when the monster has his daymare.

Duval, Kathy. 2005. *The Three Bears' Christmas*. New York: Holiday House. Illus., Paul Meisel.

Summary:

Santa Clause visits the Three Bears.

Activity:

If you have a Three Bears flannel board set or any house set, use this for the background of the story. If you don't, create your own house scene either on paper or in the room with real chairs, plates, and something for a bed. Then pretend to be shocked when the cookies are eaten, the chair is broken, and a

Santa suit is on the bed. This story can also be told using the children as the characters in the story. They will be surprised when you change the typical story they know to one where Santa and not Goldilocks is the surprise visitor.

————. 2007. *The Three Bears' Halloween.* New York: Holiday House. Illus., Paul Meisel.

Summary:

The Three Bears go trick-or-treating and are surprised by a little girl in the scary house they enter.

Activity:

Give children a paper bag and pretend to go trick-or-treating in the room or throughout the library or school. In the story, the bears get nuts from squirrels, honey from bees, and berries from birds before they come upon the scary house. Children can then run away frightened as the girl or witch surprises them.

Dylan, Bob. 2008. *Forever Young.* New York: Atheneum. Illus., Paul Rogers.

Summary:

Illustrations representing historical moments and memories accompany Bob Dylan's song.

Activity:

Play Dylan's song or any version of it to accompany the story. Have children sway or play sand blocks or some soft sounding instruments. The meanings of the illustrations, although explained at the end of the book, will be over the heads of most if not all young children. It can be used in a high school or college class for a history lesson.

Eaton, Deborah. 2005. *My Wild Woolly.* New York: Harcourt. Illus., G. Brian Karas.

Summary:

In this easy reader book, a child knows he sees a wild woolly that his mother does not see.

Activity:

Make some wild woolies, which would look like clouds with a nose, eyes, mouth, hands, and legs, out of cotton balls and construction paper. Hide some around the room. Ask the children, "Do you see a wild woolly?" when the mother tells her son there is no wild woolly around their home.

Edwards, Pamela. 2007. *Oliver Has Something to Say.* Montreal, Quebec: Lobster. Illus., Louis Pilon.

Summary:

No one lets Oliver answer questions; they always answer for him.

Activity:

Find any child puppet. Introduce him as Oliver. As you tell the story, have the puppet open his mouth and quickly shut it as people answer for him.

Edwards, Pamela Duncan. 2005. *The Neat Line: Scribbling through Mother Goose.* **New York: HarperCollins. Illus., Diana Cain Bluthenthal.**

Summary:

A squiggle turns into a line and helps the nursery rhyme characters.

Activity:

Turn this into a drawing story. Forgo the book and tell the story by drawing the baby squiggle. Then show different writing styles as the squiggle learns to become a straight line. Children can practice this on paper as well. Then recite each nursery rhyme, as I am sure you can do already by memory. After each rhyme, explain to the children why the character is in trouble, as the book does. Then draw on your chalkboard, white board, or butcher paper the object the squiggle becomes to save the day—a horn for Little Boy Blue, a path for Jack and Jill, a cloud for Mary's garden, a bird for Little Miss Muffett, and a moon for the squiggle.

———. 2008. *Jack and Jill's Treehouse.* **New York: HarperCollins. Illus., Henry Cole.**

Summary:

This cumulative tale describes building a treehouse.

Activity:

Create a board story for this book. As Jack and Jill build their treehouse, children can add the pieces to the board. They can also repeat the phrase, "... that held the treehouse that Jack and Jill built" as well as other lines if they can remember and catch on. An example of other text is, "This is the roof that was raised over the floor that was made from the wood that was hauled to the branch." You will need pictures of a branch, wood, floor, roof, light, table, treats, friends, and birds. Alternatively, use cardboard, a flashlight, and a blanket, etc., to create a more life-sized treehouse.

Ehlert, Lois. 1997. *Color Zoo.* **New York: HarperCollins.**

Summary:

Cut-outs reveal shapes and animal faces.

Activity:

Ask the children what animals the shapes represent. Then, as you flip each page, ask the children what shape is shown on the left-hand side.

———. 1997. *Cuckoo.* **New York: Harcourt.**

Summary:

This Mayan tale relates how the cuckoo lost her feathers.

Activity:

The illustrations are done in paper cutting with fasteners and papel picado. If time allows, replicate some of the images in the book as paper cuttings for a board story. Children can assemble their own out of pre-cut pieces as a craft at the end of the story as well.

————. 2004. *Pie in the Sky.* **Orlando: Harcourt.**

Summary:

A father and a child look at the cherry tree until they can make a pie.

Activity:

Read the large text that describes what the father and child are doing and witnessing. Then ask the children what they see in the pictures. It might match the text written in a smaller font, for example, "see orange and lime green balls, yellow moon and stars, a pale moth, and a dark blue sky. But no pie." Each of these statements ends with, "But no pie." Have the children repeat this phrase, or ask, "Do you see a pie?" You can even just simply ask if they see a pie for each page. In the end there is a simple pie recipe. Mix one right in front of the children's eyes, and follow this by giving them some pre-made pie or red iced or speckled cookies. End by asking students what they see out the window.

————. 2005. *Leaf Man.* **New York: Harcourt.**

Summary:

A "leaf man" is blown all around.

Activity:

Give each child a leaf to hold and twirl around while listening to the story. For a little more action, make a picture of a leaf for each child, attach it to string, and have the children wave the leaves to simulate being blown around. There is no real leaf man, although some of the leaves look as if they have eyes.

————. 2007. *Wag a Tail.* **New York: Harcourt.**

Summary:

Graduates of the Bow Wow School meet and do what dogs do.

Activity:

The words "Wag a Tail, Wag a Tail" are mentioned several times in the story. Point to the children to indicate when they should repeat these words in the story or have them repeat the words after you. Another repeated phrase is "Wig wag zig zag." Besides repetition, children can also get up and pretend to wag their tails when they say this phrase in the story. You could even give them paper cut or cloth tails to hold or attach to themselves. Paper cut tails would be especially perfect since Ehlert uses a paper cut and fabric scrap collage technique for her illustrations.

————. 2008. *Oodles of Animals.* New York: Harcourt.

Summary:

Ehlert's trademark cut-out collages are accompanied by short poems of corresponding animals.

Activity:

Give each child a picture of an animal. When you read that animal's poem in the book, he or she stands up. An example of a poem is, "In a bog,/a frog will wallow,/until he sees/a fly to swallow."

Einhorn, Edward. 2007. *A Very Improbable Story.* Watertown, MA: Charlesbridge. Illus., Adam Gustavson.

Summary:

A cat will not get off a boy's head until he wins at games of probability.

Activity:

Tell this book using storytelling. Put a cat stuffed animal on your head as the cat sits on the boy's head in the story. Then do some of the things the cat asks the boy to do, or have children try these tasks. For example, the cat must pull a dime out of a jar of coins. Next he has to pull out two matching socks without looking. Because there were 19 socks left, the odds would be 1 in 19. This is a fun book for teaching older children about probability while having them participate in the activities from the book.

Elliott, David. 2007. *One Little Chicken: A Counting Book.* New York: Holiday House. Illus., Ethan Long.

Summary:

Chickens are active in this dancing and counting book.

Activity:

Children stand up and move along with this story. For the sentence, "One chicken twirls like a top," the children twirl. For, "Two chickens do the bunny hop," the children do the bunny hop, following your lead. Kids will also do the ballet, swing, hula, ballroom dance, bump and grind, sway, cha-cha, and shake. You can also have children stand up one at a time until you have ten to complete the story.

————. 2008. *Knitty Kitty.* Cambridge, MA: Candlewick. Illus., Christopher Denise.

Summary:

A kitten knits for her family.

Activity:

Although the phrase changes a little each time, stick to one version and have the children repeat something like, "Clickety-clik./Tickety-tick./Knitty kitty sits and knits." Hold knitting needles while telling the stories, or children hold some kind of sticks as knitting needles.

————. 2008. *On the Farm*. Cambridge, MA: Candlewick. Illus., Holly Meade.

Summary:

Each double-page spread illustrates a different farm animal poem.

Activity:

Give each child the name of one of the animals in the book. Have them stand and pretend to be that animal when the animal's name is mentioned in the book. The animals that appear are a rooster, cow, pony, dog, sheep, cat, pig, snake, bee, bull, turtle, duck, hen, goose, and rabbit. Not all have poems. Alternatively, give each child a picture of an animal. If more animals are needed, make up more poems. Another possibility is not to read the animal's name or show the picture but to read the poems first and then ask the children what animals the poems describe. An example would be, "Her tail? As coy as a ringlet./In her eye there's a delicate sheen./Some look at her and see a sow;/I see a beauty queen." The answer is "pig."

Ellwand, David. 2003. *Cinderlily: A Floral Fairy Tale in Three Acts*. Cambridge, MA: Candlewick.

Summary:

The story of Cinderella is told through ugly and beautiful flowers.

Activity:

Although the outstanding feature of this book is the beautiful flowers, you can still have fun with it. Turn it into a board story by creating construction paper flowers to represent the characters. You could also use plastic flowers. A list of all the characters and the flowers that represent them are given at the back of the book. Of course, you can create your own as well. You might even have children hold the flowers and be characters in the play. Alternatively, tell the basic Cinderella story from your memory using the flowers or children. Children can make hats with a strip of construction paper, design a flower, and then select flowers for the story.

Emberley, Ed. 2007. *Bye-Bye, Big Bad Bullybug!* New York: Little, Brown.

Summary:

The itty bitty baby bugs are scared of the big bad bullybug, which is revealed bit by bit through cut-out shapes.

Activity:

Walk around the room with this book, taking turns showing the additional features that are revealed about bullybug to each child. Each page reveals more cut-out shapes that show more of this creature. Children should shriek with fear. An example of the text is, "I have two nasty pinchers for pinching itty-bitty baby bugs."

Enderle, Dotti and Vicki Sansum. 2007. *Grandpa for Sale*. New York: Flash Light. Illus., Kyle Gentry.

Summary:

An eccentric lady offers big bucks to buy Grandpa from an antique store.

Activity:

Each time the lady offers more money for Grandpa, ask the children what they could buy with $500, $1,000, $5,000, and more as in the story Lizzie tells us what she could buy—although it would not be any fun without Grandpa. Ask the children how much Grandpa is worth or how much they might sell a grandparent for. Or would they?

Ericsson, Jennifer A. 2007. *A Piece of Chalk*. New Milford, CT: Roaring Brook. Illus., Michelle Shapiro.

Summary:

A girl creates a chalk drawing with all of her colors.

Activity:

There are several possibilities for this book. One is to give each child a piece of paper and pieces of colored chalk. They can draw pictures with you as you tell the story. This could also be used in place of a craft at the end of the storytime session. You could draw the pictures yourself with chalk on a board or ask for volunteers to come up and do the drawings with the different colors as they occur in the story. The children will assist you in the order that the colored chalk they were given appears in the story. Children might also go outside to draw on the sidewalk when the story is complete. Another possibility is to give each child the chalk but not have them draw. They will just raise their piece of chalk in the air when their color is called. In the end the rain washes the colors away.

Eschbacher, Roger. 2006. *Road Trip*. New York: Dial. Illus., Thor Wickstrom.

Summary:

Poems tell the story of a family's vacation road trip to Grandma's house.

Activity:

Give children paper plates either cut as steering wheels or left alone to pretend they are holding steering wheels and driving a car as you read the poems that track the family's trip.

Evans, Cambria. 2006. *Martha Moth Makes Socks*. Boston: Houghton Mifflin.

Summary:

A moth gets larger as she eats meals of scarves and yarn covered with dust.

Activity:

Cut out a triangle for a dress and a circle for a head along with wings, and you have created Martha Moth. Next, cut out scarves, sweaters, and balls of yarn.

Pretend to have Martha eat the items. You can tape two poster boards together and drop the items in between them from the top to simulate putting them in Martha's mouth. You could also wear a really long wide skirt and hide the articles of clothing beneath you. Sprinkle confetti or glitter over the objects to replicate the dust.

Evans, Lezlie. 2006. *Can You Greet the Whole World? 12 Common Phrases in 12 Different Languages*. Boston: Houghton Mifflin. Illus., Denis Roche.

Summary:

The book describes how to say different phrases in different languages for different situations.

Activity:

Share with children some of the ways to say different phrases in different languages and have them repeat the words after you. For example, the text reads, "When offered something yummy, "please" is the word to use." Then share some of the ways to say please, such as "bitte" in German and "uxolo" in Zulu. Pronunciations are provided.

Fagan, Carly. 2008. *Thing-Thing*. Plattsburgh, NY: Tundra. Illus., Nicolas Debon.

Summary:

A selfish boy, unhappy with his toys, requests something unusual. After his father brings home stuffed Thing-Thing, the boy throws it out the window where Thing-Thing sees potential guardians.

Activity:

As Thing-Thing falls down past rows of windows, going by potential owners, have the children squat down a little further each time you turn the page. Alternatively, replicate a tall hotel building on a poster board and create a miniature picture of Thing-Thing. Either you or the children lower the stuffed animal to each floor as the story progresses.

Fajerman, Deborah. 2005. *Baa for Beginners*. New York: Barron's.

Summary:

New sheep have to learn the different meanings of and ways to say "Baa."

Activity:

Children repeat the word "Baa" in the different tones required in the story. For loud, they say "Baa" loudly, and from far away they say it very quietly. They say "Baa" softly when alone and loud when in a group. "Baa" will be more shivery when cold and wispy when windy. They can huff and puff "Baa" when out of breath. It would be said wobbly when scared, calm when sunny, and cheerily when happy and excited. Test the children with the different situations and ways "Baa" should be said in the end. You can then have them help you tell another story using the different tones they learned. Older children can be given different tones to read paragraphs from another story. For example, one child might be given the word "frightened" and another "out of breath," and they would read a paragraph from their stories in those ways.

Fallon, Jimmy. 2005. *Snowball Fight!* New York: Dutton. Illus., Adam Stower.

Summary:

The story describes the preparation for a snowball fight as well as the fight and after activities.

Activity:

As for any book about a snowball fight, crumple a bunch of white scrap paper to throw at the children when the story reads, "Spied around but didn't see . . . fifteen snowballs coming at me. Attack!" Then children can throw them at each other during the snowball fight in the book and finally into the recycling bin. Cotton balls or balloons could also be used, but crumpled paper moves faster.

Fancher, Lou. 2006. *Star Climbing.* New York: HarperCollins. Illus., Steve Johnson and Lou Fancher.

Summary:

A child who cannot sleep pretends he is with the stars.

Activity:

Set up the room as if the children are in space. Make big clouds out of large white construction paper or poster boards. Buy a machine or flashlight that projects stars onto the walls and ceiling. If you cannot do this, buy the "glow in the dark" stars or simply tape stars you have cut out onto the walls. They do not have to be the same size. Then have the children stand up with you and pretend to be in the clouds as the child in the story does. With the kids, you will tiptoe on the clouds, leap, skip, dive, toss a star (perhaps give each child a paper star to toss), soar, float, and sleep. This is a good opportunity to talk about and show pictures of constellations. The ones used in the book are identified at the back of the book.

Faulkner, Keith. 1996. *The Wide-Mouthed Frog.* New York: Dial. Illus., Jonathan Lambert.

Summary:

A frog asks other creatures what they eat.

Activity:

This is a pop-up book, so it is fun to see the animals jut out at you, especially the big frog in the end. Alternatively, use a frog puppet. Approach each child in the room, and they will pretend to be the different animals in the story. Ask them what they eat. The story includes a bird eating a worm, a mouse eating a seed and berry, and an alligator eating a fly. Have more than one child be each animal, or add more animals to the story so that everyone can have a turn. Use a gruff voice when reading the frog's part of the story.

Feiffer, Kate. 2005. *Double Pink*. New York: Simon & Schuster. Illus., Bruce Ingman.

Summary:

A girl loves pink and wants everything in her room to be pink.

Activity:

Two activities are particularly fun with this story. The first is to have children stand or raise their hands or a pink object (such as a piece of paper cut in a circle and taped on a stick) every time the word "pink" is read in the story. The second is to make everything pink. Decorate the room in pink, and give the children pink construction paper or cloth hats to wear. For a more simple version, just drape yourself completely in pink. This is especially fun when Madison's room becomes all pink and no one can determine where she is in the mess of pink.

Fenton, Joe. 2008. *What's Under the Bed?* New York: Simon & Schuster.

Summary:

A boy keeps guessing what scary thing might be under his bed.

Activity:

This is a very short story. Set up a bed with a pillow and blanket or use a doll bed and pretend to be scared and peek under it as you tell the story. Periodically ask children if they think what the child thinks in the story is true. For example, the text reads, "Is it tall? Or rather small?" Ask the children if they think it is something tall or small. Also ask the children what they think is under the bed. It turns out to be his stuffed teddy bear Ted.

Fisher, Aileen. 2005. *Know What I Saw?* New Milford, CT: Roaring Brook. Illus., Deborah Durland Desaix.

Summary:

In this counting book, a child discovers baby animals.

Activity:

This is a simple question and response story. It starts, "Know what I saw in a sprawly heap?" Flip the page and have the children look at the picture and guess. In this case, the answer is, "10 collies, and all asleep with legs and noses in comical poses." Of course, just "dogs" would be a fine answer. Children may not be close enough to identify the number of animals in the pictures.

Have them count along with you. Each page thereafter contains a response, question, or both. This can also be told as a board story, but the format is better suited to interaction.

Fisher, Valorie. 2006. *How High Can a Dinosaur Count? And Other Mysteries.* 2006. New York: Schwartz & Wade.

Summary:

Simple math word problems are provided with solutions.

Activity:

This book is best for older children with basic math skills. Ask the children three questions and show the pictures. Use this to sprig into more complex math problems. One example is, "Fatima, the fortune-teller, forecasts that Felicity will find every even number from 0 to 20 in her booth. Can you find them, too?" Use the pictures to find the answers. For some questions, you will not need the pictures.

————. 2007. *Beetle Bop.* New York: Harcourt.

Summary:

The story describes what beetles do.

Activity:

Get a beetle replica of some kind, whether a stuffed animal or a plastic toy, and move it around the room as you read facts about and descriptions of the beetle. You can provide each statement on a piece of paper for children to choose. An example would be, "Diving beetles, whirling beetles, spiraling, swirling beetles." Have the children act out the motions of the beetles. Follow by asking children what kind of beetle they are and what they can do.

Fleming, Denise. 2005. *The First Day of Winter.* New York: Henry Holt.

Summary:

Wintery things are described to the tune of "The Twelve Days of Christmas."

Activity:

Children can sing along with you to the tune of "The Twelve Days of Christmas." You could also create a board story using pictures of objects from the story, or give each child a picture or word of an item from the story and have them stand up when their word is sung or read. In the end, the song will be, "On the tenth day of winter my best friend gave to me 10 salty peanuts, 9 big black buttons, 8 orange berries, 7 maple leaves, 6 tiny twigs, 5 birdseed pockets, 4 prickly pinecones, 3 striped scarves, 2 bright blue mittens, and a red cap with a gold snap." Children will quickly catch on to the melody.

Fletcher, Ralph. 2008. *The Sandman.* **New York: Henry Holt. Illus., Richard Cowdrey.**

Summary:

A man finds a dragon's scale. He grinds it up and uses the dust to put children to sleep, which turns him into the sandman.

Activity:

Get some glitter, punched holes, confetti, or other small pieces of paper and sprinkle them on each child as you walk around the room and tell the story asking the children to fall asleep. Alternatively, put the "sand" in a bag and have the children pass it around, sprinkling some on the next child when you instruct them to. A volunteer would be helpful with this story.

Foley, Greg. 2008. *Don't Worry Bear.* **New York: Viking.**

Summary:

A bear is worried about his missing caterpillar friend.

Activity:

This is a story about a bear who doesn't realize his caterpillar friend will turn into a butterfly. Have the children repeat the phrase "Don't worry bear" throughout the text.

Fox, Mem. 2006. *A Particular Cow.* **New York: Harcourt. Illus., Terry Denton.**

Summary:

Nothing usually happens to this particular cow until this particular day.

Activity:

The word "particular" is mentioned on every page, so you can simply cue the children with a nod or some other action to guide them to say the word "particular" whenever it arises. Alternatively, turn this into a board story by creating pictures of all the characters that appear on each page, such as the cow, woman, postman, dogs, children, bridegroom, bride, sailors, boat, and flies.

France, Anthony. 2003. *From Me to You.* **Cambridge, MA: Candlewick. Illus., Tiphanie Beeke.**

Summary:

A rat receives an unsigned letter and searches for its author.

Activity:

Place stuffed animals or pictures representing all the animals in the story around the room. The animals you need are a mouse, frog, mole, and bat. Next, give each child a fake copy of the letter. Walk around the room with the children, stopping at each animal until you find the owner of the letter. Children can help decide who wrote it. You can change the characters in the story to match the puppets or stuffed animals that you have available in your library or classroom. The letter you would replicate reads, "Dear Rat, This letter is from someone who really admires you. I think you are very special, and I just want you to know how lucky I feel to have such a true and dear friend as you. All my love. . . ." You can also leave a blank and write each child's name in that space instead of the word "Rat."

Franco, Betsy. 2007. *Bird Songs.* **New York: Margaret K. McElderry. Illus., Steve Jenkins.**

Summary:

A variety of birds are described in connection with the sounds they make.

Activity:

Simply have children repeat the bird songs the number of times suggested in this counting book. For example, "A white-checked chickadee chimes in 6 times from a branch of the apple tree." Children make the sound written on the page, "dee," and repeat it six times. Model the sounds for them first. More facts about the birds are provided at the back of the book. You might also play bird songs or sounds of these birds and others during or after the story.

Fraser, Mary Ann. 2008. *Mermaid Sister.* **New York: Walker.**

Summary:

A girl who is tired of her brother seeks a sister in the sea, but finding one is not everything she has hoped for.

Activity:

Children pretend to be mermaids or mermen as you read the story. Give them messages or ask them to make their own messages in a bottle asking for a sister. Pretend to throw the bottles in the water.

Frazee, Marla. 2005. *Santa Claus: The World's Number One Toy Expert.* **Orlando: Harcourt.**

Summary:

Santa tells us how he knows what all kids want.

Activity:

To be politically correct, you may not be using a book about Santa in your storytime or class. However, if you do have a class with parents open to this activity, ask the parents ahead of time what their children want for Christmas and provide the children with a letter from Santa as you tell the story. In the book, Santa is 99.9% right about what toys the kids want. Alternatively, dress as Santa and have the children tell you what they want for Christmas and send it in a letter to their parents.

————. 2006. *Walk On! A Guide for Babies of All Ages.* Orlando: Harcourt.

Summary:

A baby learns to walk.

Activity:

Although it seems like a book for parents to read to children learning to walk, the text would be over the children's heads. The subtitle does say that it is "for babies of all ages." For young children, have each one grab onto a chair and practice the steps in the book. Tell the children you want them to pretend they are babies again. Parents will love that. You can first have them cry or act like babies. That may not be too hard. They will grab the chair or table for support, get a grip, pull themselves up, balance, let go, fall, check for hindrances, step, wobble, and walk.

Freymann, Saxton and Joost Elffers. 2002. *Dog Food.* New York: Scholastic.

Summary:

Photographs show dogs made from vegetables.

Activity:

If you think you can re-create the art of dogs made from vegetables as shown in this book, go for it. Because most of us cannot, make the vegetables used in the pictures available on a tray or table and ask the children to decide which vegetable it is. Alternatively, simply ask the children to name the vegetables shown in each picture. Instead of reading phrases such as "Dog catcher" and "Dog tag," ask the children to guess what each dog is doing in the pictures.

————. 2003. *Baby Food.* New York: Scholastic.

Summary:

Different animals are represented by real fruits and vegetables.

Activity:

Create the animals on your own and display them on a table. Children guess what the animals are. They can also guess the animals from the pictures in the books. End by providing fruits and vegetables for children to turn into animals in the fashion of Mr. Potato Head. Supply them with construction paper features and limbs.

————. 2005. *Food for Thought: The Complete Book of Concepts for Growing Minds.* New York: Arthur A. Levine

Summary:

Real fruits and vegetables are used to demonstrate shapes, colors, numbers, letters, and opposites.

Activity:

This is a simple way to test children on their concepts and their knowledge of common and unusual fruits and vegetables. Flip through each page, asking children about the shapes, colors, and sizes of the food. You can also ask children to name the fruits and vegetables represented. Some will be easier to identify, such as the orange, and some will be more difficult, such as the endive and artichoke.

Friedman, Laurie. 2005. *I'm Not Afraid of the Haunted House.* Minneapolis: Carolrhoda. Illus., Teresa Murfin.

Summary:

A boy is not afraid of the haunted house or anything in it, but he is afraid of a mouse.

Activity:

This is similar to *My Little Sister Ate One Hare* by Bill Grossman (Dragonfly, 1998). For Friedman's story, instruct the children to repeat the phrase, "I'm Simon Lester Henry Strauss, and I'm not afraid of this haunted house." Children can also substitute their own names before "Strauss." At the end, add "A mouse!" instead of "haunted house." Follow by asking the children if they are afraid of the things in the book, such as a goblin in bed, a moving floor, or a graveyard.

Fromental, Jean-Luc and Joëlle Jolivet. 2006. *365 Penguins.* New York: Abrams.

Summary:

Every day for a year a family receives a penguin by special delivery, and it starts to cause problems.

Activity:

Find a picture of a penguin and copy it multiple times on one page. Then make enough copies until you have 365. Give children envelopes containing cut-out penguins. Of course, the book does not have 365 pages. Sometimes the penguins are lumped together by numbers such as 4 piles of 15 that equal 60. This activity is also useful for older children learning to count, group, add, and multiply.

Gaiman, Neil. 2008. *The Dangerous Alphabet.* New York: HarperCollins. Illus., Gris Grimly.

Summary:

Scary things happen in this alphabet book.

Activity:

This may be too scary for some children, and the word "lovers" may evoke some questions. Because the words won't be too familiar or obvious with the pictures, ask the children to identify the letters instead. So, for, "J is the joke monsters make of their crimes," ask the children to tell you what the next letter is. In this case it is a J.

Gall, Chris. 2006. *Dear Fish.* New York: Little, Brown.

Summary:

A boy invites fish to visit, but they visit more places and for longer than expected.

Activity:

Buy some rubber fish toys or use a fish puppet and pull it out during the story when the fish attack. One comes from behind a shower curtain. Raise your voice when you read the parts of the book where the fish are exposed.

Garcia, Richard. 1986. *My Aunt Otilia's Spirits.* San Francisco: Children's Book. Illus., Robin Cherin and Roger I. Reyes.

Summary:

Demonio is frightened when Aunt Otilia's bones come apart and rise out of bed at night.

Activity:

This is a fun story to read in a spooky voice, but it may frighten young children. Children can make some of the sound effects, like knocking when Demonio awakens in the night to hear the knocking. I include this book in the multicultural children's literature course I often teach, and the students always love it even though it is an older book. Some teachers even say they have this book in their classrooms, so you may have it on your shelves too. One of my students had this book in his classroom, which makes me believe this one is still around. It is a fun and somewhat scary one if you can find a copy. The story is also excellent for storytelling.

Garza, Carmen Lomas. 1996. *In My Family.* San Francisco: Children's Book.

Summary:

Each piece of art by the author is accompanied by a bilingual description of how it relates to her family.

Activity:

This book is best for older children. Show the artwork. Ask the children to describe what they see and guess what it means to the author's family. Then read the descriptions. For example, in the picture of a woman holding a flaming rolled up newspaper over a man's ear, children might guess she is burning his ear. But, this was known to be a cure for an earache, and the bucket of water below was there to put out the fire.

Geisert, Arthur. 2005. *Lights Out.* **Boston: Houghton Mifflin.**

Summary:

In this wordless picture book, a pig devises a contraption to turn the lights out after he goes to bed.

Activity:

Because there are no words and the details of the pictures would be difficult for larger audiences to see, this is best for small groups or for older children. Read the first page, which sets up the story, so children know the pig is afraid of the dark and has to create a contraption to turn out the lights after he climbs into bed. Continue to ask the children what they think each piece of this creation, such as the dominos, broom, ball, bucket, and bicycle, will do to help turn off the lights. In the end, ask the children to create their own contraptions for turning off the lights or for completing a chore, such as doing homework or cleaning a room. They can draw out their plans as in the book. The pig even has drawings of his ideas hung on his wall in this story.

Glaser, Shirley. 2005. *The Big Race.* **New York: Hyperion. Illus., Milton Glaser.**

Summary:

A hare is on a never-ending race.

Activity:

This book never ends, because you flip the book over at the end and start it from the bottom, which is now the top and which brings you back to the beginning again. Got it? You can do several things with this story. One option is to have the children run in place or around the room while you tell the story. A second option is to find a world map or one created to resemble the map at the front of the book, and move a picture of a rabbit to the different places of the world the hare travels. Some of the descriptions of the locations are a bit stereotypical, but not much can be said on one page. A third option is to create a long strip of construction or computer paper with a slit down the middle. Make a picture of a rabbit on a stick and slide it in between the slit. Now you can slide the rabbit across the paper. If you make this paper stretch across the room, you can also write out the names of the places the rabbit runs to or objects that represent those countries. Children can help you make the rabbit run.

Goode, Diane. 2005. *Mind Your Manners!* **New York: Farrar, Straus and Giroux.**

Summary:

A not-so-proper family attends a fancy dinner, while the narrator gives advice on how one should behave.

Activity:

Each page gives a tip for using good manners. I offer two activities for this story. The first is to ask the children if they do the things mentioned while eating. Instead of reading, "Sit not down till thou art bidden by thy parents and superiors," say, "Do you wait to sit down until your parents tell you to?" You can also read the text and ask if the characters in the story are following the guidelines. "Be not the first that begins to eat." Is anyone eating first in this story? "Yes the dogs and the woman in the yellow dress." A more extravagant activity is to set up a table as a dinner table. Now read the story and glare at children or point at them in a joking way if they are not minding their manners. Provide juice and cookies for this one.

————. 2006. *The Most Perfect Spot.* New York: HarperCollins.

Summary:

A mother and her son look for a perfect spot to have a picnic.

Activity:

Have the children repeat the phrase, "The most perfect spot," when the mother and her son Jack reach a new spot each time in the story. Point to the children when it is time to say the phrase. For example, when horses gallop by and get mud on them they move to a new location. It seems like "the most perfect spot." But then another tragedy hits.

Goodrich, Carter and Clement C. Moore. 2006. *A Creature Was Stirring: One Boy's Night Before Christmas.* New York: Simon & Schuster.

Summary:

Alongside the original "Night Before Christmas" text, a boy disagrees with the way the story goes and is wide awake to experience Santa's visit.

Activity:

This is a good story for tandem storytelling. Use one adult or teenager to read the boy's part and one to read the traditional story. This would work well for a classroom where there is a teacher and an aide if Christmas stories are permitted.

Gordon, David. 2006. *Smitten.* New York: Atheneum.

Summary:

A missing sock and mitten find one another and become friends.

Activity:

Tell the story while putting a mitten on one hand and a sock on the other. Either hold the book and switch hands or tell it without the book. After the story, give the children a sock or a mitten (they can be real or paper) and have them find the matching one in the room. A fun craft would be to make a paper or mitten puppet by gluing the edges of two pictures to place on top of one another and slip their hands in. They can decorate their sock or mitten. They can also complete this craft before the story so they can participate too while you put your sock and mitten on.

Gravett, Emily. 2007. *Orange Pear Apple Bear*. New York: Simon & Schuster.
Summary:
These simple words are presented alone or separately on different pages to describe a bear and colors.
Activity:
Have children read the story to you as you point out to them the colors and objects on each page. For example, the text reads, "Orange, bear," and the picture shows a bear and a plate of orange peels. Point to the bear to get the response of "bear," and point to the orange to get the response of "orange." Some pages will show all the fruit, some will show the bear in an orange color, and some will show the bear eating the fruit, etc.

Gray, Kes. 2000. *Eat Your Peas*. New York: Dorling Kindersley. Illus., Nick Sharratt.
Summary:
A girl refuses to eat her peas despite her mom's offers of rewards.
Activity:
Turn this one into a board story. The mom offers to give the girl ice cream, extra time to stay up, no bath, a bike, an elephant, and the list gets longer. Find pictures of all these items. Pictures are used in the text to represent each reward. Slap the pictures up on the board quickly each time you mention them in the story. "I'll buy you a bike shop, a zoo, and then chocolate factories. I'll take you to super land for a week," etc. You can also give each child a paper plate with green circles for peas or perhaps green jellybeans, and have the children pretend to refuse to eat the peas. In the end the mom refuses to eat her brussel sprouts and they are even.

Grogan, John. 2007. *Bad Dog, Marley*. New York: HarperCollins. Illus., Richard Cowdrey.
Summary:
This is a very short version of the Marley story in which a dog is so bad that the family wants to get rid of him.
Activity:
The family often repeats the phrase "Bad dog, Marley!" throughout the story. Even when it is not mentioned in the book, Marley performs many more bad acts. Have the children repeat this phrase when cued every time Marley does

something bad, or just pause and ask them to say "Bad dog, Marley!" every time they think they hear Marley doing something bad in the story. In the end, Marley saves the baby and gets praise. Children for once can say "Good dog, Marley!" You can follow with a list of good and bad things dogs do, and have the children say either "Good dog, Marley!" or "Bad dog, Marley!" in response.

Grossman, Bill. 2004. *My Little Sister Hugged an Ape*. New York: Alfred A. Knopf. Illus., Kevin Hawkes.

Summary:

The story describes all the things that happen to a little sister and everything she hugs.

Activity:

If you are not uncomfortable hugging the children, take turns hugging each child while pretending they are the creatures in the book. Then pretend that you are going through the motions of the sister. For example, "My little sister hugged an EEL. She liked its slippery, slimy feel. It tied itself up in a long, icky knot, AND hung from her nose like a glob of snot." Pretend that the child is slipping from your hands or remove your hands from the child and pretend you are touching something slippery and slimy while making the faces to go with it. Rather than touching the children, you can pretend to be hugging the creatures or use pictures or stuffed animals to represent them. You will need an ape, bug, cow, deer, eel, ferret, goat, hog, iguana, jackal, kangaroo, llama, moose, newt, octopus, porcupine, quail, rat, skunk, toad, umbrella bird, vole, worm, x-ray of a bear, yak, and zebra.

Grubb, Lisa. 2003. *Happy Dog!* New York: Philomel.

Summary:

A cat paints a dog and other things to keep him company on a rainy day.

Activity:

Place a poster board or drawing paper at the front of the room on the wall, a board, or an easel. Draw the dog, castle, spaceship, and fire truck that the cat paints in the story. Alternatively, give the children their own paper and crayons and have them draw these objects as you read the story. A volunteer can help illustrate the story as well.

Guy, Ginger Foglesong. 2007. *My Grandma/Mi Abuelita*. New York: Harper-Collins. Illus., Viví Escrivá

Summary:

A trip to Grandma's overseas is told through illustrations and one single word in both English and Spanish on each page.

Activity:

This is an opportunity to teach some Spanish words to non-Spanish speakers or vice versa. Ask the children what they think each word means based on the pictures in the book. For example, the text reads, "Buenos días. Good morning." Instead, ask the children, "What do you think buenos días means in English?" The picture shows a father opening a curtain in the children's room and the children waking from bed. You can give them some hints. For Spanish-speaking children, ask them what they think "good morning" means.

Haan, Amanda. 2003. *I Call My Hand Gentle*. New York: Viking. Illus., Marina Sagona.

Summary:

The actions and uses of an unidentified hand are shared.

Activity:

Turn this into a board story by tracing a hand out of construction paper. Use other pictures such as a hammer and pencil to identify hammering and writing. Alternatively, put on gloves and act out the activities in the story. During winter, you might ask children to wear their own gloves during the story. For a craft, children can trace their hands, cut out the patterns, and glue two patterns together to make gloves. For a simpler craft, give the children precut patterns of a mitten or an adult-sized hand to glue together and wear during the story.

Harjo, Joy. 2000. *The Good Luck Cat*. New York: Harcourt. Illus., Paul Lee.

Summary:

The story describes the accidents that result in the nine lives of a cat.

Activity:

You may want to refrain from sharing this with some children, as the cat almost gets run over by a car and gets stuck in the dryer. If you use it, ask the children if they think the cat survived after each incident. For example, "The first life went when she climbed up in Mom's car to keep warm near the motor. She nearly lost the end of her tail when Mom started the car." Ask, "Do you think she survived?" Of course she did. This is a rare book by a Muskogee-Creek author.

Harley, Bill. 2005. *Dear Santa: The Letters of James B. Dobbins*. New York: HarperCollins. Illus., R.W. Alley.

Summary:

A boy writes many letters to Santa about what he wants and does not want for Christmas.

Activity:

I recommend this book if you use Christmas stories in your school or library. Pretend to open letters and read them, maybe even wearing a Santa hat. Then children can create their own letters. In between reading the letters, ask the children what they want for Christmas. Pair this book with the not-so-positive letters in *Follow-up Letters to Santa from Kids Who Never Got a Response* by Tony Medina (Just Us Books, 2003).

Harris, Trudy. 2008. *Jenny Found a Penny*. Minneapolis: Millbrook. Illus., John Hovell.

Summary:

In rhyme, Jenny finds a penny and acquires more money so that she can purchase her goal.

Activity:

Share this story with children learning to count money. Because Jenny is trying to earn or save $1, pictures of the coins she finds or makes appear on the sides of some pages. Give each child an envelope with the required coins or pictures of the coins that add up to $1, or display them in larger sizes on a board. Children can help count and add up the money. If you want to use this with preschoolers, just have the children count how many coins Jenny finds. You can add the amounts up for them, but have them tell you how many coins Jenny has found or earned.

Harshman, Marc. 2007. *Only One Neighborhood*. New York: Dutton. Illus., Barbara Garrison.

Summary:

There is only one of each location but many things that contribute to it.

Activity:

Use this book for a pause and response activity. You may have to give a few examples before the children catch on. For example, the text reads, "There may be only one bakery, but there are many kinds of . . ." Wait for children to respond "bread." They may say other bakery items as well. Children can view the pictures for assistance. They will also identify animals, toys, pizzas, vegetables, shoes, tools, food, instruments, flowers, boots, ice cream, children, and cities.

Harshman, Terry Webb. 2008. *Does a Sea Cow Say Moo?* New York: Bloomsbury. Illus., George McClements.

Summary:

Flash the space creature helps the boy Jack understand why some words in the sea are the same as words on land.

Activity:

Use this for older children. Ask the difference between the words highlighted in the book. Have the children describe, for example, what a school on land is and what a school of fish is. Other words would be cow, clown, horse, bed, and star.

Hayles, Marsha. 2005. *Pajamas Anytime*. New York: J.P. Putnam's Sons. Illus., Hiroe Nakata.

Summary:

During each month it is time to wear pajamas.

Activity:

Provide a calendar with pictures to represent the different seasons of the year. The calendar can be like a clock with hands to move. Ask the children to mark their calendars or move the hands on the "clock" when a new month is mentioned in the story. They can also repeat the phrase "time for pajamas, my pajamas, mine-o" in a singsong way.

Heck, Ed. 2005. *Monkey Lost*. New York: Simon & Schuster.

Summary:

A boy's class helps think of places where his monkey could have gone.

Activity:

When Eric tells his teacher his monkey is lost, she asks the class, "If you were a monkey, where would you go?" The class gives ideas, such as getting a haircut and going to the museum. In between these shared ideas, ask your story-time group or class where they think the monkey went. You can also ask them before you give the responses in the book to see if they answer in the way the students in the story do. Alternatively, turn it around and ask the children if they think it is likely Eric's monkey is in the places the kids suggest. "Do you think he went to get something to eat? Do you think he is at the movies? Did he go to the beach?" Next tell the children that the monkey is somewhere in the room and see who can find it, or have a picture of a monkey for each child hidden around the room and have them find one. In the end, Eric's monkey turns out to be a stuffed animal that he left on the school bus. Pull out a stuffed monkey after the story has ended, or have it hidden in the room (instead of a picture) for the children to find.

Heligman, Deborah. 2005. *Fun Dog, Sun Dog*. New York: Marshall Cavendish. Illus., Tim Bowers.

Summary:

The story is about a family dog.

Activity:

Put a dog puppet on one hand, and make it bounce and have its mouth open as you tell the story. This is a rhythmic book that makes you want to move. Children can get up and bounce with you, maybe even carrying their own

Tinka paper puppet. The text goes, "Tinka is a sweet dog, a treat dog, a jumping-up-to-greet dog. A fun dog, a sun dog, a run-and-run-and-run dog."

Henkes, Kevin. 2006. *A Good Day*. New York: Greenwillow.

Summary:

Good and bad things happen to several animals in one day.

Activity:

Even though the first half of the book shares bad things that happened to the bird, dog, fox, and squirrel and the second half shares the good, the children may not know the difference. Ask the children if each thing that happened makes it a good day or a bad day. For example, the text reads, "Little yellow bird lost his favorite tail feather." Ask the children, "Is this a good day or a bad day for the bird?" Later the text reads, "Little brown squirrel found the biggest nut ever." Then ask, "Is this a good day or a bad day?" Follow by asking children about other things that could happen to them that could make a good or a bad day. You can also ask them to offer some suggestions of things that happened to them that made a good day or a bad day.

————. 2008. *Old Bear*. New York: Greenwillow.

Summary:

A bear keeps dreaming the seasons pass until he wakes in spring.

Activity:

As you read the story, ask children which season is represented by each scene. For example, flowers are shown for the wording, "He dreamed that spring had come and he was a cub again."

Henson, Laura J. and Duffy Grooms. 2004. *Ten Little Elvi*. Berkeley: Tricycle. Illus., Dean Gorissen.

Summary:

This counting book is based on Elvis Presley.

Activity:

Although this may have a limited audience, children can count along while you play Elvis songs. "Jailhouse Rock" is a good choice for, "One little Elvis, sorting through the mail, got invited to a party at the county jail." Be careful about explaining the concept of jail to children. Children can dance along as you read to the music.

Hillenbrand, Jane and Will. 2006. *What a Treasure!* New York: Holiday House.

Summary:

A mole gets a shovel and digs for unlikely treasures.

Activity:

What the mole finds when he digs are a twig, a shell for a snail, an acorn for a squirrel, and finally another mole as a friend for himself. Get a shovel or toy shovel and pretend to dig for these objects. A brown sack works perfectly as a hole to dig in. In the bag, place the objects previously mentioned and pull them out when appropriate. Ask the children if they think these objects are treasures. If they say no, tell them how they are treasures for the animals. Then have a treasure box of small toys for the children to pretend to dig with a small toy shovel.

Hills, Tad. 2008. *Duck and Goose.* New York: Schwartz & Wade.

Summary:

This simple counting book includes a duck and goose.

Activity:

Children count along with the pictures of the backs of the animals watching three clouds, five flowers, and more until ten butterflies.

Hindley, Judy. 2006. *Sleepy Places.* Cambridge, MA: Candlewick. Illus., Tor Freeman.

Summary:

The book describes the places where different animals and humans sleep.

Activity:

Because it would be difficult to have pictures of all the places animals sleep, instead ask the children to fold their hands, lift them to one side of their heads, and tilt their heads as if sleeping every time you mention a word from the book that relates to sleeping. In "A frog takes a snooze," "snooze" is the key word. Other words include "sleeps," "snuggles," "bed," "drowse," "nap," "dream," and "lolls."

Ho, Mingfong. 2004. *Peek! A Thai Hide-and-Seek.* Cambridge, MA: Candlewick. Illus., Holly Meade.

Summary:

A game of hide and seek ensues.

Activity:

While a father looks for his baby he finds other animals that make sounds in the Thai language. Children can repeat these sounds, such as, "Swip-swip, swip-swip!" for a dragonfly, "Eechy-eecy egg, eech-eechy-egg!" for a rooster, and many more.

Hogg, Gary. 2005. *Look What the Cat Dragged In.* New York: Dutton. Illus., Mike Wohnoutka.

Summary:

A family continues to come up with ideas to use the cat for food, warmth, etc., so the cat finds alternatives to satisfy their needs.

Activity:

If you don't find the book politically incorrect because it shows a backwoods family thinking about eating a cat for food and if you believe your children won't be afraid or offended by such thoughts, this is a fun book. Have a cat stuffed animal, puppet, or picture attached to or near a big laundry or garbage bag. Each time the family suggests a way to use the cat and the cat finds an alternative, pull out from the bag what the cat drags in. For example, when the father says, "there's nothing like kitty-fur slippers," the cat drags in firewood to keep them warm instead. You will also need takeout food boxes, toys, and money. Of course, the cat calls the police in the end.

Holiday, Billie and Arthur Herzog Jr. 2005. *God Bless the Child.* Illus., Jerry Pinkney.

Summary:

Billie Holiday's song "God Bless the Child" is illustrated.

Activity:

Play the song that comes with the CD in the book or play another copy of Holiday's song while showing the pictures in the story. Follow by asking the children to tell you what the story meant. Some may not be able to use a book that mentions God in their library or classroom.

hooks, bell. 2008. *Grump Growl Groan.* New York: Hyperion. Illus., Chris Raschka.

Summary:

A few simple words help illustrate a bad day.

Activity:

Children act mad as you read the story. They can stomp and make faces and sounds that they would make when upset. Then they will calm down in the end. You might want to follow with a book on yoga or meditation.

Hopkinson, Deborah and James E. Ransome. 2006. *Sky Boys: How They Built the Empire State Building.* New York: Schwartz & Wade.

Summary:

The building of the Empire State Building is described from a boy's point of view.

Activity:

Give each child a piece of paper. Have them draw the pieces of the building as it progresses in the story. At one point you can see the almost-finished project. Alternatively, provide blocks or boxes and ask each child to take one and bring it up to the front of the room (or middle of the circle) one at a time until the end of the story when the skyscraper is done.

Horáček, Petr. 2006. *Silly Suzy Goose.* Cambridge: Candlewick.

Summary:

The story is about what a goose could do if she were another animal.

Activity:

Children can simply act out the various animals' motions or sounds. Children will do such things as squawk like a toucan, flap like a bat, waddle like a penguin, stretch like a giraffe, splash like an elephant, jump like a kangaroo, run like an ostrich, swim like a seal, roar like a lion, and honk like a goose.

Horning, Sandra. 2005. *The Giant Hug.* New York: Alfred A. Knopf. Illus., Valeri Gorbachev.

Summary:

A boy wants to send a hug to his grandmother through the mail, which sets off a chain of hugs through the post office.

Activity:

Start a chain of hugs among your storytime kids. Start by hugging one child as the first postal worker. That child would then hug the person next to him or her as the story progresses. If you are concerned about touching the children and having them touch others, walk around with a stuffed animal or one you create out of construction paper in a postal employee's uniform, or even without the uniform, and hug the animal instead. The characters are various animals, but the main character that starts it all is a pig. You can use different animals to represent those in the story.

Horowitz, Dave. 2005. *The Ugly Pumpkin.* New York: G.P. Putnam's Sons.

Summary:

An ugly pumpkin is rejected by everyone until he realizes he is a squash and finds his place at Thanksgiving.

Activity:

This is a short story. Find a squash and a nice looking pumpkin for comparison, and pretend the squash is talking to the children. Add eyes and possibly clothes to make it more real.

Hubbell, Patricia. 2005. *Trains: Steaming! Pulling! Huffing!* New York: Marshall Cavendish. Illus., Megan Halsey and Sean Addy.

Summary:

Different types of trains are described.

Activity:

Although the word "trains" is not repeated throughout, it is repeated often at the beginning and at the end. Ask children to say the word "trains" every time you point to them. You would say "passenger," and they would respond "trains." You would say "freight," and they would respond "trains." For the pages with no word "train" or throughout the story you may choose to have a few students repeat the sounds "choo choo" or "chugga chugga choo choo" or something similar. Most of the book is filled with simple words and phrases.

————. 2007. *Police: Hurrying! Helping! Saving!* Tarrytown, NY: Marshall Cavendish. Illus., Viviana Garafoli.

Summary:

The story is about what a police officer says while on duty.

Activity:

Create police badges for the children. Have them hold up their badges every time the word "police" is mentioned in the story. The word "cop" is also used. I was reprimanded by a police officer in high school for using this term. It is a matter of individual taste, in general, as to whether the word "cop" is offensive.

Hubery, Julia. 2007. *A Friend for All Seasons.* **New York: Atheneum. Illus., Mei Matsuoka.**

Summary:

A raccoon is worried his friend, Father Oak, is sad because he is losing leaves.

Activity:

Create a large tree out of construction or craft/art paper. Children gather around the tree and take turns hugging it to make it happy and lay leaves by its base to keep it warm. Have a handful of leaves yourself to let go when the tree sheds his leaves.

Hudson, Wade. 1993. *I Love My Family.* **New York: Scholastic. Illus., Cal Massey.**

Summary:

A family has a reunion.

Activity:

Give each child a nametag with the name of one of the characters in the story. Create more names if needed so that everyone can participate. Have children stand when their character's name is called. The characters are James, Hakim, Delores, Lonnie, Aunt Belle, Cousin Johnny, Aunt Nell, Little Alshon, Grandpa Lawrence, Grandma Bert, Uncle Tommy, Aunt Linda, Uncle David, Andrea, Mommy, and Daddy. Follow by having children form the family tree from the story.

Hurston, Zora Neale (Collected by). 2005. *Lies and Other Tall Tales.* **New York: HarperCollins. Adapted and Illus., Christopher Myers.**

Summary:

The book is a collection of lies.

Activity:

The lies are more like "Your mama is so fat" jokes than lies to today's audience. Therefore, each time you read one, ask the students if they believe this could have happened or if it is a lie. You may want to make cards or place cards on sticks to have the children hold up. One side will say "truth," and the other will say "lie," both words in different colors. They show the side with the answer they think is correct. Of course, they are all lies, but you could sprinkle in some true statements in between. Older children might be able to make up their own as a follow up activity. An example from the book is, "That man had a wife and she was so small that she got in a storm and never got wet because she stepped between the drops."

Hutchins, Hazel. 2007. *A Second Is a Hiccup*. New York: Arthur A. Levine. Illus., Kady MacDonald Denton.

Summary:

A father explains how long a second, an hour, a day, a week, and a month are.

Activity:

Have on hand a clock and a calendar. As the father describes how long each passage of time is, demonstrate it on the clock or calendar. For the second, the father describes it as a hiccup. Ask the children to hiccup. For the minute, ask children to do something 60 times, such as hiccup, jump, hop, or sing a short song that you have timed at a minute. For the hour, show how the clock turns to an hour. For the day, spin the clock hands longer. For the week, month, and year, show them on the calendar. Also ask children for examples of what they can do in a minute, an hour, a day, a week, and a year as the book shares examples.

Isaacs, Anne. 2006. *Pancakes for Supper*. New York: Scholastic. Illus., Mark Teague.

Summary:

In this modern version of *The Story of Little Black Sambo*, a girl gives up her clothing to animals that fight it out and turn into syrup.

Activity:

Some may still argue that *The Story of Little Black Sambo* should be laid to rest, but this is a nonoffensive version. You can wear the clothing that the girl gives away to the animals, such as a coat, sweater, dress, and mittens. Take them off as the story unfolds, handing them to children who pretend to be the animals, or create a board story using the animals and the clothing.

Isadora, Rachel. 2008. *Peekaboo Bedtime*. New York: G.P. Putnam's Sons.

Summary:

A child sees different things in a peekaboo game of his own.

Activity:

Turn this into a guessing game. Some pictures contain hints of what the child will see next. Even when there are not, children can still guess. For example, the book starts with, "Peekaboo! I see . . . " and the child is looking out the window. Ask, "What do you think he sees?" They will make their guesses. You will turn the page and find out that it is the child's grandma and grandpa. Instead of including the word "my," just say it is "Grandma and Grandpa." The next picture shows the child with his grandpa looking at a starry night. Ask the children what they think they see. This answer may be more obvious, because in the picture it is night. The answer is "the moon." Later a picture of a stroller appears with a cat's tail peeking out behind it. Observant children will be able to answer that the child sees "a cat." End with a game of your own peekaboo, perhaps seeing the children in the class and reciting their names after, "Peekaboo! I see . . ."

———. 2008. *Uh-Oh.* New York: Harcourt.

Summary:

Pictures and one simple word on every opposite page show a baby with a mishap.

Activity:

Each page is followed by the phrase "Uh-Oh." Children can repeat "Uh-Oh" each time it is mentioned. For example, the book shows a baby eating breakfast and then spilling it on his head. Your children will reply, "Uh-Oh."

Jeffers, Oliver. 2006. *Lost and Found.* **New York: Philomel.**

Summary:

A boy tries to find the lost penguin his home until the boy realizes the penguin is just lonely.

Activity:

Have a penguin puppet or stuffed animal and walk it around the room with it pretending to be the boy in the story asking children if they are missing a penguin. Ask all the children, even though in the story the boy goes to only a few places. In the end, the boy goes to the South Pole to drop off the penguin and realizes the penguin was only looking for a friend. Ask the children if they will be his friend.

Jenkins, Emily. 2008. *The Little Bit Scary People.* **New York: Hyperion. Illus., Alexandra Boiger.**

Summary:

A girl describes people who scare her but guesses that they are kind in other situations.

Activity:

Have the children repeat the word "scary" for each scenario. For example, "The cafeteria lady wears strange rubber gloves and never lets anyone take more than one milk. She's a little bit SCARY." This is a nice story about not judging people. Ask children who scares them, but be prepared for some uncomfortable responses.

Jenkins, Steve. 2006. *Move!* Boston: Houghton Mifflin. Illus., Robin Page.

Summary:

The different ways that various animals move are described.

Activity:

Have the children get up and move like the animals in the book. They will swing like a gibbon, swim like an armadillo, leap like a crocodile, climb like a praying mantis, and much more.

Jennings, Christopher S. 2008. *Animal Band.* New York: Sterling.

Summary:

Animals join together with different instruments to form a band.

Activity:

Give all children instruments and let them be different animals in the story waiting for their turn to join the band. An example from the text is, "Make way for the lion. He's one cool cat! What kind of instrument is played by a bat?" At this point, ask a child to be the lion and join in and one to be a bat and join in. You might want to wait to hand them an instrument until it is mentioned so they don't get tempted to play too soon. You can even use pots and pans, as they are mentioned as instruments in the story. Anything that makes a noise can be an instrument for this story.

Jocelyn, Marthe. 2007. *Eats.* Plattsburgh, NY: Tundra. Illus., Tom Slaughter.

Summary:

Simple text tells what different animals eat.

Activity:

There are only two words per page, and the pictures illustrate the animals and what they eat. Simply ask the children, "A worm eats what?" They will respond with "apple" either by memory or from the picture on the page. Another example is giraffes eating leaves.

Joel, Billy. 2005. *New York State of Mind.* New York: Scholastic. Illus., Izak.

Summary:

Pictures accompany Billy Joel's song.

Activity:

Most young children will not understand what a "New York state of mind" is, but the obvious activity is to play the accompanying CD or any CD with Joel's "New York State of Mind" while reading this book. Older children can use the pictures and song to describe what they think a New York state of mind is. They can follow with, "What is a Chicago state of mind? A Brookfield state of mind? A Naperville state of mind?" etc. Encourage them to create their own song, poem, or picture book.

Johnson, Angela. 2005. *A Sweet Smell of Roses*. New York: Simon & Schuster. Illus., Eric Velasquez.

Summary:

Two children participate in the civil rights marches.

Activity:

Civil rights is probably not be an issue to be addressed or understood in story-time. However, it might be approached in early elementary school. Have the children pretend to walk along with those like Dr. King. They can repeat the bold phrases in the text, such as, "We are right. We march for equality and freedom."

Johnson, D.B. 2005. *Eddie's Kingdom*. Boston: Houghton Mifflin.

Summary:

Eddie decides to draw everyone in his building.

Activity:

This is a fun story in many ways. Eddie wants to draw everyone in his building. They all confront him about his noise and complain about others in the building, but they allow him to draw them. Each time he draws someone, pull out a pad of paper and ask a different student to come up to be drawn. Of course, you will have to draw every student so that no one becomes jealous. Write the students' names on the pictures you draw. You do not have to be an expert because in the story Eddie actually draws each apartment dweller as a different animal. So, you can draw simple animals too. You can also have pictures drawn ahead of the program to save time and to make sure that they look better than your impromptu drawings. Do not reveal your pictures until Eddie does in the end. Children can alternatively draw their own pictures or each other instead even though this might not lead to the ending of animal pictures as in the story.

Johnson, G. Francis. 2004. *Has Anybody Lost a Glove?* Honesdale, PA: Boyds Mills. Illus., Dimitrea Tokunbo.

Summary:

A boy tries to find the owner of a glove.

Activity:

Walk around the class and ask each child if a missing glove is his or hers, as in the story the boy asks people in the neighborhood if a glove is theirs. To make the story more likely, place a glove under each child's seat or mat and ask the children to check if they have the matching glove. End by having everyone's matching glove hidden somewhere in the room.

Johnson, Paul Brett and Tom Glazer. 2006. *On Top of Spaghetti*. New York: Scholastic.

Summary:

A shop owner makes meatballs for his restaurant as the song "On Top of Spaghetti" is shared.

Activity:

Sing the song "On Top of Spaghetti" after each page of the story, or have the song playing in the background as you read.

Johnston, Tony. 2004. *The Worm Family*. New York: Harcourt. Illus., Stacy Innerst.

Summary:

A worm family has to keep moving when unwelcome by neighbors.

Activity:

Draw faces on your fingers to be worms. You can always add clothes, too. As you tell the story wiggle your hands as if they are the worm family. Have children pretend their fingers are worms as well. Alternatively, use or create a puppet stage and have the hand worm family tell the story from behind the stage.

———. 2005. *Chicken in the Kitchen*. New York: Simon & Schuster. Illus., Eleanor Taylor.

Summary:

A chicken runs wild in a kitchen until its eggs are hatched.

Activity:

This can be a confusing story, because some text implies that the chicken may die. "Poor old biddy! Dear old chicken! In a wink she will be stricken. She'll desist her lively kickin'. Her old hen heart will cease tickin'." Have a chicken puppet or some type of puppet to pretend to peck at the children while the chicken runs wild. When the dog homeowner begins to sweep with a broom, bring out a broom and start sweeping around. In the end, when the chicken lays eggs that hatch rather quickly, have chick pictures across the room for children to find.

Jones, Sylvie. 2007. *Who's in the Tub?* Maplewood, NJ: Blue Apple. Illus., Pascale Constantin.

Summary:

A boy can't take a bath because of all the animals in the tub.

Activity:

The short overlapping pages fold back to reveal the animals in the bathtub. This is a good story to ask the children about what is happening in the story. For example, when you turn over the shorter page that reveals turtles and a duck yet the boy responds, "MOM, I'm not in the tub. I'm not in just yet. I don't really feel like getting wet." Ask the children why the boy does not want to get into the bath to which they should respond something about the turtles and the duck in his way. Continue asking questions throughout the story, and even have children make some predictions.

Joy, N. 2007. *The Secret Olivia Told Me.* East Orange, NJ: Just Us. Illus., Nancy Devard.

Summary:

A secret passes from child to child and gets bigger and bigger.

Activity:

In the story a red balloon is used to show the secret floating and expanding from one child to the next. Give a red balloon to one child, and ask him or her to keep passing it as the balloon is passed in the story. You can also inflate instead as the secret gets bigger. Follow with questions in the author's note, such as, "Has anyone ever asked you to keep a secret?" Then follow with a game of telephone where you tell a "secret" to one child and have him or her whisper it to another child who passes it along until you find out from the last child what the secret has came to be.

Katz, Karen. 2008. *Ten Tiny Babies.* New York: Margaret K. McElderrys.

Summary:

Babies perform different actions as they are counted.

Activity:

Movement is already incorporated into this story. Have children perform the actions of the story. "3 bouncy babies jump and . . . hop!" Children jump and hop. "Along comes another . . . 4 noisy babies bang and shout!" Children bang on something or just pound on the ground and shout.

Keep, Richard. 2004. *Clatter Bash! A Day of the Dead Celebration.* Atlanta: Peachtree.

Summary:

Words and pictures show a lovely view of a Day of the Dead celebration.

Activity:

There is a rhythm to the words presented in English and Spanish. The title indicates that the book is about sound, so have children clap as you read. For example, "Yak-yak Chitter-chat ¡Qué bonito! My!" Revisit the book after one reading to explain what is happening in the pictures as described at the end of the book. More knowledgeable children can possibly explain to the group what the pictures are about.

Keller, Laurie. 2005. *Grandpa Gazillion's Number Yard*. New York: Henry Holt.

Summary:

Numbers are used in the pictures and actions in this story.

Activity:

Turn this book into a guessing game. The numbers are helpful objects in the story. For example, read, "You're buried beneath mashed potatoes and chives? What could help you?" Kids might reply, "A number five," but encourage them to explain why. In this case, the five turns into a snorkel. A six helps scoop eyebrows from soup, and a seven scrapes a bad taste from a tongue. Then continue to read the rest of the phrases in the story.

———. 2008. *The Scrambled States of America Talent Show*. New York: Henry Holt.

Summary:

The states decide to compete against one another in a talent show.

Activity:

Hang up a map of the United States. Give each child a state or two from the story. Write the names of the states (or draw their shapes so that students can more easily recognize them) on pieces of paper. Attach the papers to strings so that they can hang around the students' necks. When their state is mentioned in the story, children go up to the map and place their state where it belongs (with a little help from you if needed). If they'd like and if they can, they can also try performing the talent of their state or perform their own talent. Suggest dancing or singing. Some of the talents they can pretend to do are play a banjo, play the organ, sing, jump on a pogo stick, skate, hula, and dance.

Kelley, True. 2005. *School Lunch*. New York: Holiday House.

Summary:

A lunch lady gets letters from the students about how much she is missed.

Activity:

You can be really gross with this story and pull out icky food as new school cooks attempt to create lunch for the students at Lincoln School. Even though some of the food is good, you can pretend it is bad. Wear different hats, like a beret for the French cook and a baseball hat for the diner cook, to show the changes in the story. Alternatively, have envelopes with copies of the letters sent by the students inside. Set up a lounge chair and wear your sunglasses and sun hat and pretend to be on vacation, getting these letters and reading them instead of from the book. Use real postcards to represent the replies sent back to the school by the lunch lady.

Kimmel, Eric A. 2008. *Stormy's Hat: Just Right for a Railroad Man.* **New York: Farrar, Straus and Giroux. Illus., Andrea U'Ren.**

Summary:

Stormy the train engineer could not find an appropriate hat to face the wind until his wife helped him design one.

Activity:

The historical note indicates that this book is based on a true story. Stormy tries a variety of hats until the one his wife creates for him (based on a baseball cap) does the trick. Have a variety of hats and try them on the children, or choose one child to act as Stormy. Ask the children if they think that each of the hats will work for Stormy. After they say yes or no, read the part that corresponds to that hat. Stormy tried a derby hat, cowboy hat, pressman's hat, and fireman's hat. Use picture if you don't have any hats.

Kinerk, Robert. 2005. *Timothy Cox Will Not Change His Socks.* **New York: Simon & Schuster. Illus., Stephen Gammell.**

Summary:

Timothy Cox refuses to change his socks for a month despite the pleas of his community.

Activity:

Dangle a pair of stocks from a long stick or broom handle. Spray the socks or dunk them into something that smells unusual. Wave them around the children's heads when talking about Timothy's smelly socks. Some lines are repeated in the story. Instruct the children that when you point to them, they should say, "Timothy, Timothy, Timothy Cox, won't you consider, please, changing your socks?" You can abbreviate the phrase to "Please change your socks" and have it repeated more frequently. This story is long, so you may need to paraphrase for young audiences. There are a number of other fun things to do with the socks. Have the children make their own socks out of felt and glue or decorate cheap socks from the dollar store. These won't smell, though. Gather your old mismatched socks and throw them out to the children each time the story mentions that it is yet another day of Timothy not changing his socks. Finally, provide coloring sheets with many socks on it, and have the children color one every time you read the word "socks" in the story.

Kirk, Daniel. 2004. *Snow Dude*. New York: Hyperion.

Summary:

In keeping with *The Gingerbread Man*, Snow Dude is a snowman chased by people in the neighborhood who want him for themselves.

Activity:

There are several possibilities for this story. One is to walk in a circle pretending to chase Snow Dude. A second is to create a board story and continue to add the different characters, such as the baker and the animals, that want Snow Dude. A third is to give the children shapes cut out of white paper to create their own snow dudes as Snow Dude suggests at the end of the story. They could also create flannel board characters instead.

Kirsch, Vincent. 2008. *Natalie & Naughtily*. New York: Bloomsbury.

Summary:

Natalie and Naughtily live in their family's store and usually play, but one day they decide to help.

Activity:

Make one half of the classroom Natalie and one half Naughtily. When Natalie's name is mentioned in the story, the children who have been designated as Natalie will stand up or raise their hands or perform some other action. The same happens when Naughtily's name is mentioned. Alternatively, make a poster with a large building and nine floors. Move replicas of Natalie and Naughtily up each floor of the building when they approach those floors of the store. You can be even more creative and draw some of the items found on each floor. Follow by asking children which floor they would like to visit.

Kleven, Elisa. 2007. *The Apple Doll*. New York: Farrar, Straus and Giroux.

Summary:

A girl is afraid she will be lonely at school and creates an apple doll.

Activity:

Create an apple doll to use during the story. Children can follow up by making their own dolls out of dried apples or temporary dolls from real apples.

Klinting, Lars. 2006. *What Do You Want?* Berkeley: Groundwood.

Summary:

Flip the page to find out what each person or thing wants.

Activity:

This book is set up as a simple guessing game. Read each of the first parts of the statements, and then wait for the children's responses. Model the first one for them. Young children may have difficulty with some. The text starts, "The rooster wants . . . "; flip to the next page for the answer, "his hen." "The bumblebee wants . . . its flower." More difficult might be, "Little brother wants . . . his Band-Aid." This is a quick read that easily invites interaction.

Kloske, Geoffrey and Barry Blitt. 2005. *Once Upon a Time, the End (Asleep in 60 Seconds)*. New York: Atheneum.

Summary:

A father rushes bedtime by abbreviating stories.

Activity:

Read each shortened fairy tale and nursery rhyme. After each, ask, "Is this how the fairy tale really goes? What's missing?" You may choose not to use all the stories, as there are many. Save some for the next time you read stories to the children. Some stories included are "The Two Little Pigs," "Small Girl, Red Hood," "Sleeping Beauty," "The Old Lady's Shoe," and "Hey Diddle Diddle."

Kono, Erin Eitter. 2005. *Hula Lullaby*. New York: Little, Brown.

Summary:

A woman rocks her baby to Hawaiian sounds.

Activity:

Put on some hula music, and have the children sway to the music as you read this sweet, calming story. The first page of the book offers background about the sounds of Hawaii, including a drum and gourds. Try to obtain these instruments, or make the one out of gourds to accompany the story.

Kontis, Alethea. 2006. *Alpha Oops! The Day Z Went First*. Cambridge, MA: Candlewick. Illus., Bob Kolar.

Summary:

Z is tired of being last in the alphabet, so the letters change their order.

Activity:

Post the alphabet to remind the children of the correct order. Start with having children recite the alphabet forward and backward. Playing the "Alphabet Song" might help younger children. Start reading the story as it starts with A. Then continue reading as Z decides to start first and go backward. Have children suggest what letter will be next either by knowing their alphabet or by identifying the letters on the pages. P is tired of always being in the middle. When P starts to enter the picture after W, ask children if this is the correct order. You could also ask children what each letter stands for as indicated in the pictures in the text.

Kopelke, Lisa. 2006. *The Younger Brother's Survival Guide.* **New York: Simon & Schuster.**

Summary:

A boy has rules about how to deal with an older sister.

Activity:

Each time the sister does her brother wrong, the boy comes up with a tip to counteract it or get revenge. Read each situation to the children, for example, "My sister likes to make her favorite treat for us. Mystery Shake. For some reason mine always tastes funny." Then ask the children what he should do to get back at her, or, more politely, what advice could he give people to deal with such a sister. Wait for their suggestions, and then read Matt's tip. In this case it is, "Switch glasses when she's not looking."

Kraft, Jim. 2008. *The No-Good Do-Good Pirates.* **Morton Grove, IL: Albert Whitman. Illus., Lynne Avril.**

Summary:

Pirates are taken to court for their bad deeds but will be set free if they do a good deed before the day ends. However, they are not sure what a good deed is until they accidentally perform one.

Activity:

This is a fun story, but there is no real lesson because the pirates never figure out what they did that was good and go back to their old ways. The first half of the story presents the bad deeds. After each one, ask the children, "Was this a bad deed?" After they try to do good deeds, which were all bad, ask, "Was this a good deed?" The children should reply "no." Their good deed was scaring away other pirates, but they did not do so intentionally.

Kranz, Linda. 2006. *Only One You.* **Flagstaff: Rising Moon.**

Summary:

Some fish offer words of wisdom.

Activity:

This book works better with older children. The sayings are accompanied by pictures of fish that illustrate the words. For example, the text reads, "Find your own way. You don't have to follow the crowd." The illustration shows one fish swimming in the opposite direction from a school of fish. First ask the children what is happening in this picture. For older children, read the words of wisdom and ask children to draw their own pictures of what they mean.

Kressley, Carson. 2005. *You're Different and That's Super.* **New York: Simon & Schuster. Illus., Jared Lee.**

Summary:

A unicorn in a mix of foals is discriminated against until he is deemed special.

Activity:

Turn this into a board story with a white unicorn in a mixture of colored foals. Hold off placing the horn on the unicorn's forehead until it occurs in the story. Alternatively, make a cone with a string to attach to your head, and act as the different animals of the bunch do. Pretend to feel happy when joining the group and sad when excluded.

Kroll, Steven. 2005. *The Biggest Snowman Ever.* **New York: Scholastic. Illus., Jeni Bassett.**

Summary:

Two mice work together to build the biggest snowman ever.

Activity:

There are two options for this story. The first is to give everyone a piece of paper and ask them to draw the biggest snowman they can without going off the paper. The second is to have precut posterboard circle shapes of different sizes. Children select the correct sizes to build the biggest snowman ever.

Krosoczka, Jarrett J. 2002. *Baghead.* **New York: Alfred A. Knopf.**

Summary:

A boy goes a day with a bag on his head after trying to cut his own hair.

Activity:

Cut eyes and a mouth in a paper bag and put it over your head as you tell the story. Children can make their own masks in the end, but make sure they can breathe. Before the ending is revealed (that he cut his own hair), have the children guess why he is wearing a bag.

———. 2005. *Punk Farm.* **New York: Alfred A Knopf.**

Summary:

When the farmer isn't looking, the barnyard animals form a band and perform concerts.

Activity:

Ask each child to pretend to play one of the instruments the barn animals play. One plays electric guitar. One plays drums. One plays bass guitar. One plays the keyboard, and one sings. You can ask the children, "Who wants to be the singer in this story?" "Who wants to play guitar?" Then show them how to air guitar and air piano and drum. They can then practice along with the story. Sing "Old MacDonald" so the singers in the room can sing as the others pretend to play the instruments or make sound effects. You can also give them fake instruments to play if you have some available.

Kruusval, Catarina. 2008. *Franny's Friends*. New York: R & S.
Summary:
  A girl takes her stuffed animals for a picnic and other adventures.
Activity:
  For this story, you can create the characters in one of two ways. One is to have pictures of the animal friends mentioned in the book. The other is to use the children as the characters. The children can wear identifying masks or pictures or simply just pretend. The animals in the book are a crow, bear, bunny, giraffe, dog, hedgehog, and cat. Each has a cutesy unique name as well. In the story the girl dresses the animals and they follow her. Each time all the animals are mentioned the children can line up, follow you, or stand up according to their order. Alternatively, pictures of the animals can be added and removed from a board.

Kuskin, Karla. 2004. *Under My Hood I Have a Hat*. New York: HarperCollins. Illus., Fumi Kosaka.
Summary:
  A girl describes what she is wearing on a cold day.
Activity:
  Turn this book into a board story. Locate or draw a simple picture of a girl. You will need pictures of a hood, hat, hair, coat, two sweaters, muffler, gloves, mittens, pants, boots, shoes, and socks. Pile all the clothing on the girl and remove the pieces as mentioned in the story. You can also ask children to help remove the pieces.

————. 2005. *So, What's It Like to Be a Cat?* New York: Atheneum. Illus., Betsy Lewin.
Summary:
  A boy has a conversation with a cat about what it is like to be a feline.
Activity:
  Have a cat puppet or a cat face on a stick in one hand and a boy puppet or boy's face on a stick in the other. One child can also act out the part of the boy and another can hold the puppet so you can more easily read the book. Then simply point to the cat or move the puppet when the cat speaks and do the same for the child. For example, the boy would ask, "Do you have a kitty bed with your picture at the head?" The cat responds, "I do not have a kitty bed to rest my kitty tail and head. I'd rather sleep most anywhere that's warm and soft."

———. 2007. *Green as a Bean*. New York: Laura Geringer. Illus., Melissa Iwai.

Summary:

Questions are asked regarding different colors and words.

Activity:

This is a great book for questions. Children can answer the questions already provided in the text. The book starts, "If you could be green would you be a lawn or a lean green bean and the stalk it's on? Would you be a leaf on a leafy tree? Tell me, lean green one, what would you be?" Pause between each question to get responses. Then encourage the children to respond about what other green thing they would want to be. You will also ask questions to children about being square, soft, loud, small, red, fierce, blue, bright, and somebody holding a book.

Kutner, Merrily. 2004. *Down on the Farm*. New York: Holiday House. Illus., Will Hillenbrand.

Summary:

The story is about the activities and sounds of animals on a farm.

Activity:

Children sing the recurring phrase "Down on the Farm." For example, you say, "Horses say, 'Nay, Nay, Nay.'" The children repeat, "Down on the farm, down on the farm." There will be the sun, a rooster, crows, horses, cow, lunch, ducks, geese, turkeys, a dog, a pig, goats, sheep, chicks, and cats. Make it a song. Add your own or ask the children to add their own animal sounds and noises at the end.

Kwon, Yoon-Duck. 2007. *My Cat Copies Me*. La Jolla, CA: Kane/Miller.

Summary:

A cat copies a little girl.

Activity:

Read the text of the story and have children pretend to be cats and copy your actions. For example, "My cat copies me. We help with the laundry, and chase after flies. Smelling the flowers, or watching bugs, she always copies me." Children copy you, pretending to fold laundry, chase flies, smell flowers, and watch bugs. In the end you can create other actions that the children can copy.

LaRochelle, David. 2007. *The End*. New York: Arthur A. Levine. Illus., Richard Egielski.

Summary:

This backwards fairy tale tells how a prince and princess fell in love.

Activity:

Use this book for prediction exercises. Even though the story is backwards and you are not supposed to find out what started it all until the end, ask children to guess why they think certain events happened. For example, the text reads, "She poured a big bowl of lemonade on top of his head." Follow with, "Why did she pour lemonade on his head?" The answer is that "the knight's curly red beard was on fire." However, you may get some more creative results. Older children can follow by creating their own backwards story.

Larsen, Andrew. 2007. *Bella and the Bunny.* Tonawanda, NY: Kids Can. Illus., Kate Endle.

Summary:

Bella loves her sweater and grandma's sweaters and her bunny until her bunny and favorite sweater disappear.

Activity:

Have one sweater for children to pass and feel, or give a sweater to each child. For this part, they can feel the sweaters according to the text or identify the sweaters that you have provided according to the text. "Some are soft. Others are nubby. Some feel fuzzy. Others feel furry. Some zip up. Others button down." Then have one or more hidden sweaters around the room for children to find, or have the children turn away as one child hides a sweater to replicate the incident in the story when Bella's sweater disappears and she and her classmates look all over for it. Of course, the bunny has taken it because it is so comfortable.

Latimer, Miriam. 2007. *Shrinking Sam.* Cambridge: Barefoot Books.

Summary:

A boy thinks he is shrinking because his family is ignoring him.

Activity:

Have the children stand up. Every time Sam shrinks or the word "shrink" or "shrinking" is used, the children squat down just a little further. Model these actions for them. As Sam grows bigger in the end, stand up just a little straighter each time.

Lee, Chinlun. 2004. *Good Dog, Paw!* Cambridge, MA: Candlewick.

Summary:

A dog at the veterinarian's office shares tips for being healthy.

Activity:

April checks her dog twice a day according to a ten-step plan to being healthy. Students can bring their own stuffed animal dogs, or they can be given any puppet to pretend it is a dog, or they can be given paper dogs. Have children perform the ten items on the checklist: check the eyes, ears, nose, breath, teeth, paws, coat, tummy, tail, and whole body. Tell the children what to look for. Ask if anyone found anything wrong. If you use paper dogs, you can add some problems to some of the dogs, such as a mite in the ear. Then pretend to be the veterinarian and fix up the animals in your office.

Lee, Huy Voun. 2005. *In the Leaves.* New York: Henry Holt.
Summary:
During a trip to a farm, a boy shows his friend Chinese characters.
Activity:
This is a nice story because it shows that children have an interest in something about the Chinese culture. While reading the book, draw the Chinese characters on a paper or board, and provide paper for the children to do the same. Young children will not be able to accomplish this task, but they will have fun trying. Make sure to explain that this is how you write these words in Chinese. Words include pig, family, mouth, harmony, and rice/grain.

Lee, Spike and Tonya Lewis Lee. 2005. *Please, Puppy, Please.* New York: Scholastic. Illus., Kadir Nelson.
Summary:
Children beg their puppy to behave.
Activity:
Although the order and number of the words may change from page to page, the basic words used in each repetition reflect the book's title and read, "Please, puppy, please." Have children repeat this phrase each time the puppy does not listen. For example, read, "Away from the gate . . ." and the children would reply, "Please, puppy, please."

Leedy, Loreen. 2008. *Crazy Like a Fox: A Simile Story.* New York: Holiday House.
Summary:
Animals are described in similes.
Activity:
Even if your young children cannot define a simile, they can probably still complete one. Read one example from the book, such as the first, which goes, "In the quiet forest, Rufus is sleeping like. . . ." Then turn the page and finish, "a log." Next ask children to complete the statements. For example, "Rufus has a job to do, so he zips across the meadow as fast as. . . ." Wait for responses. The book suggests lightning, but perhaps the children can think of other responses. Ask them questions like, "What could Rufus be as fast as?" Then repeat the whole sentence. Children will soon catch on. You can also create your own similes to continue the story.

Leuck, Laura. 2007. *I Love My Pirate Papa.* New York: Harcourt. Illus., Kyle M. Stone.
Summary:
A pirate's son shares what he loves about his father.

Activity:

Make or purchase an eye patch and/or pirate hat, and give one to each child. Have them stand and march like they are pirates as you tell the story. They might want to add some "Argh"s here and there.

Levert, Mireille. 2005. *Eddie Longpants*. Toronto: Groundwood.

Summary:

Giant Eddie is teased by his classmates until they see he is more than just an extra tall boy.

Activity:

Dress a doll in a pair of your pants or another adult's pants. Dangle the doll with the long pants as you tell the story. This gives the children a visual to look at while you are reading. You can also look at the doll while reading the insults from the book. If you want the children to participate more, ask them how Eddie feels after each situation and insult.

Lewis, Paeony. 2005. *No More Cookies!* New York: Scholastic. Illus., Brita Granstrom.

Summary:

A child comes up with ways to get her mom to give her cookies until they make magic monkey bananas in the end.

Activity:

The point of this book is to make magic monkey bananas, which you can also do with your children after the story. When Florence's mom won't let her have cookies, Florence dresses as a tooth fairy and a witch, puts fake blood on her stuffed monkey, and dresses as a chef. You can also dress like these characters at the appropriate times in the story. In the end, the mom makes chocolate-covered bananas with sprinkles instead of cookies, which doesn't seem that much healthier. Provide frosting, bananas, and sprinkles for the kids to make their own, which makes this book a fun time.

Lichtenheld, Tom. 2005. *What's with This Room?* New York: Little, Brown.

Summary:

A boy's room is such a mess, but he has excuses why.

Activity:

Grab a bunch of toys and clothes from work or home and toss them about the room before children enter storytime. Start with this book and the opening words, "Look at this room, it's in such distress, you'd have to clean up just to call it a mess." Provide some of the items mentioned in the book so that you can pick them up while reading. "Your shoes in a pile, your shirts in a bunch, and there in that corner, is that yesterday's lunch?" Other items you can bring are pants, underwear if you dare, socks, a monster, various animals, blocks, a box, and a vacuum and a broom for cleaning.

Lieberman, Syd. 1994. *The Wise Shoemaker of Studena.* **Philadelphia: Jewish Publication Society. Illus., Martin Lemelman.**

Summary:

The Wise Shoemaker is confused for a beggar, so he teaches a rich man a lesson.

Activity:

This is one of my favorite stories. It is best told by Syd Lieberman either live or by a recording. For this reason, the book also makes an excellent choice for storytelling. As Lieberman does, pretend to pour the drinks and food into your clothing in order to convey the idea that a man's clothes were really what the rich man wanted if he turned the wise man away because he looked like a beggar.

Llewellyn, Claire. 2007. *Ask Dr. K. Fisher about Dinosaurs.* **Boston: Kingfisher.**

Summary:

Dinosaurs write to Dr. Fisher for advice.

Activity:

Give children envelopes containing copies of the letters from the book. Instead of reading the letters from the text, read the letters from the envelopes. Give children dinosaur hats made from a band of construction paper with a picture of a dinosaur glued to them to make the children feel as if they were dinosaurs. Then read the responses from the book. Because the letters are long, you may want to abbreviate or just select a few to read.

Lloyd-Jones, Sally. 2006. *How to Be a Baby by Me, the Big Sister.* **New York: Schwartz & Wade. Illus., Sue Heap.**

Summary:

A big sister tells her baby sibling all the bad and eventually good things about being a baby.

Activity:

Change the statements to questions, and ask your preschoolers if they think babies do these things. There is a lot in this book so you may have to skip around. For example, one sentence from the text is, "People talk to you, but you don't know what it means." Instead, ask, "When you are a baby, do you understand what people say to you?" Alternatively, have the children pretend to be babies and read the story to them as they are pretending, and talk to them as if you are the big sister. They might also bring in their own dolls or use puppets you provide and pretend to take care of the babies as you read the story. Although changing the phrases into questions will keep the children more involved, it is a cute story to just read as if it is a big sister talking.

————. 2006. *Time to Say Goodnight.* New York: HarperCollins. Illus., Jane Chapman.

Summary:

The story describes how different animals go to bed.

Activity:

For each double-page spread and verse, pause before you name each animal and have the children guess the animal from the pictures. There are bunnies, birdies, squirrels, owls, bears, fawns, and mice. In the end, when the book asks, "What about you, sleepyhead?" go around the room to each child with a verse you have created beforehand. The verse should have four lines and rhyme as in the text. For example, the book reads, "Tiny mouse, the day is done. Stop your scurrying, little one. No more squeaking, not one peep. Close your eyes now, go to sleep!" Your poem might read like this: "Little Amy, time for bed. Stop your playing sleepyhead. No more singing. No more fun. Wake tomorrow with the sun." You can probably write better than this.

Lo, Ginnie. 2005. *Mahjong All Day Long.* New York: Walker. Illus., Beth Lo.

Summary:

A family plays the game of mahjong.

Activity:

Acquire a mahjong set, and place a piece out on a table or board or by each child as you read each page of simple text. The story is written and illustrated by two Chinese sisters. Ask the children what games their families play. A brief description of the history and the game is included at the end of the book.

Lodge, Bernard. 2007. *Custard Surprise.* New York: HarperCollins. Illus., Tim Bowers.

Summary:

Two chickens open a diner only to find their patrons prefer more traditional foods according to their species.

Activity:

After the guests arrive at the diner, they are not impressed with the menu and ask for something more to their liking. At these points, ask the kids what food they think that animal would want. For example, after the chickens list their menu, the crow says, "What? No worms?" Instead, say, "The crow doesn't like the menu. What food do you think he would like to eat?" You will also ask about a mule, bear, goat, and fox.

London, Jonathan. 2007. *A Train Goes Clickety-Clack.* **New York: Henry Holt. Illus., Denis Roche.**

Summary:

The story describes a train.

Activity:

The word "train" or "trains" is mentioned on each page. Give each child a picture of a train to hold up every time the word is mentioned in the story. Ideally the trains will be laminated and taped or glued to a popsicle or craft stick, but they could also be a nametag or picture or the kids can just use their hands.

———. 2008. *Froggy Goes to Camp.* **New York: Viking. Illus., Frank Remkiewicz.**

Summary:

Froggy keeps forgetting things at camp, among other things that go wrong.

Activity:

Unlike in *Froggy Gets Dressed* (1997), this frog doesn't forget enough to make this a good board story. But because the days of the week are mentioned, it makes a good calendar story. Provide children with a calendar of the days of the week. When you read the parts of the story about what happens to Froggy each day of the week at camp, children can mark off the day on their calendar or draw a picture of Froggy's activities on each day of the week.

Lorig, Steffanie and Richard Lorig. 2008. *Such a Silly Baby!* **San Francisco: Chronicle Books. Illus., Amanda Shepherd.**

Summary:

A woman keeps leaving her baby places where it is switched with other animals.

Activity:

As in Robert Munsch's *Alligator Baby* (Scholastic, 1997), it is another wonder why anyone would leave their baby and have it switched with an animal. However, if using this story, children can repeat the phrase the baby says each time, "I'm such a silly baby." You can also give children the different animals in the story to hold and then hand off the baby to them as needed while reading the story. So the baby would be switched with a chimpanzee, bear, sow, and buffalo. You can add more animals to expand the story and allow more children to participate.

MacDonald, Margaret Read. 2006. *The Squeaky Door.* **New York: Harper-Collins. Illus., Mary Newell DePalma.**

Summary:

A boy is afraid of the dark and the sounds of the night until his grandma solves the problem.

Activity:

In this cumulative tale Grandma keeps bringing animals into her grandchild's bed so he will not be alone and frightened at night. The problem is solved by removing the animals and oiling the door. Create a bed on the floor with pillows and a blanket. Have one child be the boy in the story. Instruct the child to respond "No. Not me!" every time the grandma asks if he is scared. Alternatively, ask the whole class to respond. Then when the grandma suggests a different animal to comfort him each time, have the children respond "Yes! Yes! Yes!" as in the story. Then have each child be one of the animals in the story and bring it up to the bed. If you don't want the children moving so much, instead ask the children which animal they should bring to the bed next and use stuffed animals or puppets. If you use the children, you can make them animal masks. The author of the book suggests using different animals or adding animals to the story. Make sure each child can participate in this one.

Mack, David. 2007. *The Shy Creatures*. New York: Feiwel and Friends.

Summary:

Reminiscent of Dr. Seuss, a girl is too shy to tell the class she wants to be a doctor of shy and unusual creatures when she grows up.

Activity:

Although all the creatures are described at the beginning of the book, young children may not relate to them except for the more common ones, such as Bigfoot and the unicorn. It may work well in a high school cryptozoology lesson where students research one of the creatures from the story. If using with younger children, ask the children what each creature is and provide background on the strange animal before proceeding with the story. For example, when you come to the page with the unicorn, ask the children, "And what could this be?" Then continue to read, "What if the Unicorn broke his horn? I could tape it together so he wouldn't be forlorn." In some cases you will have to tell the children what the creature is and describe it as well. Follow the story by having children create their own unusual creatures. When the teacher in the story asks the children what career they would choose, you could also ask your children. You might ask this at the end to see if anyone else wants to be a doctor of shy and unusual creatures.

MacLachlan, Patricia and Emily MacLachlan Charest. 2006. *Once I Ate a Pie*. New York: Joanna Cotler. Illus., Katy Schneider.

Summary:

Poems relate to the temperaments of different unnamed dog breeds.

Activity:

Find different pictures of similar dogs mentioned in the book, such as a pug and a beagle. When you read each poem about a different dog, ask the children to identify each dog from the photos you provide. Follow up by asking children to describe dogs that they know.

MacLean, Kerry Lee. 2004. *Peaceful Piggy Meditation.* Morton Grove, IL: Albert Whitman.

Summary:

Peaceful Piggy talks about distractions in life and how meditation can help.

Activity:

Show students how to mediate by sitting with their legs and arms crossed and making peaceful sounds. Have them meditate throughout the story. They can listen while they have their eyes closed.

———. 2008. *Peaceful Piggy Yoga.* Morton Grove, IL: Albert Whitman.

Summary:

Yoga poses are described next to simple text about yoga.

Activity:

The note at the beginning of the book titled "How to Use This Book" suggests that you try the poses described in the text and hold each pose for three deep breaths. Demonstrate each pose to the best of your children's abilities, and read the descriptions of each pose. Then read the text as the children hold their poses. Make sure they take their three deep breaths. The book also mentions there should be no pain in the stretching. Make sure you modify the poses or skip some if too difficult for your audience.

Mahy, Margaret. 2006. *Down the Back of the Chair.* New York: Clarion. Illus., Polly Dunbar.

Summary:

A family has no money to travel in their car until the girl suggests that they look in the chair cushions.

Activity:

Although the rhyming text uses words that some children may not understand, the idea that objects can be found in the chair, including money, is a fun one. Simply pull a big comfy armchair, or as close as you can get to one, from the library, and bring it to the storytime room. Hide many objects that match those in the story under a cushion or a pillow. You can even hide other things in there as well. Items in the book include a ring, pineapple peel, spider, pins, fan, crumb, comb, cap, map, cake, snake, pearls, lion, skunk, skate, elephants, bumblebee, and finally the will that Uncle Bill left them that will get them out of their money woes. Have fun tossing things from under the pillow.

Manning, Maurice J. 2008. *Kitchen Dance.* New York: Clarion.

Summary:

Children wake up to find their parents dancing in the kitchen.

Activity:

Have the children get up and dance with you as the parents do in this book. Children can also bang on pots and pans you provide as is done in the story. Some children can be dancers and some music makers, and they can switch if they choose. Continue with a dancing march around the room.

Manushkin, Fran. 2006. *The Shivers in the Fridge.* New York: Dutton. Illus., Paul O. Zelinsky.

Summary:

A family of refrigerator magnets get stuck in the fridge and shiver until released.

Activity:

This book might not be best for preschool-aged children, as it could be confusing. It is good for older children, even high school or college ages, to teach inference. It is not revealed right away that this family is in a refrigerator and not until the end that they are magnets. Perhaps not even college students would figure out that they are magnets until it is shown in the end. However, they can have fun trying to make these inferences. Ask children to make guesses.

Marino, Gianna. 2005. *Zoopa: An Animal Alphabet.* San Francisco: Chronicle Books.

Summary:

When new letter noodles are added to the soup, new animals represented by these letters are added to the page.

Activity:

This is perfect for a board story. Create a large plate, or just use a paper plate for a small group. Reproduce all the letters of the alphabet whether by writing them out on paper, printing them from a word processing program, or using pre-made letters. Give each child in the room at least one letter. Also provide pictures of all the animals mentioned in the book: ant, butterfly, chipmunk, dog, elephant, frog, grasshopper, hedgehog, iguana, jellyfish, koala, ladybug, monkey, nanny goat, ostrich, pig, quail, rabbit, snake, turtle, unicorn, vulture, worm, xenops, yak, and zebra. Each child should also get one animal. Call out the new letters added on each page. First say, "I need an A and a B." The children with the A and B letters come up and place those letters on the plate.

Then say something like, "Now what animal starts with A?" The children might need help from the presenter or the other children. "Yes. An ant. Who has the ant? Put the ant on the plate." Continue to do this for all the letters unless it becomes too time-consuming. Instead of a board story or along with one, give all the children a paper plate or a picture of a plate and an envelope containing all the letters in the alphabet to follow along with the story.

Markes, Julie. 2005. *Shhhhh! Everybody's Sleeping.* New York: HarperCollins. Illus., David Parkins.

Summary:

The story illustrates how people in the town are sleeping.

Activity:

Children repeat the word "sleeping" throughout the story when you point to them or give them a cue. For example, "The policeman is sleeping. Everything is all right." Pause before the word sleeping so children can respond. Afterwards, point to each child, say his or her name, and say, "is sleeping." For example, "Annie is sleeping. She has been good. Bobby is sleeping under the hood."

Markle, Sandra. 2005. *A Mother's Journey.* Watertown, MA: Charlesbridge. Illus., Alan Marks.

Summary:

The story describes the activities of penguins.

Activity:

This is a children's version of the film *March of the Penguins.* If possible, show clips from the film or show a short scene to accompany the text of this similar story. Even the photo book *March of the Penguins* (National Geographic, 2006) would demonstrate the reality of these events through actual photographs. Without any visuals, this story will be too slow for a large storytime audience. It might work better for an older audience.

Martin, Bill Jr. 2007. *Baby Bear, Baby Bear, What Do You See?* New York: Henry Holt. Illus., Eric Carle.

Summary:

Different animals are asked what they see with the response of another animal performing an action relating to its species.

Activity:

For this book, as with others in a similar format by Bill Martin Jr., ask the children the questions, show the next picture, and wait for a response. For example, "Prairie Dog, Prairie Dog, what do you see?" would be followed by the question to the children, "I see a what strutting by me?" Then flip the page and the children will respond by picture, which in this case is a skunk.

Martin, Bill Jr. and Michael Sampson. 2008. *Kitty Cat, Kitty Cat, Are You Waking Up?* Illus., Laura J. Bryant.

Summary:

A rhyme takes kitty from waking up to leaving the house.

Activity:

Although the whole phrase changes each time, children can still repeat the phrase, "Kitty Cat, Kitty Cat" and then fill in the rest, such as ". . . now we have to go!" "Okay, Mother, I'm sorry I'm so slow."

Martin, David. 2005. *We've All Got Bellybuttons.* Cambridge, MA: Candlewick. Illus., Randy Cecil.

Summary:

Each animal shares a distinguishing feature and asks children if they have the same body part.

Activity:

This is a simple story for movement. It starts with a picture of elephants and reads, "We've got ears, and you do too. We can pull them. Can you?" Then ask the children if they can pull their ears. They will also be asked to clap hands, stretch necks, kick feet, close eyes, open moths, and tickle bellybuttons.

McBratney, Sam. 2006. *Yes We Can!* New York: HarperCollins. Illus., Charles Fuge.

Summary:

Little Roo and Duck argue over what they can and can't do.

Activity:

Children can repeat the phrase "Yes I can," every time it is mentioned in the story. Be sure to signal children when it is time to say this phrase. It occurs when one animal challenges the other over things he can or cannot do.

McCarthy, Meghan. 2003. *George Upside Down.* New York: Viking

Summary:

George likes to do everything upside down, which often lands him in trouble.

Activity:

Use a puppet to demonstrate the actions of George upside down. Tell the story while leaning backward or against the wall. Ask the children to tilt their heads forward or to the side or stand up and bend forward to pretend they are upside down. Ask them to repeat some of the actions in the story, such as being an astronaut, bat, or dog; riding in a plane; yo-yoing; reading; playing the trumpet; painting pictures; and flying a plane.

————. 2006. *Aliens Are Coming! The True Account of the 1938 War of the Worlds Radio Broadcast.* New York: Alfred A. Knopf.
Summary:
> The story describes how people reacted to the radio play *War of the Worlds* in 1938.

Activity:
> Have a microphone and pretend to be the announcer. You might have a radio set to static nearby. Because this is a play, it would be best to have several people reading parts. It mostly alternates between Announcer and Phillips, with an occasional part for Voices. There is also some commentary at the beginning and end of the story. Tell the background of the story to the children and ask if they would have believed it. Was it scary? You might ask older children if they have seen the movie. This could be a good way to introduce the story to middle or high school students reading the book in their classes or any book by H.G. Welles.

McClements, George. 2008. *Night of the Veggie Monster.* **New York: Bloomsbury.**
Summary:
> A child turns into a shaking monster when he has to eat peas or other vegetables until he realizes they aren't so bad.

Activity:
> Children act out the motions of the boy (aka Veggie Monster) when he has to eat a pea. They will have wiggly fingers, watery eyes that they rub, and twisted and curled up toes. They will squirm in their seats and swallow the pea.

McClintock, Barbara. 2006. *Adele and Simon.* **New York: Frances Foster.**
Summary:
> A young boy keeps losing his belongings on the streets of Paris.

Activity:
> This story is best suited for a small audience that can sit close around the book. The activity is already incorporated in the story, as in most pictures the objects that the boy loses can be found hiding on the pages. To involve a larger group, select items from the story, such as a knapsack, crayons, and gloves, and hide them somewhere in the room. Children can search for them after each page is complete. The end of the story gives more information about the early twentieth-century street drawings, so an older audience can use this as an introduction to the architecture or geography of Paris.

McDonnell, Patrick. 2006. *Art.* **New York: Little, Brown.**
Summary:
> Art creates art.

Activity:

One possibility is to put butcher paper, poster board, or other paper on the walls. As you tell the story, draw the art that Art creates. Make squiggles and splotches, zigs and zags, scribbles, squiggles, dots, splotches, blotches, curly cues and doodles of a house, tree, car, dog, moon, and stars. Another option is to lay out the paper all over the floor for children to sit on and draw on. They can draw the objects and designs that Art draws in the book while you read the story. They can end with their own creative paintings.

──────. 2007. *Hug Time.* **New York: Little, Brown.**

Summary:

A kitten wants to give the whole world a hug.

Activity:

Every time the word "hug" or a variation of it is mentioned in the story, ask children to hug themselves. End with a group hug. For example, "He hugged an elephant/and a chimpanzee . . . ./A giraffe,/a hippo,/a baobab tree." You can also have stuffed animals for children to hug, or each time the word "hug" is mentioned, pass a stuffed kitten around to hug.

McGinty, Alice B. 2007. *Thank You, World.* New York: Dial. Illus., Wendy Anderson Halperin.

Summary:

Illustrations of children around the world accompany a thank you message.

Activity:

Although some of the illustrations might be considered stereotypical, they are not identified with any specific countries. With this book, have children simply repeat the phrase "Thank you" each time you signal them. For example, the text reads, "Thank you breeze, for lifting up my kite wings." The accompanying illustration shows children around the world holding kites.

McGuirk, Leslie. 2008. *Lucky Tucker.* Cambridge: Candlewick.

Summary:

A dog's luck turns when he rolls in clovers and meets a leprechaun.

Activity:

Give each child a green four leaf clover created from construction paper or any green paper. Have the children hold up the clover leaf every time the word "lucky" is mentioned in the story or any time the children think that the dog Tucker is lucky. Have them hold it down or behind their backs when he is unlucky.

McKissack, Patricia. 2005. *Where Crocodiles Have Wings.* **New York: Holiday House. Illus., Bob Barner.**

Summary:

The story describes things you wouldn't normally expect an animal to do.

Activity:

In this odd story, "crocs have wings" and "minks wear rings," and other animals do other crazy things. Ask the children if they think the actions are possible. "Do turtles go fast?" "Do coyotes sneeze?" To avoid interrupting the flow of the story, first read each page and then ask questions. You can also assign all the children different animals mentioned in the story and have them stand when their animal name is called.

McKissack, Patricia C. and Onawumi Jean Moss. 2004. *Precious and the Boo Hag.* **New York: Atheneum. Illus., Kyrsten Brooker.**

Summary:

Precious's mother leaves her alone and tells her not to let anyone in. Her brother warns her of the Boo Hag she must avoid.

Activity:

In this somewhat scary story for younger children, have the children repeat the lines, "Pruella is a Boo Hag—she's right outside my window. She's tricky and she's scary, but I won't let her in." Make sure to have the children practice this phrase a few times as it is rather long. The children will see it coming as it is highlighted and in printed rather than typed text. Precious outsmarts the Boo Hag five times.

McLeod, Bob. 2006. *Superhero ABC.* **New York: HarperCollins.**

Summary:

In this ABC book, unique superheroes with corresponding names are described in alphabetical order.

Activity:

Meet Astro-Man, Bubble-Man, Captain Cloud, and more. Bubble man "Blows big bubbles at bullies" "He's bald." "He's a bad boy." "He wears boots." Ask children what other "b" words describe Bubble Man. Do the same for each letter. Then go through the alphabet again, inventing even more superheroes.

McMullan, Kate and Jim. 2006. *I'm Dirty.* **New York: Joanna Cotler.**

Summary:

A backhoe loader describes what he does.

Activity:

Because the story can get a bit confusing, have the children crawl on hands and knees while the story is read. Some of the backhoe's actions they will be able to replicate, and others they will just continue to crawl with. Some actions that they can copy include showing arms, going down the ramp, cleaning up, dumping, making noises, chomping, loosening up, moving tires, and shifting. If you prefer to have children not crawl around, they can sit and act the motions out with their hands.

McNamara, Margaret. 2006. *Fall Leaf Project.* New York: Aladdin. Illus., Mike Gordon.

Summary:

When children find out that leaves don't change colors in every state, they decide to send some leaves to a class where leaves do not change.

Activity:

Collect or create leaves from paper, and scatter them around the room. When the children collect the leaves for the other school, have them collect some off the floor. If time, weather, and opportunity permit, have them collect real leaves from outside to send to another school or library. You can also ask children to pick up leaves off the floor that match the descriptions in the book, such as yellow, orange, red, oak, maple, and chestnut. If you are in one of the states where leaves do not change their colors, you can make your own or pretend to be the recipient of such a package.

McNulty, Faith. 2005. *If You Decide to Go to the Moon.* New York: Scholastic. Illus., Steven Kellogg.

Summary:

A boy tells you everything you need to know if you decide to go to the moon.

Activity:

Have children sit and pretend they are getting ready to go to the moon. You can prepare them by making them a space helmet and playing a video of a spacecraft taking off or just the sound of a rocket launching. Then have them hold on for liftoff. As you read the story you will pretty much just be describing what the boy sees and experiences in the story, and children should feel like they are experiencing the same. Instead of a helmet, you can cut circles for windows and have children hold them throughout the story as if they are viewing the moon from their rocket.

Meade, Holly. 2005. *Inside, Inside, Inside.* New York: Marshall Cavendish.

Summary:

Two siblings play a game where they hide items or containers in other containers.

Activity:

This is a very easy story for which to locate props. It starts with a girl who asks her brother if she could put a marble in a saltshaker. Then the girl and her brother have to put the salt somewhere, so they choose a cereal box. Then the cereal box goes in the recipe box. The recipe box goes in the hat, the hat in the pillowcase, the pillow in a jacket, and so forth. As you can see, the props are every day items the children find around the house. After you tell the story, have the children walk with you through the room or library where you have placed other objects and containers for them to continue the story, taking turns deciding what objects to put in which containers. Because the text is written in two parts for the brother and the sister, you can also tell this story in tandem with another librarian, parent, or volunteer.

Melling, David. 2003. *The Tale of Jack Frost*. New York: Barron's.
Summary:
Goblins kidnap Jack Frost and make him perform his magic.
Activity:
When it is time for Jack Frost to trick the Goblins, they sit in a circle around the lake. You can have the children gather around blue poster board you have cut into the shape of a lake. Hold hands and watch the water turn to ice. To make it turn to ice, simply flip over the blue water to the side you have cut from white poster board. You might also have hidden under the water a container of ice cubes for the children to grab. Alternatively, have a bag of ice cubes, and, when Jack turns something into ice in the story, hold the hand of a child and place an ice cube in his or her hand as if you are turning the hand into ice. You can also do this with other objects in the room and present an ice cube each time you touch an object in the room.

Milgrim, David. 2006. *Time to Get Up, Time to Go*. New York: Clarion.
Summary:
The story is about what a boy does all day.
Activity:
This is a perfect book for bingo or a clock game. Create all the things that the boy does as pictures on a clock or a bingo card. Perhaps a bed or sun for waking up, food for eating, stroller or bike for strolling, pool or water for swimming, a slide, a toy for stopping, a car for riding, unopened food for shopping, pan for cooking, book, trashcan for picking up, broom for sweeping, mouth for chatting, toy for paling, bandage for healing, a full meal for eating dinner, a bathtub for cleaning, a pillow for bedtime stories, and a cloud for dreaming. Arrange the pictures on a card or clock. Each time you read a page, ask the children which picture they think goes with that page in the story. When they guess correctly, ask them to mark it off on their card or clock. Everyone can be a winner by having the same bingo card. Alternatively, they can make it around the clock with the different activities of the day.

————. 2006. *Young MacDonald.* **New York: Dutton.**

Summary:

A boy creates mixed up animals.

Activity:

Either in his mind or in his workshop, young MacDonald combines two animals to create one, such as a "hig" for a horse and a pig, a "deese" for a donkey and goose, a "shicken" for sheep and chicken, "mucks" for mice and ducks, a "cowl" for a cow and an owl, and a "bog" for a boy and a dog. Make these creature combinations out of pictures from patterns or clip art. Pull them out when you arrive at that point of the story. Children can also help out by singing the new verses, such as, "with an Oink-Neigh here, and an Oink-Neigh there." Afterwards, give children patterns from paper bag puppet books or patterns that are mixed up for children to create and name their own new animal.

Miller, Pat. 2008. *We're Going on a Book Hunt.* Fort Atkinson, WI: Upstart Books.

Summary:

The "Bear Hunt" rhyme is adapted to be about finding a good library book.

Activity:

Give all children a book, or let them choose their own. As you tell the story have the children perform the actions on and with their books. They will first tip toe. Then they will look inside the book, look at the size, count fingers, hug it, and turn the pages. They can also repeat the words, "We're going on a book hunt. We're going to find a good one. We know how. Not too easy. Not too hard. But just right." This is a useful book to teach library care to children, but some things, such as shelf markers and counting words to determine reading level, will not be used by all schools.

Mitton, Tony. 2007. *Playful Little Penguins.* New York: Walker. Illus., Guy Parker-Rees.

Summary:

Playful penguins enjoy many activities.

Activity:

Children can stand up and act out the moves of the penguins in this story. They will do such things as slip on ice, squeak, waddle, slide, sled, jump, leap, shout, swirl, whirl, twirl, splash, eat, swim, dance, wiggle, giggle, yawn, and cuddle. You can act as a model, demonstrating the moves they should copy.

Monks, Lydia. 2004. *Aaaarrgghh! Spider!* Boston: Houghton Mifflin.

Summary:

A spider wants to be a part of a real family as a pet.

Activity:

Because the phrase "Aaaarrgghh! Spider! Out you go!" is repeated several times, have children repeat it is well. This occurs only in the first half of the book, because the family does take the spider as a pet until he brings all his spider family and friends.

Montijo, Rhode. 2006. *Cloud Boy.* New York: Simon & Schuster.

Summary:

A cloud boy makes other clouds into shapes to keep him company.

Activity:

Although the book's pictures are lovely, tell the story without the book or continue telling the story after the book is read. Cut out cloud shapes from white paper or poster board and hold them up, asking the children to name the shapes. You will need a butterfly, bunny, boat, and anything else you would like. Next have children create their own cloud shapes from cotton balls or cotton stuffing.

Mora, Pat. 1999. *The Rainbow Tulip.* New York: Puffin. Illus., Elizabeth Sayles.

Summary:

A girl feels awkward when she is the only one in a dress with multiple colors.

Activity:

In this story, Estelita wants a multicolored dress for her school's performance, but when she sees everyone else's clothing has only one color, she doubts her decision. You can either keep adding different colors of scraps of material with Velcro onto a Velcro belt you have on to demonstrate her dress or give each child scraps of colorful material to hold to illustrate the creation of her outfit.

Mortensen, Denise Dowling. 2006. *Ohio Thunder.* New York: Clarion. Illus., Kate Kiesler.

Summary:

It is a stormy day in Ohio.

Activity:

This is a quiet story except for the thunder. You can liven up the rhyming text by having the children make the sound of thunder when similar words are mentioned in the story. You can also play a thunder sound effect or wave a piece of metal to simulate thunder. The sounds children can make include "crackle," "boom," "kaboom," and "roar." The words in the book that indicate the thunder are "storm," "zap," "boom," and "crash." You can also have water to emulate the rain and a flashlight to copy the lightning.

Mozelle, Shirley. 2005. *The Bear Upstairs*. New York: Henry Holt. Illus., Doug Cushman.

Summary:

> A female bear is upset about the noise the new upstairs neighbor bear is making until she realizes how nice he is and that she makes noise too.

Activity:

> Use a dollhouse or playhouse of any kind. Find two bear dolls, animals, or pictures and put one on the first floor and one on the second. You can also draw a house or create one for a flannel board or use a house in a flannel board set. Then point to the upstairs bear or downstairs bear as you tell the story. Alternatively, have the children stand up when you say "upstairs bear" and sit down when you read "downstair's bear."

Muecke, Anne. 2008. *The Dinosaurs' Night Before Christmas*. San Francisco: Chronicle Books. Illus., Nathan Hale.

Summary:

> To the "Night Before Christmas" rhythm, the tale is retold about a boy witnessing dinosaurs in the nearby museum come to life.

Activity:

> This book comes with a CD of dinosaur songs, and lyrics to two of the songs are included at the back of the book. Play the music softly in the background as you read the story. For this book, focus on you as the story reader, because this is a tale that is mostly read to children on the night before Christmas. Act out the motions of the dinosaurs, such as, "Back and forth the bones shook," and have the children emulate you.

Müller, Birte. 2007. *I Can Dress Myself!* New York: NorthSouth.

Summary:

> A bunny insists on trying different clothes to dress herself.

Activity:

> Turn this into a board story. Make a picture of a bunny to tape to a board or wall. Then create clothing out of plain paper in the designs mentioned in the book, or alternate designs to attach to the bunny as she tries on the clothes in the story. Some examples are a yellow dress with flowers and red overalls. Children can also repeat the phrase "I can dress myself!"

Munsch, Robert. 2005. *The Sand Castle Contest*. New York: Scholastic. Illus., Michael Martchenko.

Summary:

> A boy's sand castle is so real that the judges don't believe it is a sand castle.

Activity:

Give each child a piece of paper to draw their own sand castle. Then accuse some of the children of bringing a real house to the beach as in the story. The children can bring the pictures to the front of the room to show off. If you want to use this as a craft and you have a space that can get messy, children can create sand pictures instead.

———. 2008. *Kiss Me, I'm Perfect!* **New York: Scholastic. Illus., Michael Martchenko.**

Summary:

A girl has nothing to wear to school so she wears a grandma gift that says, "Kiss Me, I'm Perfect!" which causes her to be kissed multiple times that day.

Activity:

Make a shirt that has a heart and that reads, "Kiss Me, I'm Perfect!" unless you already own one. Then either act out the story pretending to be kissed by multiple animals as you move your head and cheek in reaction or have puppets that you make kiss your cheek. The animals that will kiss you are a cat, dog, eagle, and a moose, and a boy will kiss you too.

Muntean, Michaela. 2006. *Do Not Open This Book!* **New York: Scholastic. Illus., Pascal Lemaitre.**

Summary:

A pig scolds the reader of the book, who was warned not to open it.

Activity:

There used to be an old Oscar the Grouch book that may still be available in which Oscar warned people not to open his garbage can. As you tell the story, walk around and have a different child turn the page each time. They will laugh when you read words such as, "Aaaargh. Why are you still here?" Then children are warned that if they sit still and quiet it will be okay but that the schoolchildren should not turn the page. Have the children do what the pig asks, such as sit quiet and still, but then have another child open the book.

Murphy, Liz. 2007. *ABC Doctor.* **Maplewood, NJ: Blue Apple.**

Summary:

Words associated with a doctor's visit and health accompany each letter of the alphabet.

Activity:

There are several options for this story. One is to create a bingo game with pictures or words representing the words from the book, such as "germs," "knee brace," and "thermometer." Another is to give children pictures representing the words, and have them stand up and show the pictures when the words are read. Alternatively, simply ask the children what the pictures represent, such as "stethoscope." Then read the short descriptions of each word. Some of the words are a stretch and will be harder to represent with pictures or for the children to identify.

————. 2007. *A Dictionary of Dance.* Maplewood, NJ: Blue Apple.

Summary:

Words related to dance are defined and illustrated.

Activity:

Read each word and definition, model the dance movements when applicable, and have the children copy your dance moves. Some of the words are not types of dances, but most are. For example, children will arabesque, break dance, gallop, and hula.

Myers, Christopher. 2007. *Jabberwocky.* New York: Hyperion.

Summary:

Lewis Carroll's poem takes on a new interpretation about basketball.

Activity:

After each page, ask the children to look at the pictures and listen to the words and guess what they think the poem means. For example, there is a large arm and hand with a basketball in the palm over a basketball net. The text reads, "The jawsa that buite, The claws that catch!" Children can make their own interpretations. At the end ask children for more silly and gibberish words.

Nakagawa, Hirotaka. 2006. *Sumo Boy.* New York: Hyperion. Illus., Yoshifumi Hasegawa.

Summary:

Sumo Boy fights for justice.

Activity:

If you are willing to add a little violence to storytime, here is the book. Don boxing gloves and fake punch as you tell the story. At one point Sumo Boy "punches" a bully harassing a girl. The end offers pictures of different wrestling moves. I'd save this one for non-storytime moments, but if children love wrestling, they will love this book.

Napoli, Donna Jo. 2005. *Pink Magic.* New York: Clarion. Illus., Chad Cameron.

Summary:

A boy wants mail, especially something pink and especially something that shows love.

Activity:

The postal worker delivers mail every day. Have a mailbag. Inside of it keep the objects that the mail carrier has with him. You will need regular mail for the beginning of the story. Then when Nick decides he wants pink mail and it is actually delivered to him, you will need a watermelon, flamingo, pink pigs, and a pink letter from his sister.

Nedwidek, John. 2008. *Ducks Don't Wear Socks*. New York: Vilking. Illus., Lee White.

Summary:

A serious girl is confused by a duck who wears clothes.

Activity:

Ask children to identify the clothing that the duck is wearing, such as boots, socks, underwear, and a hat, in each picture. In the end, the girl wears a duck outfit to tease the duck.

Nelson, Kadir. 2005. *He's Got the Whole World in His Hands*. New York: Dial.

Summary:

Nelson's beautiful artwork illustrates this popular song.

Activity:

Sing the song or play a version of the song as you read this story. You may even remember the hand motions you learned as a child or easily locate them on the Internet, even on YouTube.

Neubecker, Robert. 2007. *Wow! School!* New York: Hyperion.

Summary:

Simple text describes what happens at a school.

Activity:

Ask children to identify the activities occurring on each double-page spread. For example, for the pages that read, "Wow! Classroom!" ask the children what it is and then what they see in the classroom. For, "Wow! Art!" ask the children what the kids in the story are creating and have them be specific, such as, "decorating letters" and "painting a picture of a fish."

Nevius, Carol. 2004. *Karate Hour*. New York: Marshall Cavendish. Illus., Bill Thomson.

Summary:

A karate practice session is described.

Activity:

The art of karate should be respected, so the goal is not to exaggerate. Instead, simply have the children try to copy the images and words of the story. Have them stand and move to the best of their ability as if they were in their own karate class. First they will bow and then bend and touch their toes. They will stretch and kick. Make sure they have plenty of space. The descriptions of the belts and their colors at the end are interesting.

Newman, Jeff. 2006. *Hippo! No, Rhino.* New York: Little, Brown.

Summary:

A rhinoceros is misidentified as a hippo because of a signage error.

Activity:

Begin by showing the picture in the book and asking the children, "Is this a hippo?" They may say yes, but the answer is "no." For each page, tell the children that the people see the sign and think it is a hippo. Ask them if they know what the sign says. Continue to ask them, "Is this a hippo? What could it be?" In the end tell them it is a rhino, and ask if it is a porcupine-o as the sign now reads.

Niemann, Christoph. 2007. *The Police Cloud.* New York: Schwartz & Wade.

Summary:

A cloud wants to be a police officer but does not have much success.

Activity:

Simply create a cloud out of a big piece of white poster board as your prop. Create a police hat and a firefighter's hat. Although the cloud fails as a police officer, he excels as a firefighter in the end. Just add the hat when he becomes a police officer and change it to a firefighter's hat later in the story.

Nobisso, Josephine. 2005. *The Numbers Dance: A Counting Comedy.* Westhampton Beach, NY: Gingerbread House. Illus., Dasha Ziborova.

Summary:

Numbers dance in various ways.

Activity:

This is the perfect story for movement. As in a dance competition, attach a number with string or tape to each contestant (storytime participant). Use the numbers 1 to 10. Assign more than one child a number if you have more than ten children. The earlier numbers are used more often in the story. Instruct children that when their number is mentioned in the story they should act out the dance that that number is performing. For example, the book begins, "And-a-1, And-a-2, And-a-3, And-a-4, Four dainty numbers waltz across the floor." Numbers 1 to 4 will then dance across the floor. They may need some encouragement and modeling. "1 spins elegant, straight and true. 2 tiptoes from shoe to shoe. 3 swirls 'round, so curvy and plump. With 4 on one leg, glide and jump!" Therefore, 1 will spin, 2 will tiptoe, 3 will swirl and 4 will glide and jump on one leg. Some activities will be a little more difficult to decipher. Children may not always act on turn, but it will still be a fun time.

Norac, Carl. 2007. *Monster, Don't Eat Me!* Berkeley: Groundwood. Illus., Carll Cneut.

Summary:

A pig's overeating leads him into the arms of a monster.

Activity:

Each time it seems like the monster is about to eat the pig, the pig says, "Monster don't eat me." Even though there is more text surrounding this sparsely written phrase, cue children as when to say this phrase in the story.

Norworth, Jack. 1993. *Take Me Out to the Ballgame.* New York: Four Winds. Illus., Alec Gillman.

Summary:

The popular song is illustrated.

Activity:

Flip the pages, and have children sing along. Pause at places like the crowd and peanuts and point to the pictures so children know which words to sing next if they are unfamiliar with the song. Then sing the song as you play a game of baseball by having children toss a ball or swing a bat or run to bases. You can also make up a song about going somewhere else, like, "Take me out to the library," and ask children for suggestions about what to sing next. Also try the version by Jim Burke.

O'Connor, Jane. 2005. *Fancy Nancy.* New York: HarperCollins. Illus., Robin Preiss Glasser.

Summary:

Nancy tries to get her family to dress and act as fancy as she is.

Activity:

Bring out the dress-up clothes or make long scarves out of scraps of material or buy cheap feather boas. You might want some ties for the boys. Hats will be helpful even if they are made from construction paper. When Nancy trains her family to be fancy, have the children start putting on fancy clothes. Then have them pretend they are going to the restaurant as the family does and lift their pinkies as they drink.

———. 2008. *Fancy Nancy's Favorite Fancy Words: From Accessories to Zany.* New York: HarperCollins. Illus., Robin Preiss Glasser.

Summary:

Fancy Nancy illustrates fancy words.

Activity:

Show the pictures and say the words on each page. Ask children what the words mean. For example, for the word "Monogram," the picture shows Nancy's initials on a bathroom rug. Students may see this and guess the meaning of the word. Then read the descriptions. This is a good for vocabulary for older children.

O'Connor, Joe. 2006. *Where Did Daddy's Hair Go?* New York: Random House. Illus., Henry Payne.

Summary:

A boy thinks his father has "lost" his hair, so he tries to find it.

Activity:

The first thing you can do is have the children follow you around the room looking for Jeremiah's dad's hair. Pretend to look in the places mentioned in the book, such as cupboards, drawers, the bathtub, garage, toilet, trash cans, rocks, front yard, and backyard. Alternatively, pretend to look in places in the library because Jeremiah's dad had been there. When Jeremiah imagines his dad with different hair styles, place various wigs or cut-out hair pieces over your own head, a child's head, doll's head, or a picture on a board. In the end, Jeremiah realizes that everyone is different.

Oelschlager, Vanita. 2008. *Let Me Bee.* Akron, OH: Vanita Books. Illus., Kristin Blackwood.

Summary:

A bee and a child alternate claims that they are more afraid of the other.

Activity:

Locate a bee finger puppet, or create one yourself. Make the bee talk during the bee's parts in the story, and you will pretend to be the child responding to the bee. You can also use a volunteer to take parts in this story.

Ogburn, Jacqueline K. 2005. *The Bake Shop Ghost.* Boston: Houghton Mifflin. Illus., Marjorie Priceman.

Summary:

A baker dies and haunts the bakery and future bakers.

Activity:

Cora Lee wants no one else to run her bakery and scares them all off except for Annie. You might pretend to be a ghost and have different children act out the parts of the bakers. They can run back to their seats when you scare them away. When Cora Lee wants Annie to bake a cake better than any other, Annie tries many different kinds. Give children cookies or pieces of cake to try or just pictures of cakes. It is actually a birthday cake that Cora Lee wants.

Children can guess what kind of cake will make Cora Lee happy. After Annie fails many times, ask the children, "What cake do you think Cora Lee might like?" Answers might be chocolate or banana, etc. Then pull out a picture of a birthday cake or an actual cake.

O'Malley, Kevin. 2004. *Lucky Leaf.* New York: Walker.

Summary:

A mother makes her son go out to play instead of playing video games, and he finds a lucky leaf.

Activity:

In the story, a boy and his friends try to grab the last leaf off of a tree because they believe it will be lucky. Dangle a leaf on a sting attached to a stick over the heads of the children or place one high and have each child take a turn at reaching for it. Ask the children what else might lucky, such as a rabbit's foot. Have leaves hidden around the room for children to find so they can each have their own lucky leaf. These can be made from construction paper or actual leaves that children can then use in a craft.

————. 2005. *Once Upon a Cool Motorcycle Dude.* New York: Walker. Illus., Carol Heyer and Scott Goto.

Summary:

Two children make up a fairy tale they don't always agree with to tell in class because they can't decide on a favorite real one.

Activity:

The boy and girl each take turns telling their version of a fairy tale. The girl's tale involves a princess, of course, and the boy's involves a motorcycle and giant, of course. Have a boy and a girl puppet, or make boy and girl heads to place on sticks. Use the girl puppet when the girl tells her story and the boy when the boy tells his. You can also use props and make quick clothing changes. Wear a wig for the girl and a baseball hat for the boy, or wear a princess hat or drape yourself in silky or lacy fabric when talking about the girl's story and maybe a leather jacket when talking about the boy's story. Either way, show whose turn it is by what you wear or hold. Different voices will help too.

Orloff, Karen Kaufman. 2006. *If Mom Had Three Arms.* New York: Sterling. Illus., Pete Whitehead.

Summary:

A boy wonders what his mom could do with up to 20 arms.

Activity:

This is a counting book that goes up to 20, so have children count with you. Just pause and ask children, "If Mom had how many arms could she make good art?" Children can keep track or count the arms in the picture on their own or with you. In this case, the answer is six. Alternatively, read the number of arms the mother has and ask the children to guess by the pictures what the mother would do with those arms. In this case, the answer would be to make art although children might say paint or draw. You can also make 20 arms out of paper or material or socks and pull them out each time mom has more arms. Get even more creative and crafty and Velcro the arms to a shirt.

Osborne, Will and Mary Pope Osborne. 2005. *Sleeping Bobby.* New York: Atheneum. Illus., Giselle Porter.

Summary:

The story of *Sleeping Beauty* has a male lead.

Activity:

This story is very similar to the tale we all know. If children are not familiar with *Sleeping Beauty,* you may first want to tell it to them or read it to them. Then, while reading *Sleeping Baby,* ask, "Did this happen in *Sleeping Beauty*? For example, "Did the king and queen name their baby Bob in *Sleeping Beauty*?" "No" they should answer. "Did the queen keep out the thirteenth wise woman in *Sleeping Beauty*?" Or, simply, "Did this happen in *Sleeping Beauty*?

Page, Gail. 2006. *How to Be a Good Dog.* New York: Bloomsbury.

Summary:

Bobo learns to be a good dog so he can stay at the house.

Activity:

When the cat teaches the dog to shake, fetch, heel, sit, lie down, roll over, and stay, children can bring their own stuffed animal to give these commands to. If no animals are available, ask the children to repeat the commands. This is a good story to use with a pet parade or fake pet parade.

Paratore, Coleen. 2004. *26 Big Things Small Hands Do.* Minneapolis: Free Spirit. Illus., Mike Reed.

Summary:

Describes all the big things little hands can do using the letters of the alphabet.

Activity:

The children can act out all the different actions with just their hands. For example, have the children join hands for "and small hands join." Children can pretend to be planting something for "small hands plant," and they can fold their hands together to pretend to open a book for "small hands open books and travel far." Keep the kids active and using their imagination on every page with this book.

Park, Linda Sue. 2004. *Mung-Mung: A Foldout Book of Animal Sounds.* **Water-town, MA: Charlesbridge. Illus., Diane Bigda.**

Summary:

Different animal sounds from different parts of the world are shared.

Activity:

The book is already set up to ask the children questions. It starts, "What kind of animal says . . . Mung-Mung," which is Korean. On the next page it shares "Bo Bo" in Hindu, "Wow Wow" in Spanish, "Gav Gav" in Russian, and "Woof-Woof" in English. Share all these sounds, and maybe make it more difficult by leaving out the English sound. Then flip the page and read, "It's a dog." Continue using the same approach with each animal.

Parr, Todd. 2003. *The Family Book.* **New York: Little, Brown.**

Summary:

Different families are described.

Activity:

I like this book because it includes families with two Moms and two Dads. If it will not cause any controversy and all children can be included, ask the children to stand up when their type of family is mentioned in the story. For example, when the text reads, "Some families are big," children with big families can stand. The text will also read, "Some families have one parent instead of two," and then children with only one parent stand. Most likely children will get confused and try to stand as often as possible. This would work best in a school with slightly older children where they have a variety of different living arreangements. At least one category should apply to each child.

Parsons, Garry. 2005. *Krong!* **Wilton, CT: Tiger Tales.**

Summary:

An alien arrives in a boy's backyard and he does not speak English, so the boy must figure out his language.

Activity:

Have the children repeat the English, French, Spanish, and Japanese greetings as well as the words in Noobanese after you. So, when the alien says, "Krong!" ask the children, "Can you say 'krong'? Can you guess what it means?"

Patricelli, Leslie. 2007. *The Birthday Box.* **Cambridge, MA: Candlewick.**

Summary:

A boy gets a box with a puppy in it for his birthday.

Activity:

Bring out a cardboard box with holes on the side and a stuffed dog inside. Children can gather around the box and be surprised at every moment as the boy is in the story. In the story they stand on the box, but this would not be a good action to replicate. The boy does hug the box, too, which the children can all do. They can peek in the hole to guess what is inside or simply guess without looking in the hole. As in the story, they can each take turns sitting in the box with the dog if the box is big enough. They can pretend it is a ship or a sled or a robot and then pretend to sleep next to the box as the boy in the story sleeps in it.

Paul, Ann Whitford. 2004. *Manana Iguana*. New York: Holiday House. Illus., Ethan Long.
Summary:
Iguana is having a party, but the other creatures claim they are too slow or too fast to help.
Activity:
Tell the students that every time you say the word "fast" when the rabbit claims to be too fast to help, they are to run in place and move their arms like they are running. Tell them that every time you say the word "slow" when the turtle claims to be too slow to help, they are to walk in place in slow motion. Then tell them to hold their hands behind their backs every time the snake claims he cannot do something because he has no arms. Demonstrate the actions for them. You can also ask the children to tell you what the names of the week are in English, as they are written in Spanish in the book. In the end, the creatures all help clean up. This is a good way to have children start cleaning up the storytime area.

Penner, Fred. 2005. *The Cat Came Back*. New Milford, CT: Roaring Brook. Illus., Renée Reichert.
Summary:
Illustrations accompany Fred Penner's song about a cat that keeps returning.
Activity:
Children can simply repeat or sing the refrain, "But the cat came back the very next day. The cat came back—we thought he was a goner. But the cat came back. He just couldn't stay away." Find a copy of the song to play along while you show the book. Keep covering up and revealing a cat puppet, or have a hidden stash of paper cats that you keep pulling out and giving to the children each time the cat is sent away.

Perkins, Lynne Rae. 2007. *Pictures from Our Vacation*. New York: Greenwillow.
Summary:
A boy and girl take pictures of a vacation to the family farm.
Activity:
The children in this story are given cameras that print instant sticky pictures to add to their journal. They are quite bored on this vacation but learn to savor the memories in the end. Give each child pages that look like a journal with room to draw pictures at the top and write words at the bottom. Younger

children will obviously not be writing words. Children can illustrate the journal with pictures of this family's trip as you read the story. In the end they can create pictures from their family's trips or visits.

————. 2008. *The Cardboard Piano.* **New York: Greenwillow.**

Summary:

A girl, inspired by the story of a composer who practiced on a fake piano, shares a cardboard piano with her friend so that they can learn together, but it doesn't work out as planned.

Activity:

Create a cardboard piano for children to try and play. It can be one large one that children can stand on, as in the movie *Big*, a smaller one for children to play with their hands and take turns on or pass around, or each child can get his or her own copied on paper. Children can play along in the story. This would be for a slightly older than preschool audience, because younger children might not understand the story of the comppser and how someone could play a fake piano as the girls in the story could not quite grasp.

Peters, Bernadette. 2008. *Broadway Barks.* Maplewood, NJ: Broadway Barks. Illus., Liz Murphy.

Summary:

Based on an actual yearly event, dogs are auctioned for adoption, especially a stray dog from a park.

Activity:

Conduct your own dog adoption with pictures of dogs or stuffed animals or puppets. During the story hold up dogs to auction off, and give one to each child to hold.

Phillips, Sally Kahler. 2006. *Nonsense!* New York: Random House.

Summary:

The author describes silly things and instructs readers to say "Nonsense!" at such things.

Activity:

This is a simple game of repetition. Instruct the children to say "Nonsense!" when you ask, "What would your answer be?" or similar phrases. "What would you say if dogs grew on trees, if rhinos could fly, and chickens laid cheese?" "Nonsense!" they'd say.

Philpot, Lorna and Graham Philpot. 2006. *Find Anthony Ant.* New York: Boxer.

Summary:

Using the "The Ants Came Marching" song, the book demonstrates counting to ten while asking children to find Anthony Ant on each page.

Activity:

This may not be best for large groups, because the pictures of Anthony Ant are small. It is also a little confusing because it is hard to tell if the ants really resemble Anthony when they are so small. However, you can assume if the ant is doing what the question asks, such as, "Anthony stopped . . . To eat a plum? or To buy bubble gum? or To beat a drum?," that the ant is Anthony. Alternatively, ask the children which of those three activities Anthony partook in or walk around the room with the book giving children a chance to find him.

Pickering, Jimmy. 2007. *Skelly the Skeleton Girl*. New York: Simon & Schuster.
Summary:

A skeleton girl asks all the ghoulish creatures around her if a lost bone is theirs until she finds the owner, a skeleton dog.

Activity:

Walk around the room pretending each child is a character in the book. Hold a bone and ask the children one by one if the bone is theirs. If they say no, as they should, continue with the statements in the book. If they say yes, respond with something like, "Are you sure? I thought you said. . . ." An example from the text is, "'I asked my MAN-EATING plants.' 'No, my dear, we wouldn't eat THAT!'"

Pilutti, Deb. 2008. *The City Kid & the Suburb Kid*. New York: Sterling. Illus., Linda Bleck.
Summary:

The book tells two similar stories about a boy's visit to the city and his friend's visit to the suburbs. When the reader reaches the end of one story, the book must be flipped over to begin the next one.

Activity:

Use this for a compare and contrast lesson in any grade, even high school and college. First read the suburban kid's adventure to the city. Then, as you read the city kid's adventure to the suburbs, ask the children what happened in the city in the same or similar way. For older children, read each half of the book first and then compare and contrast later by memory.

Pinkney, Jerry. 2007. *Little Red Riding Hood*. New York: Little, Brown.
Summary:

The traditional story of *Little Red Riding Hood* is shared.

Activity:

Children act out the parts of the wolf, grandmother, and Little Red Riding Hood as you tell the story. They can repeat the classic lines, "what great eyes you have," "what great teeth you have," etc.

Plourde, Lynn. 2005. *Pajama Day.* New York: Dutton. Illus., Thor Wickstrom.
Summary:
A boy forgets everything he needs for pajama day but finds it all in unusual places.
Activity:
Have children wear their pajamas to pajama day. Prepare a box of items that can be used for slippers, a pet, and a pillow. In the book, the boy uses mittens as slippers and a balloon as a pillow.

————. 2007. *A Mountain of Mittens.* Watertown, MA: Charlesbridge. Illus., Mitch Vane.
Summary:
Children are told not to lose their mittens, but they keep using them for other purposes.
Activity:
The rhyme "Mittens, Mittens. My, oh, my! A mountain of mittens piled up high" is repeated throughout the text after more and more mittens are left behind. Have children repeat this phrase when cued. Alternatively, give children real mittens left behind at your home or in the library or found at a thrift store and have them stack them in piles as in the book. You can give children paper mittens to create a pyramid on a wall or board to replicate the images from the text. After the story, have children find hidden mittens or pictures of mittens throughout the room.

Poole, Amy Lowry. 2005. *The Pea Blossom.* New York: Holiday House.
Summary:
Five peas tell where they would like to go, but only one gets his wish.
Activity:
Create a pea pod and peas out of construction paper or purchase a pea pod puppet. You can also use real peas or small objects that resemble peas. If you use real peas or pea-sized objects, take a straw and spit one across the room one at a time as happens in the story. If you use balloons or construction paper peas, simply throw them across the room. To make them move better, attach green circles to small Frisbees. In the end, the last pea finds him useful on the windowsill where he provides strength for a sick girl and gets to live.

Portis, Antoinette. 2006. *Not a Box.* New York: HarperCollins.
Summary:
An unidentified voice asks a bunny about his box, and the rabbit is adamant that it is not a box but all of these other wonderful objects.

Activity:

Instruct children to repeat the phrase "It's not a box" when signaled. Alternatively, show them the pictures and ask them what the object is if it is not a box. They will see that the box is a car, peak, building, robot, boat, and more. Another possibility is to give the children a box or have them share a box and have them pretend their "box" is the things in the story and hold it like the pig does in each scene.

————. 2008. *Not a Stick.* New York: HarperCollins.

Summary:

An unidentified voice asks a pig to watch out for his stick, but the pig is adamant that it is not a stick but all of these other wonderful objects.

Activity:

Instruct children to repeat the phrase "It's not a stick" when signaled. Alternatively, show them the pictures and ask them what the object is if it is not a stick. They will see that the stick is a fishing pole, baton, paintbrush, weight, riding stick, and sword. Another possibility is to give the children blunt-edged sticks, such as rhythm sticks or paper towel tubes, and have them pretend their "stick" is the things in the story and hold it like the pig does in each scene.

Postgate, Daniel. 2007. *Smelly Bill.* New York: NorthSouth.

Summary:

The family can't rid their dog of his stink until Aunt Bleach comes over.

Activity:

Give children a picture of a dog and a black or gray crayon. Ask them to draw or scribble a puff of smoke every time the story mentions the smell of the dog. Words that would trigger this response include "smelly," "stink," and "smell."

Prap, Lila. 2004. *Animals Speak.* New York: NorthSouth.

Summary:

The book describes the sounds animals make in different countries.

Activity:

Ask children what sounds each animal makes, and then ask them, "Yes, but did you know that in the (insert language) language, the people say the sound (insert animal sound)?" Have the children repeat the sounds. "The sheep bleats Baa. Do you know what sound a sheep makes in Spanish? Bee." Other language alternatives are also provided for each word, although only one is highlighted.

————. 2005. *Why?* La Jolla, CA: Kane/Miller.

Summary:

Questions about various animals are asked and answered.

Activity:

Simply ask the children the questions to see if they know the answers. "Why do hyenas laugh?" A funny answer is provided. Ask the children, "Do you think it is because it tickles them to walk barefoot on the grass?" They may reply no, and you can provide the correct answer, which in this case is that they do not laugh. However, they make a giggling sound when attacked. Continue with other questions of your choice. Other possibilities are, "Why are zebras striped? Why do whales spout water? Why do rhinos have horns on their noses?" And many more.

Prose, Francine. 2005. *Leopold, the Liar of Leipzig.* New York: HarperCollins. Illus., Einav Aviram.

Summary:

A man tells stories of places that do not exist.

Activity:

The townspeople love to hear Leopold's story but question him when a professor says these places do not exist. After reading each page about a different place, ask the children if they think the place exists. "Is there really a Lusitana? Do you think there is a place where ladies look like lizards?" You can even ask about the true places the professor talks about. In the end, ask the children to make up a place and things about it that all start with the same letter. Give them a silly example.

Pulver, Robin. 2006. *Nouns and Verbs Have a Field Day.* New York: Holiday House. Illus., Lynn Rowe Reed.

Summary:

A classroom of nouns and verbs has fun with and without the children.

Activity:

This should be used with older children who are familiar with parts of speech and spelling. Younger children may get confused. There are many activities you can do throughout the book; select one for each day, or select only a few. "Each day in Mr. Wright's classroom, the kids searched the room for nouns and verbs." Have children identify nouns and verbs in the room, including on signs and book covers. Mr. Wright decides the children will abandon this game for one day and go outside to play. Next, each part of speech says a word that relates to itself. "'Look!' said a verb." Ask the children which other words the verb might say, which words would the nouns say, etc. "Verbs wanted to be with other verbs. Push, pull, yank, and tow said they belonged together."

Ask the children what other verbs belong in this category. Make other categories not listed on the page, or have the children fill in the blank. Then the verbs and nouns realize they need one another. "Mike and Ting were throwing and catching." Make up combinations for kids in your class, or have them do it themselves. At the end there is a fill-in-the-blank Mad Libs–type letter. Follow up with a game of Mad Libs that you have purchased, gotten online, or created yourself.

————. 2008. *Silent Letters Loud and Clear.* New York: Holiday House. Illus., Lynn Rowe Reed.

Summary:

Children don't want to use silent letters, thinking they are useless until they disappear from a letter to the editor that they write.

Activity:

The letter to the editor with the missing silent letters reminds me of English meme where you can still read words even if vowels are excluded if you are familiar with the words already. Pair this book with an article on English meme for high school and college students. For younger students, ask them to identify the silent letters within the text of the book. They are either outlined or in a different color.

Ransom, Jeanie Franz. 2007. *What Do Parents Do? (When You're Not Home).* Atlanta: Peachtree. Illus., Cyd Moore.

Summary:

Two children speculate about what their parents do when the kids are not home.

Activity:

This is a fun story in which the children think their parents play their video games and jump on the bed when they are gone. To make this book more interactive, ask the children after each page if they think their parents do these things. For example, the text reads, "At least mom and dad can agree on one thing, They both think it's a lot of fun to dress up the dog. I don't know how the dog feels, but those better not be clean clothes he's wearing!" Then ask the children, "Do you think your parents dress up your pets when you are gone?" You can follow by asking children what else they think their parents do when they are away. Hopefully they will say rest, clean, and watch TV.

Raschka, Chris. 2006. *Five for a Little One.* New York: Atheneum.

Summary:

Words describe the five senses.

Activity:

Name the senses, read the examples from the book, and then ask the children to provide their own examples of the senses. For example, the text reads, "Hearing is 2. Happy ears, pay attention! Did we mention sounds surround you? Catch the honking, barking, sinking." Then you could ask the children, "What else can you hear?"

Rayner, Catherine. 2006. *Augustus and His Smile.* Intercourse, PA: Good Books.
Summary:

A tiger looks for his smile.

Activity:

Have children follow you around the room as they pretend to help Augustus the tiger find his smile. You can have a tiger mask or tiger puppet to follow. Act out the story as Augustus searches. Creep under bushes, climb trees, climb a mountain, swim the ocean, prance through the desert, dance in the rain. Finish by looking in a mirror to see that your smile is there wherever you are.

Reid, Barbara. 2005. *The Subway Mouse.* New York: Scholastic.
Summary:

A mouse ventures out to Tunnel's End.

Activity:

Reid uses Plasticine to create the mice and scenery in this story. She also adds found objects. Find your own objects that students can collect as the mouse does in the story or that can be displayed on a board. Use a raisin box and gum wrapper, for example, and place objects such as these around the room for children to collect and hoard. Then they can walk around the room with you as they pretend they are in the subway looking for the way out.

Rex, Adam. 2007. *Pssst!* New York: Harcourt.
Summary:

A child goes to the zoo and gets requests from the animals to bring them unusual things.

Activity:

This is a clever book. In the end it turns out that all the items the animals need are to help them build a car as an escape or form of entertainment. In the story, the animals get the attention of a child by saying, "Pssst!" Have the children say this word when they are signaled. Pass out pictures of the objects the girl needs to bring back to the zoo, and have them bring them to you when mentioned. The items are a tire, trash can, flashlights, paint, helmets, corn, and a wheelbarrow.

Rex, Michael. 2007. *You Can Do Anything Daddy!* New York: G.P. Putnam's Sons.
Summary:
A boy asks his dad what he would do to save him in unusual situations.
Activity:
Have children finish the sentences for you. Instead of the boy asking things like, "What if they took me up a high cliff?" you could say, "What if they took me up . . ." and have the children complete the question. Then you respond as the father and say, "I would put on my boots and climb up." Finish by having children ask their own questions about what Daddy would do to save them.

Reynolds, Aaron. 2007. *Buffalo Wings.* New York: Bloomsbury. Illus., Paulette Bogan.
Summary:
A rooster looks for a buffalo to make buffalo wings for a football game.
Activity:
This is an obvious book that would have been funnier if the rooster were a chicken when he found out that that is where buffalo wings come from. The phrase "But not a single buffalo" is repeated several times in the story when the rooster goes looking for one. Signal the children when to repeat this phrase.

Reynolds, Peter. H. 2003. *The Dot.* Cambridge, MA: Candlewick.
Summary:
A boy doesn't think he can draw until a teacher gets him to draw a dot, which leads to more creativity.
Activity:
Place a piece of paper on a wall or board. Draw a simple dot, and sign it as the teacher has the boy do in the story. When Vashti starts to draw more colorful dots, replicate the pictures by drawing more and more dots with different colored markers or pulling out pre-made pictures. Alternatively, give children paper and crayons and have them create their own dots or come to the board and create some for you.

Ries, Lori. 2004. *Super Sam.* Watertown, MA: Charlesbridge. Illus., Sue Ramá.
Summary:
Sam entertains his brother by wearing a cape and pretending to be "Super Sam!"
Activity:
Have children perform the actions of Sam, such as run, fly, show strength, leap, climb, hide, escape, and save the day while yelling "Super Sam!" Kids can also use their coats or towels you have brought to drape around them as their capes.

————. 2007. *Fix It, Sam*. Watertown, MA: Charlesbridge. Illus., Sue Ramá.

Summary:

Sam can fix anything for his brother.

Activity:

There is not much text in this story. After Sam fixes something for his brother, such as toys that are a mess, a blanket that is stuck, or books that are out of place, and before his brother praises Sam for his help, can ask the children, "Did Sam fix it?" Children can look at the illustrations to make their decisions.

Rinck, Maranke. 2008. *I Feel a Foot!* Honesdale, PA: Lemniscaat. Illus., Martijn van der Linden.

Summary:

Using the folktale made popular by Ed Young's *Seven Blind Mice*, a group of animals guess what the creature before them really is. It is an elephant.

Activity:

Turn this into a guessing game. For example, when the turtle thinks he feels a foot, ask the children what they think this could be. When the bat feels the wings, ask the children what they think this might be. You will also ask them after the octopus feels a tentacle, the bird feels a beak, and the goat feels a goatee. You could also use a blanket or hammock to have children sit on and pretend to be the animals in the story or place stuffed animals there instead.

Robinson, Fay. 2005. *Faucet Fish*. New York: Dutton. Illus., Wayne Anderson.

Summary:

Fish keep coming out of a girl's faucets.

Activity:

There are two possibilities for this story. The first is to have a fish bowl and various types of fish cut out of construction paper. When different fish come out of the faucet and Elizabeth puts them in bowls, you can pull out fish and place them in the bowl. Alternatively, have children grab fish from around the room and put them in the bowl. You can even make a fake faucet and hang fish from a bag beneath it from which children can select. Another possibility is to turn the story into a flannel board story.

Rohmann, Eric. 2005. *Clara and Asha*. New Milford, CT: Roaring Brook.

Summary:

Clara invites Asha and other imaginary creature friends into her room at night.

Activity:

Because Clara invites creatures into her room, make a window out of cardboard or poster board. Sit behind the window while you tell the story. Either prop it up, hold it up, or have two children hold it up. Give children stuffed animals or pictures to pass through the window throughout the story. Even though only two creatures actually enter the window in the story, Clara says she has many friends, so you can end with all the children bringing their creatures through the fake window.

Root, Phyllis. 2006. *Looking for a Moose.* Cambridge, MA: Candlewick. Illus., Randy Cecil.

Summary:

Children go looking for a moose that they do not expect to find.

Activity:

Have children walk around the room or even the library with you pretending to look for the moose. Children can act out the actions in the story along the way, such as, "TROMP STOMP!" in the woods, "squeech squooch!" in the swamp, "scritch scratch! In the bushes!" and "TRIP TROP!" in the hillside. Older children can play a game that I remember playing at a friend's church event during high school called the "Blue Gnu." We had to go to a mall and ask people if they were the blue gnu. We never did find him but suspected it was the pastor. Children can ask library staff if they are the moose and then find one with antlers at the end of their walk.

Rosenthal, Amy Krouse. 2005. *Little Pea.* San Francisco: Chronicle Books. Illus., Jen Corace.

Summary:

A little pea doesn't want to eat his candy.

Activity:

Simply hold a large round green circle cut out of construction paper to represent a pea, or give each child one to hold and move as you tell the story. You can give children candy too, if allowed, although the pea rejects the candy in the story until he can eat spinach.

———. 2006. *Christmas Cookies: Bite Size Holiday Lessons.* New York: Harper-Collins. Illus., Jane Dyer.

Summary:

Life lessons, such as tradition, appreciation, and responsibility, are taught through the idea of baking and sharing cookies.

Activity:

You can approach this story in a number of ways to teach the valuable lessons of the book. One is to give each child a piece of paper with words on it from the book to convey a lesson in one of the themes, such as anticipation, tradition, disappointed, celebrate, appreciative, prosperity, charitable, responsible, moderation, reciprocate, frustrated, perseverance, selfish, thoughtful, lonely, sharing, gratitude, family, gracious, believe, joy, peace, and hope. For younger children, tell them their lesson and/or write it on large paper so you can see who has which lesson. As the story progresses, children can stand when their lesson is mentioned. Ask slightly older children to define what each lesson means, or give an example for each life lesson and ask if this is what the lesson means. Another option is to read the scenarios in the story without telling the children what the lesson is, and they can stand up if they think their paper names the lesson. Some of these words will be too difficult for most preschool children to grasp, so simply having them stand when appropriate would work best for this age.

———. 2006. *Cookies: Bite Size Life Lessons.* **New York: HarperCollins. Illus., Jane Dyer.**

Summary:

Life lessons, such as envy, respect, and compassion, are taught through the idea of baking and sharing cookies.

Activity:

You can approach this story in a number of ways to teach the valuable lessons of the book. One is to give each child a piece of paper with the name of a lesson written on it, such as cooperate, patient, proud, modest, respect, trustworthy, fair, unfair, compassionate, greedy, generous, pessimistic, optimistic, polite, honest, courageous, envy, loyal, open-minded, regret, content, and wise. For younger children, tell them their lesson and/or write it on large paper so you can see who has which lesson. As the story progresses, children can stand when their lesson is mentioned in the story. Ask slightly older children to define what each lesson means, or give an example for each life lesson and ask if this is what their lesson means. Another option is to read the scenarios in the story without telling the children what the lesson is, and they can stand up if they think their paper names the lesson. Some of these words will be too difficult for most preschool children to grasp, so simply having them stand when appropriate would work best for this age.

Rosenwald, Laurie. 2007. *And to Name but Just a Few: Red Yellow Green Blue.* Maplewood, NJ: Blue Apple.

Summary:

The book describes many things in various colors.

Activity:

The text reads something similar for each color. For yellow, it says, "I'm the middle of a Daisy! The canaries call me crazy! I'm bananas I'm a joke! Sunshine, LEMONS and a YOLK!" Give children a piece of construction paper for each color mentioned in the book. Have them hold up the color when it is seen or identified in the story. You will need the colors of red, blue, green, orange, purple, yellow, pink, and black.

Rueda, Claudia. 2006. *Let's Play in the Forest.* **New York: Scholastic.**

Summary:

Forest animals taunt the wolf to come out while he dresses.

Activity:

Children can repeat the phrase "Wolf, are you there?" for every page. The wolf replies that he is putting on an undershirt, pants, a T-shirt, socks, shoes, and a jacket; combing his hair; and putting on a backpack. Then he announces he is ready and very hungry, and the animals look worried. After the children ask if wolf is there, add the piece of clothing to a wolf doll or paper clothing to a picture of a wolf on a board. Luckily the wolf wants pancakes to eat and not the other animals.

Rumford, James. 2007. *Don't Touch My Hat.* **New York: Alfred A. Knopf.**

Summary:

A cowboy can't do his work without his ten gallon hat until he accidentally takes his wife's hat one night.

Activity:

"Don't touch my hat!" is repeated several times in the story. Have children repeat this phrase when signaled.

Ryder, Joanne. 2006. *Won't You Be My Hugaroo?* **Orlando: Harcourt. Illus., Melissa Sweet.**

Summary:

Different animals demonstrate different hugs.

Activity:

Ask children to bring a stuffed animal, and have extras for those who forget. The children can practice their different hugs on the animals. They can also just hug themselves if there is not time to ask the children to bring a toy with them. The different hugs include a twirly hug where children can twirl around, a tickle hug where a stuffed animal is tickled, and a cuddly hug with a big hug. Other hugs will be gentler or more active. This makes a nice bedtime storytime book.

————. 2006. *Won't You Be My Kissaroo?* **Orlando: Harcourt. Illus., Melissa Sweet.**

Summary:

Different animals demonstrate different kisses.

Activity:

Because you probably can't kiss the children and they can't kiss each other, have children kiss their hands. You can also make two pairs of lips or two paper bag puppets for each child to pretend they are kissing each time you describe a new kiss. Some of the kisses are, "A morning kiss is full of sun and wishes for the day to come." And "A breakfast kiss is nice and sweet. It's fun when sticky lips can meet." Instruct children to make their puppets or paper lips kiss every time you say the word "kiss."

Rylant, Cynthia. 2005. *If You'll Be My Valentine.* New York: HarperCollins. Illus., Fumi Kosaka.

Summary:

A child says what he will do if different animals and people will be his valentine.

Activity:

Have a stack of valentine cards to give out to the children as you tell the story, pretending that the children in your room are the characters in the book. For example, hand a valentine to a child or two when you say, "If you'll be my valentine/I'll sit with you today./We'll read a book about some frogs/if you don't want to play."

————. 2008. *Baby Face: A Book of Love for Baby.* New York: Simon & Schuster. Illus., Diane Goode.

Summary:

The story is about what a baby does.

Activity:

Use this book on a day children are requested to bring a doll or stuffed animal. They pretend they are taking care of their "baby" as in the story, such as washing and feeding the baby.

Saltzberg, Barney. 2005. *Cornelius P. Mud, Are You Ready for Bed?* Cambridge, MA: Candlewick.

Summary:

Mom asks Cornelius if he has done all the things to prepare for bed.

Activity:

This is a short and simple book, so just ask the children to respond "Yes" to each question. "Have you put your toys away?" Children respond "Yes." "Did you feed your fish?" "Have you used the bathroom?" You may skip this one, although the picture shows Cornelius on top of a shut toilet seat. When Cornelius' mother asks him if he is ready for bed, Cornelius says "No," so you may have to correct the children here unless they catch on or can read the word themselves. He is not ready because he wants a hug. Have the children hug themselves. This is a good story for a bedtime storytime.

————. 2006. *Goodnight Kisses*. New York: Harcourt.

Summary:

Questions ask what kinds of kisses different animals like.

Activity:

Although children would likely never guess the answer to the questions determining which animal likes what kind of kisses, you can still ask them and have them guess. In reality, the "me" in the book is the child and not the animal, and this book was meant more for home use. However, you can adapt it for a storytime too. For example, the text begins, "Who likes fluffy goodnight kisses?" Flip the page and it shows a zebra with a fuzzy belly and a bubble, indicating the zebra is responding, "Me!" Children can repeat the word "Me!" after you.

Sayre, April Pulley. 2007. *Vulture View*. New York: Henry Holt. Illus., Steve Jenkins.

Summary:

A vulture soars through the air looking for food.

Activity:

Children can spread their arms and move around the room as if they are vultures looking for food. Put pictures of the animals around the room that the vulture considers for food. Children can stop by the animals and respond if they would eat them. You need a snake, fox, bear, and deer. Children can answer "No, no" when the story questions if the vulture would eat it. "That snake overe there?/No, no."

Schaefer, Carole Lexa. 2005. *The Bora-Bora Dress*. Cambridge: Candlewick. Illus., Catherine Stock.

Summary:

A girl is invited to a fancy party at her aunt's home but doesn't like the idea that she will have to wear a dress until she finds the perfect one.

Activity:

In the book, the girl tries on several dresses at the store. Bring in some old dresses and hold them up to see if the children would say they should wear them. You can also have one child come to the front and hold the dresses and ask if he or she should wear this dress until you find the perfect Bora-Bora dress.

Schaefer, Lola. 2007. *Frankie Stein*. Tarrytown, NY: Marshall Cavendish. Illus., Kevan Atteberry.

Summary:

Frankie is born into the scary Stein family, but he is not scary so his family tries to teach him to be so.

Activity:

Draw a picture of a child that resembles Frankie, and have the children help you make him scary by adding black teeth and purple hair as happens in the story. Children could also have their own Frankie pictures to make scary in their own ways. Then children can practice the movements of being scary, such as walk with wide steps and arms stretched out or with their arms up and fists shaped like claws. In the end, a normal-looking Frankie turns out to be scariest for the Stein family.

Schaefer, Lola M. 2008. *What's That, Mittens?* New York: HarperCollins. Illus., Susan Kathleen Hartung.

Summary:

Mittens hears noises on the other side of the fence only to find a friend in a dog.

Activity:

For this easy reader, have children repeat the phrase, "What's that, Mittens?'" For example, "What's that, Mittens? What's barking behind the fence?"

Schafer, Susan. 2005. *Where's My Tail?* New York: Marshall Cavendish. Illus., Doug Cushman.

Summary:

A lizard loses his tail and asks other animals if they have lost theirs.

Activity:

Use this book as an opportunity to teach a small lesson. The back of the book tells you about how each animal mentioned in the book needs its tail. Draw or cut out of construction paper the tails of all the animals mentioned in the book. When it is time for the lizard to ask a new animal if he can have his or her tail, ask the students if they think the animal needs his or her tail. Why? Then tell them the answer from the book index and the endnote if they do not guess or answer correctly. You will need the tails of a lizard, frog, raccoon, bear, opossum, skunk, and snake. You can also ask children which tail they think belongs to each animal before you begin each section of the story. In the end, the lizard finds that his own tail has grown back. Finally, you can also make lizard tails as crafts to show the children that their tails have grown back too.

Schertle, Alice. 2007. *Very Hairy Bear.* New York: Harcourt. Illus., Matt Phelan.

Summary:

The story describes all the things a hairy bear can do, even withstanding the weather.

Activity:

Every time the phrase "A very hairy bear doesn't care" is repeated, ask the children to repeat it with you or after you. You can also wear a wig and pretend to be a very hairy bear. Children can make their own wigs by cutting strips from a long piece of brown construction paper, leaving one long uncut strip lengthwise. They can attach it to their heads like a headband to be the hairy bear.

Schneider, Josh. 2007. *You'll Be Sorry.* New York: Clarion.

Summary:

A girl makes her brother cry, which causes a flood of tears in town.

Activity:

Every time the word "cry" or "water" or any variation appears in the story, have the children make fists and move them back and forth under their eyes to simulate crying.

Schroeder, Lisa. 2005. *Baby Can't Sleep.* New York: Sterling. Illus., Viviana Garofoli.

Summary:

A father counts sheep to help his baby go to sleep.

Activity:

Have the children count sheep with you. Ask children to identify how many sheep are on each page and count together. You can also give them sheep pictures or paper finger puppets to count. This makes a good board story too. Make ten sheep and have the children count the sheep as you place them on the board or have the children help you place or remove them from the board.

Schwartz, Amy and Leonard S. Marcus. 2006. *Oscar: The Big Adventure of a Little Sock Monkey.* New York: Katherine Tegen. Illus., Amy Schwartz.

Summary:

A sock monkey saves the day.

Activity:

Use a sock monkey (which can be found at many stores) or make your own. Use it as a prop to help tell the story.

Scieszka, Jon. 2008. *Smash! Crash!* New York: Simon & Schuster.

Summary:

Two dump trucks crash against one another.

Activity:

As different trucks arrive and situations occur, the two truck friends smash and crash. Have the children repeat the words "Smash! Crash! Smash-Crash!"

each time they are used in the text either by giving the children a signal or having them repeat after you.

Scieszka, Jon and Lane Smith. 2004. *Science Verse*. New York: Viking.

Summary:

Different concepts are represented by different rhymes.

Activity:

For older children, turn this into a guessing game. Instead of reading the titles and each rhyme completely, skip the titles or topic words in the poems and have children guess what science concept the rhymes are about from the clues in the rhymes. This can also be used for a lesson on inference. The book comes with a CD, so alternately play the CD and show pictures that represent the concepts, such as the food chain and evolution, in the book.

———. 2005. *Seen Art?* New York: Viking.

Summary:

A boy is looking for his friend Art but keeps being taken to different areas of the Museum of Modern Art.

Activity:

This one might be difficult for young children to understand and would probably be best used as an introduction to an elementary art lesson. Ask children if the pictures of art in the book are the boy's friend Art. Show children other sculptures you create, other objects, and other pictures and ask them if they are art, or put these objects in the room and ask them if they have seen Art.

Scillian, Devin. 2007. *Brewster the Rooster*. Chelsea, MI: Sleeping Bear. Illus., Lee White.

Summary:

Brewster crows more frequently than usual until it is determined he has a vision problem and does not know when the sun is out.

Activity:

In this rhyming book, each time the rooster crows, instruct children to crow when you point at them. For example, "And Grandma Pearl was down in the kitchen. It was awful how they would find her. While she was cooking, no one was looking when Brewster strolled up behind her. She was there at the stove, flipping a hotcake when Brewster sent the old woman reeling. She shrieked at the sound, started slipping around, and got batter all over the ceiling." After the word "reeling" children can crow. You might even use a rooster puppet to add to the story.

Seeger, Laura Vaccaro. 2004. *Lemons Are Not Red.* Brookfield, CT: Roaring Brook.

Summary:

Cut-outs show objects in the wrong color until the page is flipped.

Activity:

Rather than making the statements in the book that are incorrect, ask the students if these objects are really these colors. Instead of "Lemons are not red" say "Are lemons red?" Children will respond "No." Say, "But they are red here. Are you sure lemons are not red? Then what color are they?" Then flip the page. "Ah, you were right. Lemons are yellow. Apples are red." Then flip the page and begin again. You can create more examples using magazine pictures or construction paper to keep the story going. Older children might make their own with the same supplies.

————. 2007. *First the Egg.* New Milford, CT: Roaring Brook.

Summary:

Cut-outs reveal what comes first and next like the chicken and the egg.

Activity:

Ask the children what comes next after each cut-out. For example, the text reads, "First the TADPOLE." Ask what comes next. If they do not reposnd, the answer is "then the Frog." You can continue the story with your own pictures you have made from magazines. Children can make their own from magazines as a craft.

Segal, John. 2006. *Carrot Soup.* New York: Simon & Schuster.

Summary:

A rabbit looks for the carrots he grew to make soup.

Activity:

When the rabbit asks different animals if they have seen his carrots, ask the children. "Mole, have you seen my carrots?" Continue by asking all the children if they have seen his carrots. In the end, reveal a covered table of carrot soup or perhaps bowls of corn candy or actual carrot sticks to be healthier. Yell "Surprise!" as they do in the book when rabbit finds his friends and family have made him soup from the carrots. You can also hide pictures of carrots around the room for children to find.

Serfozzo, Mary. 2007. *Whooo's There?* New York: Random House. Illus., Jeffrey Scherer.

Summary:

An owl continues to ask "Whooo's there?" as he has questions what animals have done certain things.

Activity:

Instruct children to ask "Whooo?" like an owl when you point to them as that point arrives in the story each time. For example, "'Whooo!' said Old Owl. "Who has turned on the light? Fireflies glowed, a bright show at night.""

Shannon, David. 2008. *Too Many Toys.* New York: Blue Sky.

Summary:

Spencer has too many toys that just get in the way.

Activity:

Give children a copied picture of a room or a toy box. Have them scribble on it every time you mention the word "toys" or the phrase "too many toys" or anything about toys in the book. Alternatively, have them stand and sit when these words are read.

Shannon, George. 2005. *White Is for Blueberry.* New York: Greenwillow. Illus., Laura Dronzek.

Summary:

Each color represents only a piece of the object or animal shown.

Activity:

The book begins, "PINK/is for crow. . . ." Then turn the page to see pink baby crows with the words, "when it has just hatched/from its egg." Begin by asking children if pink is really for crow. Then read the rest and ask if pink is still for crow. Ask again why it says that pink is for crow to make sure your children understand.

Shaw, Charles. 1947. *It Looked Like Spilt Milk.* New York: HarperCollins.

Summary:

Are different blobs of white spilt milk or something else?

Activity:

This is an older book, but when I came across it in a library I thought it would still be fun for children today. Each blob of white on a dark blue background is a picture of something else. Ask the children what each picture represents. For example, the text might read, "Sometimes it looked/like a Tree./But it wasn't a Tree." Ask the kids, "What was it then?" even though it obviously looks like a tree. However, the answer at the end of the book is that they are cloud shapes. Instead of reading the text as is, say, "Sometimes it looked like what?"

Shindler, Ramon and Wojciech Graniczewski. 2005. *Found Alphabet.* Boston: Houghton Mifflin. Illus., Anita Andrzejewska and Andrzej Pilichowski-Ragno.

Summary:

Found objects are put together to form new objects for which poems are written.

Activity:

Have your students bring in objects they find from home, or provide some for them. Show some pictures from the book, ask students what the objects are and what they were made from. For example, a queen appears to be made with leaves for a skirt, wire for arms, and a fastener for a nose. An igloo is made of sugar cubes, and the poem ends, "My dentist thinks it's much too sweet." Then children can make their own objects and share them with the group to guess. It is important to know that the term "Eskimo" should not be used to generalize or represent all Native Americans from Alaska and Canada. However, you also don't need to share all the poems in the book.

Shulman, Mark. 2006. *A Is for Zebra.* New York: Sterling. Illus., Tamara Petrosino.

Summary:

Each letter of the alphabet represents the last letter of a word or phrase.

Activity:

Ask the children if the letter on each page is for the picture represented. Basically, you will switch each statement to a question. "A is for Zebra" becomes "Is A for Zebra?" Children should respond "No." If they don't, write out a letter A and a letter Z on a board for them to see. Then say, "No, A is not for Zebra. But is there a letter A in the word Zebra?" Write out the complete word, and have them match the letter you have drawn to the letter A in the word Zebra. Continue for each letter of the alphabet where you will have such words and phrases as "B is for rub-a-dub-dub" and "C is for tic and tac, but not toe." For older children, you can read a few first and ask the children what they think is going on here.

Siegelson, Kim L. 2003. *Dancing the Ring Shout!* New York: Hyperion. Illus., Lisa Cohen.

Summary:

A family prepares their instruments to play at a ring shout.

Activity:

Toby is searching for an instrument he could bring that speaks from the heart. In his search he keeps repeating that his sister is bringing a gourd, his mama tin pans, his papa a hoop drum, and his grand a cane. Provide children with pans, a gourd or shaker, a drum or container, and a cane or stick to play each time that instrument is mentioned in the song, or they can all play their instruments each time one is mentioned in the book. In the end, the children form a circle for the ring shout. The author explains that a ring shout was a sacred dance tribute to ancestors or performed after a funeral.

Sierra, Judy. 2007. *Mind Your Manners, B.B. Wolf.* **New York: Alfred A. Knopf. Illus., J. Otto Siebold.**

Summary:

Wolf is invited to a library tea and must practice his manners.

Activity:

Crocodile helps Wolf learn some manners, which he turns into a song to help him remember. Although this song is repeated a few times in the story, it is not frequent. Teach the children this song in your own melody and have them repeat it more frequently throughout the book when you give them your signal. The song goes, "Sip your tea and never slurp, say 'Excuse Me' if you burp. Smile and have a lot of fun, but don't go biting anyone."

Silverman, Erica. 2008. *There Was a Wee Woman . . . .* **New York: Farrar, Straus and Giroux. Illus., Rosanne Litzinger.**

Summary:

A wee woman who lives in a shoe takes her family to find a larger living place.

Activity:

Read the story and ask the children if each home the woman finds would be a good home, such as a birdhouse or bucket. You can also place pictures of the potential homes around the room and walk with the children pretending to find each home and decide if it would be a good place to live. You would need a barrel, birdhouse, cradle, bucket, and dollhouse. Children can also run from the animlas they see along the way.

Simmons, Jane. 2007. *Together.* **New York: Alfred A. Knopf.**

Summary:

Two dogs who were once friends can no longer get along because their interests are different.

Activity:

For this book, use two dog stuffed animals as props. As the dogs complain about the other's interest, use each dog to tell his side of the story. Pictures will work just as well. Children can hold the dogs and be a part of the story too.

Singer, Marilyn. 2007. *City Lullaby.* **New York: Clarion. Illus., Carll Cneut.**

Summary:

City sounds are presented in a counting rhyme while baby sleeps.

Activity:

The pictures of the objects in the story are crammed together in busy city scenes. Ask a child to come to the front of the room for each page and count the objects in the hustle. For example, when the text reads, "Garbage truck, wheezing, mashing!/7 trash cans clanging, bashing," have a child count all the trash cans on the page to make sure there are seven. The children can also repeat the phrase "in the stroller, Baby's sleeping" when cued.

Siy, Alexandra. 2008. *One Tractor: A Counting Book*. New York: Holiday House. Illus., Jacqueline Rogers.

Summary:

This counting book features a boy's transportation toys.

Activity:

As you read the story pause before you say either the number or the mode of transportation in this simple counting book. Children can fill in the blank with the number of items on the page or with the type of transportation on the page. For example, "Three boats float below/sailing fast,/docking slow."

Skalak, Barbara Anne. 2005. *Waddle, Waddle, Quack, Quack, Quack*. San Francisco: Chronicle Books. Illus., Sylvia Long.

Summary:

Ducklings follow their mother until one duckling gets lost.

Activity:

The text is too complicated for repetition, because you would have to instruct children of the new phrases to repeat each time. However, the text lends itself to a fast-paced reading. So, instead of repetition, simply have children follow you in a circle around the room and act out what you can. For example, the book begins, "What's that pecking? *Tap, tap, tap!* Eggs start splitting. *Crack, crack, crack.* Mama paces up and back. Waddle, waddle, *quack, quack, quack.*" In this case the librarian, teacher, or children can pace, waddle, and quack. Other pages will have you wobbling, swooping, and plopping. So, if you walk briskly around the room and read quickly, this will be a fun time. In the end, one duckling gets separated and looks for his mother. Here you can have the children search for the mother all over the room where you might have a picture or a stuffed animal hidden.

Sklansky, Amy E. 2007. *The Duck Who Played the Kazoo*. New York: Clarion. Illus., Tiphanie Beeke.

Summary:

A duck plays the kazoo for friends, when he is bored, and almost any time.

Activity:

Purchase inexpensive kazoos, and give one to each child to make sounds with during the story. If this is not possible, have one kazoo for yourself or have the children make some out of toilet paper rolls with wax paper or tissue paper attached to one end. Although the sounds of the kazoo alternate in the story, you can keep them consistent and just have the children make kazoo sounds when you signal them. If kazoos are not a possibility at all, have the children speak the kazoo sounds, which would go, "La ditty, da ditty zu zu."

Slater, Dashka. 2006. *Baby Shoes.* New York: Bloomsbury. Illus., Hiroe Nakata.

Summary:

Baby moves around in new shoes as colors are added to them.

Activity:

There are two activities you can use with this book. The first involves movement. The phrase "Those white, high-jumping, fast-running, dizzy-spinning shoes!" is repeated on almost every double-page spread except that "dizzy-spinning" is replaced with a new phrase each time. Children can jump, run in place, and perform the final action, such as spin or kick, for each page. A second activity is to have children participate with the colors. They can either have a picture of a shoe and different color crayons that they use to color the shoes when different colors are mentioned in the story or get a different color crayon or circle cut from construction paper to hold up when their color is mentioned in the story. Colors needed are red, green, purple, yellow, and brown.

Sloat, Teri. 2006. *I'm a Duck!* New York: G.P. Putnam's Sons.

Summary:

A duck discovers he is a duck.

Activity:

Simply have the children stand and pretend they are ducks while you tell the story. At some points they could act out parts of the story. They will quack and waddle and spread their wings and fly and flap. They will have to settle down when the duck gets a wife and builds a nest.

Slonim, David. 2005. *He Came with the Couch.* San Francisco: Chronicle Books.

Summary:

A family buys a couch that comes with a creature that refuses to leave.

Activity:

You will need a prop for this book. Try to find a doll couch or chair. If not, a cushion or pillow will work. This of course could also be done with paper or cardboard. Attach a creature of any kind, such as a monster puppet or any odd-looking toy or picture of a friendly monster-like creature. Replicate the activities in the book. For example, a boy asks the creature who he is. You can do the same. The dad and child try to move the couch and get the creature off with a plunger. You can tip the couch over or pull out a plunger. Show the children you are pretending to remove this creature from your couch. You can finally separate the creature from the couch and throw the couch to the side when the boy in the family falls from a tree and the creature throws the couch out the window to save him.

Smallman, Steve. 2006. *Bumbletum*. Wilton, CT: Tiger Tales. Illus., Tim Warnes.
Summary:
A strange stuffed animal asks for help from the other toys to figure out what he is.
Activity:
There are two things you can do with this story. One is to keep asking the children what they think the toy is. Another is to have the children act out what the other toys in the story can do. In this case, children can squeak, stand on paws (touch the ground with hands), wag tail (shake behind), drink something wet (show motion of drinking), jump, and hug.

————. 2006. *The Lamb Who Came for Dinner*. Wilton, CT: Tiger Tales. Illus., Joelle Dreidemy.
Summary:
A wolf can't seem to eat a cute lamb.
Activity:
The wolf can't eat the lamb because it is too cold, has hiccups, and hugged him. Throughout the story keep asking the children if he should eat the lamb.

Smith, Will. 2001. *Just the Two of Us*. New York: Scholastic. Illus., Kadir Nelson.
Summary:
The book illustrates Will Smith's song about a father and son.
Activity:
Play Will Smith's song "Just the Two of Us" as you turn pages and show pictures of the story. In the end, ask children what the book was about and what they remember the father saying to and about his child.

Sockabasin, Allen. 2005. *Thanks to the Animals*. Gardiner, ME: Tilbury House. Illus., Rebekah Raye.
Summary:
A family accidentally leaves their baby behind when he falls from the sled, but the animals protect him.
Activity:
Although it is disturbing that the family does not immediately notice their child is missing, have a baby doll and pretend it fell from the sled. Pile a variety of stuffed animals or puppets over the baby as they protect the child in the story. You can also use this as a board story and do the same on the board with pictures of any animals. Because the author is a Passamaquoddy

storyteller, you can also tell this story without the book. The author also reads this book with his daughter in English and in the Passamaquoddy language online. Locate this recording at www.tilburyhouse.com and play it for the children.

Soto, Gary. 1996. *The Old Man and His Door.* **New York: Putnam & Grossett. Illus., Joe Cepeda.**

Summary:

A man confuses the Mexican word "puerco" for "puerta" and therefore takes a door instead of a pig.

Activity:

Make a piece of poster board or cardboard look like a door. Hunch over and hold it on your back as you pretend to be the old man in the story and walk around with the door on your back, which you have confused with the word "pig." Then use the text of this book for storytelling.

Sperring, Mark. 2003. *Find-a-Saurus.* **New York: Scholastic. Illus., Alexandra Steele-Morgan.**

Summary:

A boy wants to find dinosaurs but instead finds strange creatures until a dinosaur finally appears.

Activity:

Show the pictures of the creatures, and, before you tell them what they are, ask the children to identify them. Children will identify a monster, elves, dodo, alien, a something-or-other, thinga-ma-jig, sea monster, unicorn, footprint, and giant and finally a dinosaur.

Spinelli, Eileen. 2004. *Do You Have a Hat?* **New York: Simon & Schuster. Illus., Geraldo Valerio.**

Summary:

The hats of famous people are described.

Activity:

Each description of what a famous person's hat looks like or is used for it is followed by the statement, "Do you have a hat?" Ask students to bring a hat to this session or provide some play hats for them. Then they can answer "Yes" when you ask if they have a hat. After the story is over, ask each child to describe his or her hat.

————. 2005. *City Angel.* **New York: Dial. Illus., Krysten Brooker.**

Summary:

A City Angel watches over and cares for the people of a city.

Activity:

An angel with wings appears on each page, so have children raise their arms as wings and pretend to fly and float around the room as you tell the story. You will have to be careful if you fear children might take the flying seriously or if parents might worry about the use of the word "angel." You can also have the children make construction paper wings.

————. 2007. *Heat Wave.* New York: Harcourt. Illus., Betsy Lewin.

Summary:

The story describes what happens each day during a heat wave and how it finally ends.

Activity:

Use a calendar or post the days of the weeks. Point to each day as you read the story and describe what happens on each even hotter day. You can also tape the names of the days of the week to the children, tell them their day, and have them stand when their day arrives in the story. Alternatively, give children fans or have them make a fan as a pre-craft. They can then fan themselves throughout the story of this heat wave.

————. 2008. *The Best Story.* New York: Dial. Illus., Anne Wilsdorf.

Summary:

A girl takes suggestions from her family about what to write in a story for a contest until she realizes her own story is best.

Activity:

Ask children to help with the story. When the girl asks her family for suggestions, ask the children for suggestions and try to incorporate the ideas into the stories in the book. You can also ask the children if they like each story using the family's suggestions.

Spiridellis, Gregg and Evan Spiridellis. 2007. *The Longest Christmas List Ever.* **New York: Hyperion.**

Summary:

A boy forgets to ask for what he really wants for Christmas, so he writes a very long list for the next year.

Activity:

There are two possibilities for this book. The first is to read each of the things the child wants for Christmas and ask children if they would want these things. A second idea is to have a long scroll of paper and unroll it to represent the very long list the boy has created. Follow by asking children what they would ask for and writing it on the list.

Spohn, Kate. 2004. *By Word of Mouse.* **New York: Bloomsbury.**

Summary:

Two sisters welcome some mice into their homes until the mice want to eat the the sisters' cookies.

Activity:

Give each child a brown mouse copied on brown paper or cut from construction paper. When the mice do things in the story like slide down sculptures or eat cookies, have children take turns bringing their mice up to you. You can give them back in the end.

Steffensmeier, Alexander. 2007. *Millie Waits for the Mail.* **New York: Walker.**

Summary:

Millie the cow attacks the mail carrier every day until the mail carrier has a surprise for Millie.

Activity:

There are two possibilities for this book. The first is to have the children run around the room with you pretending to be Millie and chasing the mail carrier each time he visits. Another is to create fake letters to deliver to the children while the story is told. In the end, Millie delivers the mail with the carrier.

Steggall, Susan. 2008. *The Life of a Car.* **New York: Henry Holt.**

Summary:

The life and maintenance of a car are described in simple words.

Activity:

Ask children what is occurring in each picture. For example, in one picture workers are building a car. Children should respond as the text is worded, with, "Build the car." However, anything similar will suffice. Another picture shows a car wash. Children should respond, "Wash the car."

Steig, Jeanne. 2008. *Fleas!* **New York: Philomel. Illus., Britt Spencer.**

Summary:

A man trades his fleas for an uncle. He keeps trading but finds that each thing he trades something for is worse than the last.

Activity:

Give each child something to represent everything the man trades for in the story. Have them pass the items on to one another as the man trades the items. Alternatively, have just one object, such as a ball, to represent all the things the man trades and pass the ball around each time.

Stein, David Ezra. 2007. *Leaves.* **New York: G.P. Putnam's Sons.**

Summary:

A baby bear is confused by the seasons and falling leaves.

Activity:

When the seasons change, before you read the name of the season, ask children to identify what season is next by the pictures. For example, they will see snow for winter.

————. 2008. *The Nice Book.* New York: G.P. Putnam's Sons.

Summary:

Simple words describe nice behavior.

Activity:

After you read each comment about being nice, such as, "hear what someone has to say," ask the children if they do these things. So, you would ask, "Do you always listen to what people have to say?" Older children can create their own statements of things they think are nice.

Stevens, Janet and Susan Stevens Crummel. 2005. *The Great Fuzz Frenzy.* New York: Harcourt.

Summary:

A group of prairie dogs find a tennis ball and get greedy over its fuzz.

Activity:

Find a tennis ball, place it in the middle of the storytime circle or group of children, and stare at it in fascination. Ask the questions and make the comments in the book to the children. "What is it?" "A thing." "A good thing or a bad thing?" "A round thing." "A strange thing." "A scary thing." "What should we do?" "Don't touch it!" "Is it alive?" Approach the ball and examine it with curiosity. Pass it around for the children to touch. When the prairie dogs take the fuzz off to cover themselves, pass out pieces of pillow stuffing for children to do the same. In the end, collect it all and put it over yourself as the one prairie dog does after he steals all the fuzz from everyone when they collapse in exhaustion after a fight.

————. 2008. *Help Me, Mr. Mutt! Expert Answers for Dogs with People Problems.* Illus., Janet Stevens.

Summary:

Dogs write to Mr. Mutt for advice.

Activity:

Give each child a fake letter representing one of the letters in this book so they can pretend that they are the dogs with the human problems. Some of the problems are owners putting a dog on a diet, having no one to play with, and being a barker. Ask the children if they think Mr. Mutt's advice is good and if they have any other advice for the dogs in the letters, such as how to get food or how to get people to play with them.

Stiegemeyer, Julie. 2006. *Cheep! Cheep!* **New York: Bloomsbury. Illus., Carol Baicker-McKee.**

Summary:

Simple text accompanies pictures of terrycloth chicks peeping and cheeping.

Activity:

Because the text is simple, have your children repeat the words "Cheep? Cheep? Cheep? Cheep!" They will also peep, creep, eep, leap, and heap. Ask children what they think is happening in the story.

Stimson, James. 2005. *Thirteen O'clock.* **San Francisco: Chronicle Books.**

Summary:

Strange events occur when the clock strikes 13.

Activity:

As the clock strikes each number up to 13 strange creatures appear. First of all, you will need a clock that goes to the number 13. You will also need a bell or something to make the different ringing sounds of the clock's chimes. You can also create pictures of the creatures that come out at each ring, such as the monster and ghosts. Change the clock as you read the story.

Stinson, Kathy. 2008. *A Pocket Can Have a Treasure in It.* **New York: Annick. Illus., Deidre Betteridge.**

Summary:

Questions and statements ponder what is inside something else.

Activity:

Ask children for their questions, and turn the questions into statements. For example, two pages read, "Can a sock have a head in it?/No!/But a sock can have . . . / . . . a toe in it." First ask children if a sock can have a head in it. When they respond, "No," ask, "But a sock can have a what in it?" The answer is, "a toe."

Stroud, Bettye. 2005. *The Patchwork Path.* **Cambridge, MA: Candlewick. Illus., Erin Susanne Bennett.**

Summary:

A girl learns how quilts were used to guide people along the Underground Railroad.

Activity:

The book shows different types of quilt patterns and explains what they represent, such as "follow the *stars.*" Ask the children what each one means. The patterns also begin each page. Wait until each pattern is shown on a different page to ask the children what direction they think the slaves should travel. Prepare some patterns for children to color. You could do this first and then have children line up in the correct order while you tell the story. The authenticity of quilts having been used to find the way to freedom is debatable.

Sturges, Philemon. 2005. *Waggers.* New York: Dutton. Illus., Jim Ishkawa.
Summary:
The story explains why dogs chase one another's tails.
Activity:
A cat infiltrates a meeting of the dogs. The dogs complain about the cats and vice versa. Divide the group into cats and dogs. You may even indicate this by their name tags or craft activities or who owns or likes cats or dogs. Have the child cats stand or raise their arms every time you say "cat" and those representing dogs stand or raise their hands when you read "dog" in the story. The craft might be making dogs and cats on popsicle sticks to hold up during the story or paper bag puppets. End by asking children to tell you some good and bad things about cats and dogs.

Suen, Anastasia. 2003. *Raise the Roof!* New York: Viking. Illus., Elwood H. Smith.
Summary:
A home is built in simple steps.
Activity:
Children can act out the motions of pouring concrete, sawing wood, hammering, painting, etc. You might even have them color and cut or provide for them some of the different tools necessary in building a house. They could end by designing their own house with construction paper pieces.

Swados, Elizabeth. 2005. *The Animal Rescue Store.* New York: Scholastic. Illus., Anne Wilson.
Summary:
Poems are about the animals in a pet rescue store.
Activity:
Start by reading the opening poem about the rescue store. Use the Table of Contents to find pictures or toys to represent the animals in the store, such as a frog, ferret, puppy, cat, snake, buzzard, rat, butterfly, cockatoo, poodle, dove, turtle, llama, guinea pig, rabbit, tarantula, lobster, mutt, and fish. Instead of reading all the poems, because they are lengthy, ask the children to select the animals they want to hear about. Then end with the last poem, "My Vagabond Zoo . . . ."

Swallow, Pamela Curtis. 2005. *Groundhog Gets a Say*. New York: G.P. Putnam's Sons. Illus., Denise Brunkus.

Summary:

After Groundhog Day, Groundhog experiences a letdown and talks up facts about himself to the other creatures.

Activity:

Read the facts as presented by the groundhogs and ask the kids if they think these things are true. For example, Groundhog says, "We're related to the squirrels." Ask the children, "Is this true? Are groundhogs related to squirrels?" The wisecracking squirrel and other creatures chime in with their insults to accompany his facts.

Swanson, Susan Marie. 2008. *The House in the Night*. Boston: Houghton Mifflin. Illus., Beth Krommes.

Summary:

Things in the night are highlighted in this story.

Activity:

This is already a lovely story and the illustrations are part of the appeal. Even though you still want to show the illustratiuons, you can also have the objects in the same orange color taped to the walls. Children can walk around with you to experience the book live. You will need a key, light, bed, book, bird, song, moon, sun, and house.

Symes, Ruth. 2008. *Harriet Dancing*. New York: Scholastic. Illus., Caroline Jayne Church.

Summary:

The butterflies won't dance with Harriet, so she finds a friend to dance with instead.

Activity:

Although there is not continuous dance in this story, have the children get up and dance when Harriet dances with the butterflies and then dance with the flowers and then with her frined. Children can dance throughout the book anyway by twirling amd moving in any way they'd like or by copying your moves.

Taback, Simms. 2008. *Simms Taback's Safari Animals*. Maplewood, NJ: Blue Apple.

Summary:

Fold-out pages reveal the identities of different animals.

Activity:

Slowly fold out the pages as children guess what animal is in question. For example, the words read, "Who am I?" The illustrations show part of a mane and two feet. The clue then reads, "I have a big, furry mane." Most children will be able to identify the animal already, but you can ask, "Are you sure?" and continue. Fold open again. The illustrations reveal a tail, two more legs, and the behind of an amnimal. The text reads, "I can ROAR!" You can then ask, "Do you still think it is a lion? What else can it be?" Or "What do you think it is now?" Fold one more time for a full-page picture of a lion with the text, "I am a LION!"

Tafolla, Carmen. 2008. *What Can You Do with a Rebozo?* Berkeley: Tricycle. Illus., Amy Córdova.

Summary:

The story describes everything you can do with this Mexican shawl.

Activity:

Use a long shawl or an actual rebozo to demonstrate the many things you can use it for. For example, you can spread it like a butterfly, play hide-and-seek, twist in your hair, hold a baby, keep warm, wipe up spills, use as a blindfold, make a tunnel, cape, or bandage, or dance.

Tafuri, Nancy. 2005. *Goodnight, My Duckling.* New York: Scholastic.

Summary:

A mother duck sends her ducklings home to bed, but one gets distracted.

Activity:

Create a situation in which it seems like the ducklings are swimming home to bed while one gets lost. Set up a pool with rubber ducks or a fake blue construction paper pond. The easiest way may be to have duckling pictures taped around the room. Have more at one end when the ducks are all together and then soon have one on the next section of the wall. Walk the children around the room saying things from the story, like, "Hurry home, little duckling."

————. 2006. *Five Little Chicks.* New York: Simon & Schuster.

Summary:

The story is about what newborn chicks might eat.

Activity:

Use a chick puppet or make one from a paper bag or from other materials. Locate or create pictures of the chick's food, such as a worm, bug, butterfly, strawberry, trout, and corn. Make enough copies so all the children can have one picture. When it is time for the chicks to find a worm to eat, for example, move around the room to the children who have worms and have the chick's mouth move to eat them up. Children can also recite the repetitive phrase, "Peep! What can we eat?" when it occurs.

Tarpley, Natasha Anastasia. 2004. *Destiny's Gift*. New York: Lee & Low. Illus., Adjoa J. Burrowes.

Summary:

Destiny's favorite bookstore may be closing.

Activity:

The story begins with Mrs. Wade showing Destiny a game to find out the definition of new words in the dictionary. Have a children's dictionary available, and let children take turns opening the book and putting their finger to a page with their eyes closed just as Destiny does in the story. Ask every child to select a word and discuss the meaning of the words and how they relate to the children. For example, if a child selects "apple," ask the children if they like apples. Write the words on paper to give to each child as their own special word. Tell the children that if their word is mentioned in the story, they should raise their word in the air. This will keep them paying attention even if their words are not included. In the end the neighborhood shows support for the store and raises money. Hold up signs of protest as in the book that read, "Save our store." Have the children march and chant with you. You may even have them enter the library to give these chants.

Taylor, Aaron. 2008. *The Pumpkin Goblin Makes Friends*. Austin: Emerald.

Summary:

The Pumpkin Goblin terrorizes a town until he befriends a lonely boy.

Activity:

A stranger, especially one with a pumpkin head, might not be easily forgiven for hanging out with a boy at a park at night. Still, if you use this book, you can make a pumpkin mask and pretend to be the goblin in the story. Children can wear or make their own masks too.

Teckentrup, Britta. 2007. *How Big Is the World?* New York: Boxer.

Summary:

A mole searches to find how big the world is by asking other animals.

Activity:

Have children repeat the question, "How big is the world?" every time the mole asks another animal. Toward the end the mole meets a whale who takes him all over the world. Until then, the mole believes the world is as big as each of the animals he asks, such as spider, mouse, horse, and seagull.

Tellis, Annabel. 2007. *If My Dad Were a Dog*. New York: Scholastic.

Summary:

The story describes what a dad would do if he were a dog.

Activity:

Have children complete your sentences as they view the pictures and predict what it is a dad would do if he were a dog. For example, the text reads, "If my dad were a dog, just for a day,/I'd tell him to sit/and I'd tell him to stay." Pause for the children to fill in the blanks. For example, "I'd tell him to . . ." The children will reply "sit" when they see the picture of a sitting dog.

They Might be Giants. 2003. *Bed Bed Bed*. New York: Simon & Schuster. Illus., Marcel Dzama.

Summary:

Bedtime songs are presented in words and on a CD.

Activity:

Play the song "Bed, Bed, Bed, Bed, Bed" and show the pictures in the book or just have the children march around the room with you. Children can do some of the motions as they walk, such as stretch, yawn, eat, pretend to ride a bike, form a conga line with friends, pretend to play guitar, etc. This is perfect for a bedtime storytime.

Thomas, Jan. 2007. *What Will Fat Cat Sit On?* New York: Harcourt.

Summary:

Different animals respond to the question, "What will fat cat sit on?"

Activity:

Ask the children the questions in the book, such as, "Will Fat Cat sit on . . . the CHICKEN?" The children may answer yes or no.

Thompson, Lauren. 2004. *Polar Bear Night*. New York: Scholastic. Illus., Stephen Savage.

Summary:

The moon beckons a polar bear away from home.

Activity:

Create a moon from poster board or other sturdy paper, and place it on a stick. Hold it in front of you as you walk the children around the room reading the story as the bear comes across other animals, stars, and more until he reaches home again.

———. 2007. *The Apple Pie That Papa Baked*. New York: Simon & Schuster. Illus., Jonathan Bean.

Summary:

This cumulative tale tells how a pie was created.

Activity:

Turn this into a board story, adding what was needed to make this pie possible. You will need pictures of a pie, apples, tree, roots, rain, clouds, sky, sun, and world. Children can also help you place the pictures on the board. Children could instead draw pictures of the things in the story that were necessary to create this pie.

Thong, Roseanne. 2000. *Round Is a Mooncake: A Book of Shapes.* **San Francisco: Chronicle Books. Illus., Grace Lin.**

Summary:

A girl identifies shapes in her environment.

Activity:

Give each child the shapes of a circle, square, and rectangle. Have them hold the correct shape up in the air when it is mentioned in the story. For example, "Round is a mooncake/Round is the moon/Round are the lanterns/ outside my room." This is a Chinese story, so, because the children may not recognize some of the objects, the story will expose them to something new.

————. 2004. *One Is a Drummer: A Book of Numbers.* **San Francisco: Chronicle Books. Illus., Grace Lin.**

Summary:

A girl identifies numbers in her environment.

Activity:

The numbers one through ten are used to describe different objects in a girl's world. Give children pieces of paper with the numbers one through ten. They should hold up the correct number each time it is mentioned in the story. Alternatively, they can count the objects on each page or tell you what number comes next each time the number changes.

Tildes, Phyllis Limbacher. 1998. *Baby Animals Black and White.* **Watertown, MA: Charlesbridge.**

Summary:

Black and white pictures show animals.

Activity:

Ask the children to name each animal pictured. This is best for toddlers. The animals represented are a panda, seal pup, bunny, zebra, cat, dog, calf, and lamb.

Tokuda, Yukihisa. 2006. *I'm a Pill Bug.* **La Jolla: Kane/Miller. Illus., Kiyoshi Takahashi.**

Summary:

The story provides facts about the pill bug.

Activity:

Even though the book shows the size of a pill bug as being very small, you can create a pill bug of any size and walk around to show children as you tell the story. The book is written as if the pill bug is telling the child facts about himself, with words like, "See?" So you can approach each child with a different fact. You might even put the facts out of order and have them copied on strips of papers that the children select. Then read the facts as the pill bug visits each child.

U'Ren, Andrea. *Pugdog*. New York: Farrar, Straus and Giroux.
Summary:
A dog wants to act like a dog, but when his owner finds out he is a she, new rules apply.
Activity:
Throughout the story ask the children if they think the behavior of the pugdog is appropriate for a female dog. For example, the text reads, "That evening, Pugdog rolled on top her back and exposed her big belly." Ask the children, "Is that ladylike behavior?" and "Should a girl dog be able to do that?" Do the same when the owner makes the dog do more feminine things. Only then ask them if they think the dog should have to go to a salon, etc.

Vail, Rachel. 2008. *Jibberwillies at Night*. New York: Scholastic. Illus., Yumi Heo.
Summary:
A girl can't sleep because the jibberwillies are in her room until her mother gets rid of them in a bucket.
Activity:
I'm still not quite sure what the jibberwillies are, but they are something imaginary that puts fear in this girl. In the book, every time the word "jibberwillies" is used, children can repeat it. You can also give the children slips of paper with the word on it and have them put it in a bucket to collect and pretend to throw away or out a window.

Valckx, Catharina. 2005. *Lizette's Green Sock*. New York: Clarion.
Summary:
Lizette finds one green sock.
Activity:
Cut green socks out of green construction paper. Tape them around the room. When Lizette looks for the match to the sock she found, children can search the room for either one green sock you have hidden or for one of many green socks so they can all have one. Alternatively, use real dyed or undyed mismatched socks you have lying around or cheap ones from a dollar store so children can pretend to use them as a cap. For a craft, children can create a cap or sock out of plain green construction paper if you believe in the idea that crafts and art should be original and not cookie cutter.

Van Dusen, Chris. 2005. *If I Built a Car.* New York: Dutton.
Summary:
   A boy describes the fancy car he would build that even goes in water and air.
Activity:
   If you have access to a child's car that can actually be peddled or pushed, borrow or bring that along. If not, create one out of boxes or poster board. Walk around the car as you describe and point out all of its features to the children. However, because the illustrations are so fun, children might enjoy seeing the pool and fireplace in the book instead. You can also make this a board story and continue to add pictures of the features of the car onto a basic model. Children can also tell you what features they would like on their car and draw or create their own.

Waddell, Martin. 2005. *It's Quacking Time!* Cambridge, MA: Candlewick. Illus., Jill Barton.
Summary:
   A duck questions the egg from which his sibling will hatch.
Activity:
   When Grandpa and Aunt and other characters enter the story, the duck asks them if they came in an egg like the one his sibling will soon hatch from. Make a large egg out of construction paper or a more creative form, place it in the center of the room, and look at it curiously as you tell the story. So, for example, when Duckling asks, "Did I come in one of those eggs?" point to it and raise your arms as if questioning and focus your question toward the students. Students can decorate their own eggs when finished even if it's not Easter time which would be controversial for non-Christians . . .

Waldman, Maya. 2007. *To-Do List.* Long Island City: 4N.
Summary:
   The list contains 20 fun things to do.
Activity:
   Ask the children if they would like to do the things on this to-do list. Give them paper so they can pretend they have a to-do list. Some of the things on the list are make friends, go on vacation, and dance like an octopus. You can turn this into a truth-or-dare type of game. Use each of the to-dos and ask each of the children if they would like to do this thing now or answer the truth. So, I would ask one child if he would like to take the dare and dance like an octopus or if he wants to answer my question truthfully. The questions would, of course, be appropriate for preschoolers, such as, "What is your favorite color?" or "What is your favorite food?" You could also relate the questions more to a to-do on the list, such as, "Would you hug an octopus?"

Walker, Alice. 2006. *There Is a Flower at the Tip of My Nose Smelling Me.* **New York: HarperCollins. Illus., Stefano Vitale.**

Summary:

A lovely poem describes various objects and ideas that touch the body.

Activity:

Although the poem is meant to be read rather than acted out, have the children stand and touch the body parts mentioned in the story. As in the title, they can touch their nose when you read, "There is a flower at the tip of my nose smelling me." They will touch their eyes, feet, fingers for leash, head, skin, tongue, body, bones, shoulder, hand, and arms. They will be exposed to a beautiful poem while paying attention to the words as they connect the poem to their own bodies.

Walker, Rob D. 2005. *Once Upon a Cloud.* **New York: Blue Sky. Illus., Matt Mahurin.**

Summary:

Clouds contain a child's thoughts.

Activity:

As you read this lyrical story, have some white balloons floating in the air for children to gently bounce, tap, and toss throughout the story to represent clouds. If no white balloons are available, perhaps try some stuffing or a small white pillow. An example from the text is, "Are clouds whirling wind/in a swirl-away rush?/I hope they'll slow down/for my paper and brush!"

Watson, Richard Jesse. 2005. *The Magic Rabbit.* **New York: Scholastic.**

Summary:

A rabbit from a magic hat is lonely until he pulls out another magic hat.

Activity:

Pull out your magic set or make one. You will need two top hats that fit inside one another. Make them or use any hats if you don't happen to have two top hats lying around. Inside the hats you will need two rabbits, two balls to juggle, scarves tied together, a little car, picnic food like carrots and apples (as in the picture), a frog, mice, and birds. Pull them out at the appropriate times in this short story. Of course you can use pictures instead, or you could make a flat paper hat with the pictures to pull from behind it or, for a board story, put onto it. Glue the bottom and side edges of two flat hats to make a pocket to slide the objects in in order.

Watt, Melanie. 2007. *Chester.* **Tonawanda, NY: Kids Can.**

Summary:

A story of a mouse is interrupted by the big cat Chester and his red marker.

Activity:

Give the children a picture of a room with a window and a chair and have them draw the red marking that Chester draws in the story. In black text, the story of a mouse is being told, but Chester the cat comes in with a red marker and changes the story and the illustrations so he can live alone without the mouse. Children might draw things like a plane, sun, ball of yarn, and fish. Alternatively, have the chair and window drawn on a large board and you or one child at a time can add pictures and cross outs according to the story.

Weaver, Tess. 2007. *Cat Jumped In!* New York: Clarion. Illus., Emily Arnold McCully.

Summary:

A cat enters a window and creates a mess in a house.

Activity:

Children can act like a cat and try to act out parts of the story. They can jump when the cat jumps. They can sniff, snoop, dive, dash, creep, fall, race, sneak, hiss, twitch, and more.

Weeks, Sarah. 2006. *Overboard!* Orlando: Harcourt. Illus., Sam Williams.

Summary:

A bunny keeps throwing things and yelling "Overboard!" as he does.

Activity:

Gather all the items in the book and throw them from your lap or desk as you read them in the story. You can also give each of the children an object in the book and instruct them to yell "Overboard!" and throw their items at the appropriate times. Children can yell "Overboard!" either way. You will need peaches, a rubber duck, pajamas, a stuffed lamb or other toy, wipes, diapers, and raisins. This may promote bad behavior even though it is supposed to be describing what a baby might do. You might want to clarify that this book is about a baby. It also concerns me that a picture shows a window shade with the phrase "Pull the cord" because of the many instances where young children are strangled by window cords in their rooms.

Weiss, George David and Bob Thiele. 1997. *What a Wonderful World.* New York: Atheneum. Illus., Ashley Bryan.

Summary:

The popular song is illustrated.

Activity:

Play Louis Armstrong's "What a Wonderful World" while sharing the pictures of this story with different hand and face colors from around the world. I was once at a workshop where they swirled colors in a bowl on an overhead to also help illustrate this story.

Wells, Rosemary. 2004. *Bunny Mail*. New York: Viking.

Summary:

Max tries to write to Santa, but Grandma gets the letters and can't interpret what he wants from his drawings.

Activity:

Lift the flaps to open the letters to Santa from Max. Just as Grandma has trouble interpreting what tire tracks and a red splotch might be, children may not easily figure it out either. Don't let on what he wants, and ask the children to look at the letters and make a guess as to what gift Max is asking for.

———. 2006. *Max's ABC*. New York: Viking.

Summary:

The alphabet is related to ants in Max's pants.

Activity:

Cut little black circles for ants out of construction paper, and pour them out of your hand each time the ants appear in the story. You can also ask the children to identify all the words in the story for each letter. "Max Kicked his feet. But the ants Kicked their feet, too." Say, "What words in that sentence started with the letter K?" and repeat the sentence.

———. 2007. *Max Counts His Chickens*. New York: Viking.

Summary:

The Easter Bunny hides marshmallow chicks all over the house for Max and Ruby to find.

Activity:

This is an obvious one. Purchase packages of Peeps marshmallow chicks and hide them throughout the room for children to find as the story is told. For example, when Ruby finds a second chick in her dollhouse, send a child to look in the room and bring one more back. Because the Peeps will have been touched by children, you will want to throw them away, but you can give each child a Peeps in a plastic bag to take home, with their parents' permission. Instead of real marshmallow chicks, you can instead cut chicks out of pink paper to look like the chicks in the story.

West, Jim and Marshall Izen. 2004. *The Dog Who Sang at the Opera*. New York: Harry N. Abrams. Illus., Erika Oller.

Summary:

Based on a true incident, a dog sings at an opera although unasked.

Activity:

Play opera music while reading this story in which a dog is needed on stage at an opera and is so conceited that he sings along and is removed from the stage. When Pasha sings, make a howling dog sound or ask the children to help. This is a longer story. Two opera dogs also become friends, so you might have a stuffed dog dressed more like a clown and one with jewelry to resemble Pasha.

Wheeler, Bernelda. 1992. *Where Did You Get Your Moccasins?* **Winnipeg, Canada: Peguis. Illus., Herman Bekkering.**

Summary:

A boy answers questions from his classmate about his moccasins.

Activity:

This is an older book from a small publisher (available from http://Oyate. org). Children can either repeat the questions the children in the story ask or you can ask the children what they think the answers are. For example, "My Kookum used leather to make my moccasins for me./Where did she get the leather?" Children can either repeat "Where did she get the leather?" or you can ask them where they think she got the leather. The answer is "My Kookum made the leather." This nice simple story combines older and newer traditions.

Wheeler, Lisa. 2007. *Jazz Baby.* **New York: Harcourt. Illus., R. Gregory Christie.**

Summary:

Baby and his family make music.

Activity:

All you have to do for this one is have the children get up and clap and dance and make noise. An example from the text is, "So they BEAT-BEAT-BEAT and they STRUM-STRUM-STRUM and the bouncin' baby limbos with a RUM-TUM-TUM!"

Wiesner, David and Kim Kahng. 2005. *The Loathsome Dragon.* **New York: Clarion. Illus., David Wiesner.**

Summary:

A king marries an enchantress, who puts a spell on his daughter.

Activity:

Although this story is not conducive to participation throughout, have children repeat the spells the enchantress casts. Have a picture of a dragon or a dragon puppet to pretend to scare the children as the dragon does those in the kingdom. Even though early on we know that it will take three kisses from the brother to turn the dragon back into the princess, you can continue to ask the children what should be done to get the princess back. They may offer other suggestions or repeat "three kisses."

Willems, Mo. 2006. *Don't Let the Pigeon Stay Up Late!* **New York: Hyperion.**

Summary:

The reader is instructed to not let the begging pigeon stay up late.

Activity:

Read the questions or statements by the pigeon, and then ask the children if you should let the pigeon stay up late. Sometimes they will say yes and sometimes no. For example, the pigeon says, "How about five more minutes?" and "I'll go to be early tomorrow night instead." For each, children can respond.

————. **2007.** *There Is a Bird on Your Head!* **New York: Hyperion.**

Summary:

An elephant keeps asking what is on his head only to find out it is a bird that eventually has babies.

Activity:

Ask children to answer the elephant's questions about what is on his head. For example, elephant says, "Is there a bird on my head now?" and the pig replies, "Now there are two birds on your head." This is a fun book and an easy reader.

————. **2008.** *Are You Ready to Play Outside?* **New York: Hyperion.**

Summary:

Elephant and Piggie want to play outside until it rains.

Activity:

Children can act out the motions in the story. As Elephant and Piggie play outside, the children can run, skip, and jump. When it starts to rain, they can splish, splash, run, skip, and jump.

Willey, Margaret. 2008. *The 3 Bears and Goldilocks.* **New York: Atheneum. Illus., Heather M. Solomon.**

Summary:

The traditional story of *Goldilocks and the Three Bears* is retold.

Activity:

We may be used to Goldilocks breaking chairs, but in this case she sleeps on the blankets of the more realistic looking bears. Give some children bear masks and have one be Goldilocks and one be the father, and have them all act out the story as you read or tell it.

Williams, Sam. 2005. *Talk Peace.* **New York: Holiday House. Illus., Mique Moriuchi.**

Summary:

This book promotes peace no matter where you are or what you are doing.

Activity:

This is a simple case of repetition. The phrase "Talk peace" is repeated throughout. Even when the word "peace" alone is used, the children can still repeat, "Talk peace." Instruct them to do so. "In the day or at night, in the light of a dream, talk peace." Pause and point to the children when you want them to repeat the phrase.

Wilson, Karma. 2003. *A Frog in the Bog.* New York: Margaret K. McElderry. Illus., Joan Rankin.

Summary:

A frog gets bigger as he meets a variety of bugs.

Activity:

Turn this into a board story by having a frog on your bulletin board and placing all the insects he eats under the frog pattern or through a slit in his mouth. You can also use a green sheet and cover yourself with it. Then have students give you the insects to pretend to eat and hide under your green shawl. You will need a tick, two fleas, three flies, four slugs, and five snails. You will also need an alligator. When you pretend to finally notice the alligator, scream and let all the animals go, or have an alligator for your board story to frighten the frog away.

———. 2004. *Never, Ever Shout in a Zoo.* New York: Little, Brown. Illus., Doug Cushman.

Summary:

A girl imagines what would happen if you shout in a zoo.

Activity:

The first thing that would happen if you shout in a zoo is that a bear might escape. Locate stuffed animals or puppets for the animals in the book that escape and chase the girl, such as a bear, moose, ape, hippo, lion, tiger, kangaroo, snake, flamingo, crocodile, and "EVERY single beast in the zoo!" If you do not have enough animals, turn this into a board story. If you use toys, toss them to your audience as you read the story, or have them in a circle around the room and pretend to run from them. In the end, walk to the corner or toss a sheet or blanket over the children as if they were trapped in a cage as the girl is at the end of this story.

———. 2007. *Bear Feels Sick.* New York: Margaret K. McElderry. Illus., Jane Chapman.

Summary:

Bear feels sick even though his animal friends try to help.

Activity:

Every time the word "sick" is mentioned in the story, instruct children to pretend to be sick. Practice first with looks of pain, shivers, moans, and whatever else children can think of. Have them practice their sickness first.

————. *How to Bake an American Pie.* New York: Margaret K. McElderry. Illus., Raúl Colón.

Summary:

The ingredients of a pie are all that make an American and America.

Activity:

Give each child a spoon or rolling pin or bowl, etc., and have them pretend to make a pie. Give them each a word to add to the pie when it is read in the story. Older children can read their own words. Tape the words to younger children or place the words in front of them so you can signal the chilren when they should add their words to the bowl.

————. 2008. *Where Is Home, Little Pip?* New York: Margaret K. McElderry. Illus., Jane Chapman.

Summary:

Pip the penguin wanders off and searches for home.

Activity:

When Pip asks others for help finding home and they offer their own homes, he responds, "But that's not the home I know." Signal children when they should repeat this phrase.

Wing, Natasha. 2007. *Go to Bed, Monster!* New York: Harcourt. Illus., Sylvie Kantorovitz.

Summary:

A girl draws a monster who demands more and won't go to bed.

Activity:

There are several possibilities to this story. One is to color a bag green and cut out eyes and a mouth. Make it look like the monster in the story, and wear it as a prop as you read. Because the girl draws the monster, children could have their own paper to draw the monster and the other things the monster wants or needs. You can also draw them on a board or paper taped to a board or wall. After Lucy draws a monster and he won't go to bed, Lucy tries to appease him in other ways. Children or you can draw meatballs for his hunger, water for his thirst, a bathroom for his needs, a bear for his fear, pajamas for his cold, a moon for the dark, and a book for his energy.

Winter, Jeanette. 2003. *Nino's Mask.* **New York: Dial.**

Summary:

Nino wants to make a mask for the fiesta, but his father thinks he is too young.

Activity:

Create different masks to represent those that Nino thinks about making in the story, such as a conejo, buho, calavera, ciervo, caiman, tigre, and a perro. When he creates his mask, as in the story, piece it together on the board by the nose, ears, mouth, eyes, coat, and tongue. Children can make their own masks at the end of the story. A glossary is provided in the back so you know the animals' names.

Winthrop, Elizabeth. 2005. *Squashed in the Middle.* **New York: Henry Holt. Illus., Pat Cummings.**

Summary:

A middle child leaves without anyone knowing.

Activity:

Children often interrupt storytime, a situation handled differently by librarians. This time let them talk, but ignore them. In the story, the girl feels ignored because she is the middle child and even leaves without anyone noticing. Pretend your kids are the middle children in the family and you aren't going to listen. Point this out when they ask a question. You can also play the telephone game as a further example of what it is like when someone doesn't listen properly. Whisper a phrase in one child's ear and have that child whisper it to the next.

Wolf, Sallie. 2008. *Truck Stuck.* **Watertown, MA: Charlesbridge. Illus., Andy Robert Davies.**

Summary:

A truck gets stuck under a viaduct, causing a traffic jam.

Activity:

In my experience, people aren't as joyful when a truck gets stuck and blocks traffic. For this story, create an arch or put a pole, stick, broom, yarn, etc., over two chairs to create a viaduct. You can be the truck that gets stuck, or instruct another student to do so. Then have each child act as a different truck from the story that is added behind you and can't get through because of the traffic jam. You can also use this as a board story and add pictures of the different vehicles that get stuck behind the truck. You will need a truck, recycling truck, excavator, limousine, exterminator van, street sweeper, tree chipper, delivery van, and produce van. You can add more if needed.

Wong, Janet. 2003. *Knock on Wood: Poems about Superstitions.* New York: Margaret K. McElderry. Illus., Julie Paschkis.

Summary:

The poems are about superstitions.

Activity:

Describe what a superstition is, and give an example. For each poem, first ask the children what they think the superstition is. If they get it right, read the poem. If not, ask more and give hints or just reveal the superstition. One poem is "Clover." "If you find a four-leaf clover in the grass,/you know a horse was born there/sometime./In the days of fairies?/Fame, a faithful friend, wealth, good health./These will be yours, doubled, they say—/if you give your clover to me."

———. 2004. *Alex and the Wednesday Chess Club.* New York: Margaret K. McElderry. Illus., Stacey Schuett.

Summary:

Alex becomes interested in participating in the school chess club.

Activity:

Create a chessboard for children to see. You can even create one out of white and brown bread as Alex's mother does in the story. You can also copy a picture of a chessboard for all the children in the class and give them paper pieces or other objects as the chess pieces. Every time a chess move is mentioned in the story, the children can move a piece to part of the board. When Alex does join the chess club, they are given chess puzzles. Simply print out a page for a chess puzzle as the game board. Many children learn to play chess at an early age. This book may begin to spark an interest. You can also ask children to predict if Alex will win or join the chess club after certain scenes in the book, such as getting mud in his face at football practice and peeking in the library to watch the chess club.

———. 2005. *Hide & Seek.* Orlando: Harcourt. Illus., Margaret Chodos-Irvine.

Summary:

While waiting for cookies to be ready, a child lists ten do's and don'ts of hide-and-seek.

Activity:

Have the children pretend to make the movements in the book for the game hide-and-seek. "Hide-and-seek means find a fat tree, stand behind it tall and thin, don't scratch, don't sneeze—hide and freeze." Children can pretend to stand behind a tree without moving, or one child could be the tree with his or her branches out and another child could pretend to hide. You could also be the tree. Ask children their rules of hide and seek. Alternatively, set up an obstacle course and have children walk with you as you find places to hide the objects mentioned in the book, such as a box, trash can, desk, lamp shade, and blanket. End with a true game of hide-and-seek, or ask one child to hide while the others keep their eyes closed, as I am sure they all will.

————. 2007. *The Dumpster Diver.* **Cambridge, MA: Candlewick. Illus., David Roberts.**

Summary:

A boy jumps in the trash and encourages others to do so as well to find treasures.

Activity:

Prepare a box or trash can of random junk from the library and your house. As you tell the story, pull out items that you have pretended to pull from the trash as the boy does in the story. Other options are to have children take turns pulling out the "trash" or to put pictures of junk around the room and have children look for them or pull them out of a box or trash can to pretend they have found these treasures. If you use real objects that you had planned to get rid of, children can make a found object collage at the end of the session.

————. 2007. *Twist: Yoga Poems.* **New York: Margaret K. McElderry. Illus., Julie Paschkis.**

Summary:

Each double-page spread contains a poem relating to different yoga shapes and positions.

Activity:

Even the youngest of children can benefit from simple yoga. Show the children some basic yoga moves, and read the poems as they stretch and bend. One example of a short poem is "Cobra." "Darkness pushes Cobra up from damp soil. She lifts herself higher, to dry out her heart." You might even share a short yoga video clip with children first.

Wood, Audrey. 2004. *Ten Little Fish.* New York: Blue Sky. Illus., Bruce Wood.

Summary:

This is a simple fish counting story until there is one left.

Activity:

Use eleven children to be the fish in the story. Have ten of them stand up and then sit down one at a time as the fish are eliminated in the story. This can also be a board story or finger rhyme. An example from the text is, "Seven Little Fish, swimming through sticks. One gets lost, and now there are . . ."

————. 2005. *The Deep Blue Sea: A Book of Colors.* New York: Scholastic. Illus., **Bruce Wood.**

Summary:

This book of colors focuses on a rock at sea.

Activity:

This book is perfect for a very simple board story. The story starts with a blue sea and a red rock. Cut a lump out of red construction paper and a pool of water out of blue construction paper. Put the red rock on the blue water. Next, add a green tree, brown nut, purple parrot, orange butterfly, black spot, yellow sun, white cloud and gray cloud. You can even add a rainbow that appears after the storm, and have the children recite all the colors used in the story. Children can take turns adding the pictures to the board, or you can add them as you read the story. This is perfect for very young children.

————. 2007. *A Dog Needs a Bone.* New York: Blue Sky.

Summary:

A dog tells his mistress what he would do if he could get a bone.

Activity:

Use a dog puppet as a prop pretending to tell this story. Some of the things the dog says are, "I'll sweep your floors. I'll answer your phone." Ask the children what other things the dog could do for its owner to get a bone. Follow by hiding pictures of bones throughout the room and having the children find them to "feed" the dog puppet.

Woodson, Jacqueline. 2005. *Show Way.* **New York: G. Putnam's Sons. Illus., Hudson Talbott.**

Summary:

A woman shares the family tradition of creating freedom quilts for the Underground Railroad.

Activity:

This is one of many stories about the quilts although with a different slant. The focus of this story is on family. Create a quilt replicating some of the pictures from the quilt in the story. You can even make a quilt representing different parts of the story and point to the appropriate squares while telling the story. For example, use a fire, light, stars, line of people, or anything else you find significant in the story.

Yarrow, Peter and Lenny Lipton. 2007. *Puff the Magic Dragon.* **New York: Sterling. Illus., Eric Puyabaret.**

Summary:

The book illustrates the popular song about Puff.

Activity:

Simply play the song that accompanies the book, find another version, or sing it to the children. You can play the song a few times before you read so children pick up on the melody if it is unfamiliar to them and then have them sing along with you. Hopefully parents won't object to the alternate meaning of this story.

Yolen, Jane. 2007. *Baby Bear's Big Dreams.* New York: Harcourt. Illus., Melissa Sweet.

Summary:

A bear shares his dreams for the future.

Activity:

Ask children if they have the same dreams as the bear. For example, the text reads, "When I grow up/in a year or two,/I know just what/I'm going to do./I'll live in a shop that's filled with toys—/a few for girls and LOTS for boys." Follow by asking children if this is their dream too or if they think that is a good dream. Do this for each dream the bear shares.

Yolen, Jane and Heidi E. Y. Stemple. 2007. *Sleep, Black Bear, Sleep.* New York: HarperCollins. Illus., Brooke Dyer.

Summary:

Rhymes are about what different animals do to sleep.

Activity:

Children can repeat the changing phrases after you, which would include such statements as, among others, "Sleep, little one, sleep." "Hang, little bat, hang." "Snooze, box turtle, snooze." Even though the sentence is repeated only at the beginning and end, you can have children repeat right after you so they know what to say, as it changes from page to page.

Yolen, Jane and Mark Teague. 2003. *How Do Dinosaurs Get Well Soon?* New York: Scholastic.

Summary:

The story asks what a dinosaur does when he gets sick.

Activity:

Ask students the questions in the book about what a dinosaur does to get well when he or she is sick. Wait for responses. Questions are similar to, "Does he push back each drink, spit his pills in the sink?" Follow up by asking students what they do to get well.

Yorinks, Arthur. 2005. *Happy Bees.* New York: Harry N. Abrams. Illus., Carey Armstrong-Ellis.

Summary:

The story describes all the things happy bees do.

Activity:

The phrase "happy bees" is repeated many times, so have children repeat this phrase with you. Prepare little bee pictures to put on tongue depressors or popsicle sticks or attach them to a string and have the children wave the bees in the air and say "happy bees" each time the phrase is repeated. You might have the children stand and dance around to pretend to be happy bees. The book also comes with a CD and the song "Happy Bees." You can also forgo the props and have the children just pretend to be bees.

Zalben, Jane Breskin. 2005. *Hey, Mama Goose.* New York: Dutton. Illus., Emilie Chollat.

Summary:

An old woman asks Mama Goose where she can move, which begins the displacement of another fairy tale or nursery rhyme character.

Activity:

Test the children's knowledge of fairy tales and nursery rhymes. Let them fill in the blanks with the correct character's name. For example, "She (Snow White) rented a room from a gnome who said, 'I can spin your hair into pure golden thread.'" Who is he? Who can spin her hair into gold? "Rumpelstiltskin remarked, 'I'm tired of tresses! The time is now ripe for changing dresses.' He yearned to spin sugar, not spools of fine metal." Where do you think he will go to spin sugar? Look at the picture. Whose house is made of sugar? Yes. It is Hansel and Gretel.

Zane, Alexander. 2005. *The Wheels on the Race Car.* New York: Orchard. Illus., James Warhola.

Summary:

Similar to "The Wheels on the Bus," this story is about the wheels on the race car.

Activity:

As you would for a "Wheels on the Bus" activity, sing this book to the same tune. "The wheels on the race car go ROUND and ROUND, ROUND and ROUND, ROUND and ROUND. The wheels on the racecar go ROUND and ROUND. All around the track." Children can make a steering wheel out of paper plates or be given one to simulate the race car experience. They can make the sound effects and motions, such as "Vroom-VROOM-VROOM." They can yell "GO-GO-GO." They can steer and speed. They can even stand up and move around the room.

Zemach, Margot. 2005 *Eating Up Gladys.* New York: Scholastic. Illus., Kaethe Zemach.

Summary:

Two sisters get revenge on their older sister by pretending to eat her for dinner.

Activity:

When the two girls get the pot and try to get her sister to sit in it so they can pretend to cook her and eat her, pull out a pot. It might offend some parents, but you could walk around the storytime room and see if any children would get into the pot. You can also pretend to be the sister who falls in the pot and gets stuck. Children will be amused as you pretend you cannot get out.

Ziefert, Harriet. 2005. *The Big Red Blanket.* New York: Sterling. Illus., David Jacobson.

Summary:

No one in her family will play with a girl until she creates a fun game of being covered in a red blanket.

Activity:

One activity for this book is to have children repeat the word "later" when you cue them as the girl in the story keeps asking people in her family to play and this is their response. Another activity is to pull out a red blanket and have children hide under it and jump up and down. In the story they run, but, because the kids won't be able to see, jumping in place would be best. You can ask each child if they want to play and have them join under the blanket even though in the story it is the family who asks to join the fun.

———. 2005. *Circus Parade.* Maplewood, NJ: Blue Apple. Illus., Tanya Roitman.

Summary:

A circus parade comes to town.

Activity:

This simple story describes what people see at a circus parade. Get the children up and walk around the room in a circle pretending to be part of the parade. Encourage them to act out what is happening in the story with you leading. "Flags are waving! Horns are blowing! Hear the cheers. The crowd is growing." Have children pretend to wave a flag, blow a horn, and cheer. You might also want to give each child something represented in the story, such as a whistle to blow and a flag to wave. Occasionally the phrase "A-rum-a-tee-tum! A rum-a-tee-tum!" is repeated. Instruct the children to repeat this phrase with you every time you turn the page and add it to the story. Follow with a parade around the library or school.

Zolotow, Charlotte. 1972. *William's Doll.* New York: HarperCollins. Illus., William Pène Du Bois.

Summary:

This is the classic story about a boy who wants a doll.

Activity:

Instead of reading this story, play the song "William's Doll" from the *Free to Be You and Me* album, I must admit that I have this song memorized and could sing it without the music. You can also use a doll and sporting equipment as props throughout the story.

Zweibel, Alan. 2005. *Our Tree Named Steve.* New York: Puffin. Illus., David Catrow.

Activity:

A father writes a letter to his children, who are away at Grandma's, about their beloved tree and how the tree will no longer be with them when they return.

Activity:

This is a sad story like *The Giving Tree* by Shel Silverstein (1964). Create a large cardboard tree, and tell the story as your children sit by the tree. The story is about a father telling his children in a letter all the great things Steve the tree has been to them before he gave his life to save their house by getting hit in the storm. The tree would greet them, be a swing holder, hold clothes to dry, and be a place to camp under, a holder of snow, and a hammock rest. Steve also had to be trimmed when he was older. Copy pictures of some of the things Steve was to the family and have the children take turns taping them to the tree as you tell the story.

Theme Index

If you choose to use themes or want to use this book to enhance your themes, what follows are topics represented in the picture books included in this book. Most are included in more than one category. Not every book is listed under every possible theme.

Adventure

You Can Do Anything Daddy! (Rex), 157

Aliens

Aliens Are Coming (McCarthy), 132
Beegu (Deacon), 73
Krong! (Parsons), 148

Alphabet

A Is for Zebra (Shulman), 169
ABC Doctor (Murphy), 140–141
Adventures of Wonder Baby from A to Z, The (Chin), 66
Alpha Oops! The Day Z Went First (Kontis), 116–117
Bad Kitty (Bruel), 62
Campbell Kids Alphabet Soup, 64–65
Dangerous Alphabet, The (Gaiman), 93–94
Dog's ABC (Dodd), 76
Fancy Nancy's Favorite Fancy Words (O'Connor), 144
Found Alphabet (Shindler), 168–169
Little Bitty Mousie (Aylesworth), 50
Superhero ABC (McLeod), 134
26 Big Things Small Hands Do (Paratore), 147
Zoopa (Marino), 129–130

Architecture/Buildings

Art

Aunts

Babies

Basketball

Bath

Bears

Bedtime

Birds

Chickens

Children

Christmas

Circus

Concepts

Cookies

Counting/Numbers/Math

Dogs

Be Gentle with the Dog, Dear! (Baek), 51
Birthday Box, The (Patricelli), 148–149
Broadway Barks (Peters), 150
Carl's Sleepy Afternoon (Day), 72
Digby Takes Charge (Church), 66–67
Dog Needs a Bone, A (Wood), 197
Dog Who Sang at the Opera, The (West), 189–190
Dog's ABC (Dodd), 76
Fun Dog, Sun Dog (Heligman), 101–102
Good Dog, Paw! (Lee), 121–122
Happy Dog! (Grubb), 98
Help Me, Mr. Mutt! Expert Answers for Dogs with People Problems (Stevens), 177
How to Be a Good Dog (Page), 147
If My Dad Were a Dog (Telis), 182–183
Juggling Pug, The (Bryan), 62
Lucky Tucker (McGuirk), 133
My Father the Dog (Bluemle), 58–59
Naptime for Slippers (Clements), 68
Nobody's Diggier Than a Dog (Bartoletti), 53–54
Once I Ate a Pie (MacLachlan), 127–128
Please, Puppy, Please (Lee), 122
Pugdog (U'Ren), 185
Smelly Bill (Postgate), 153
Stella, Unleashed (Ashman), 49
Together (Simmons), 170
Wag a Tail (Ehlert), 82
Waggers (Sturges), 179
What's That, Mittens? (Schaefer), 164

Dragons

Loathsome Dragon, The (Wiesner), 190
Puff the Magic Dragon (Yarrow), 197–198
Sandman, The (Fletcher), 90

Dreams

Dream Hop (Durango), 78–79

Ducks

Duck Who Played the Kazoo, The (Sklansky), 171–172

Family

Food/Eating

Football

Friendship

Frogs

Lost

Magic

Mail/Letters/Lists

Manners/Lessons

Matching

Mermaids

Messes

Mice

Mittens

Money

Monkeys

Monsters/Creatures

Moose

Mothers

Alexander's Pretending Day (Crumpacker), 70
Cornelius P. Mud, Ate You Ready for Bed? (Saltzberg), 162
Eat Your Peas (Gray), 97
Mabel O'Leary Put Peas in Her Ear-y (Delaney), 74
No More Cookies! (Lewis), 123

Movies/TV/Celebrities

Silent Movie (Avi), 50
Ten Little Elvi (Henson), 102

Multicultural

Adventures of Wonder Baby from A to Z, The (Chin), 66
Alex and the Wednesday Chess Club (Wong), 195
Can You Greet the Whole Wide World? (Evans), 86
Clatter Bash! A Day of the Dead Celebration (Keep), 112–113
Cuckoo (Ehlert), 81–82
Destiny's Gift (Tarpley), 182
Empanadas That Abuela Made, The (Bertrand), 57
Gift of Gracias (Alvarez), 48
God Bless the Child (Holiday), 104
Has Anybody Lost a Glove? (Johnson), 110–111
Hide & Seek (Wong), 195–196
How Chipmunk Got His Stripes (Bruchac), 61
I Lost My Tooth in Africa (Diakite), 74
I Love My Family (Hudson), 106
In My Family (Garza), 94
In the Leaves (Lee), 122
Jabberwocky (Myers), 141
Kikiriki/Quiquiriríqui (De Anda), 72–73
Kitchen Dance (Manning), 129
Lion's Share, The (Ahmed), 46
Little Red Riding Hood (Pinkney), 151
Mahjong All Day Long (Lo), 125
Mung-Mung (Park), 148
My Aunt Otilia's Spirits (Garcia), 94
My Cat Copies Me (Kwon), 120
My Grandma/Mi Abuelita (Guy), 98–99
Old Man and His Door, The (Soto), 174
One Is a Drummer (Thong), 184
Patchwork Path, The (Stroud), 178–179

Museums

Music/Songs

Parties

Nature

Neighborhood/Community

Night

Occupations

Opposites

Owls

Parades

Penguins

Pets

Picnic

Pigs

Pirates

Plants/Seeds/Flowers

Poetry

Police

Presidents

Grace for President (DiPucchio), 75

Questions

Green as a Bean (Kuskin), 120
Pocket Can Have a Treasure in It, A (Stinson), 178
Simms Taback's Safari Animals (Taback), 180–181
There Is a Bird on Your Head! (Willems), 191
What Will Fat Cat Sit On? (Thomas), 183
Why? (Prap), 154

Rabbits/Bunnies

Bella and the Bunny (Larsen), 121
Bunny Mail (Wells), 189
Carrot Soup (Segal), 167
Little Rabbit Who Liked to Say Moo, The (Allen), 47
Magic Rabbit, The (Watson), 187
Not a Box (Portis), 152–153
Race of the Century (Downard), 77

Raccoons

Friend for All Seasons, A (Hubery), 106
Raccoon's Last Race (Bruchac), 61–62

Rain

Are You Ready to Play Outside? (Willems), 191
Ohio Thunder (Mortensen), 138
Rain Stomper, The (Boswell), 59

Rainforest

Frog with the Big Mouth, The (Bateman), 55

Reptiles/Amphibians

Frog in the Bog, A (Wilson), 192
Where's My Tail? (Schafer), 164

Roosters

Brewster the Rooster (Scillian), 166
Buffalo Wings (Reynolds), 157
Cock-a-Doodle Quack! Quack! (Baddiel), 51

Royalty

Scary Stories

School

Science

Seasons

Senses

Shapes

Sheep/Lambs

Shoes/Socks

Siblings

Sickness

Germs (Collins), 68

Silliness

Nonsense! (Phillips), 150

Size

Shrinking Sam (Latimer), 121

Snow

Biggest Snowman Ever, The (Kroll), 118
Frosty the Snowman (Bedford), 56
Snow Dude (Kirk), 115
Snowball Fight! (Fallon), 87

Sounds

Animals Speak (Prap), 153
Baa for Beginners (Fajerman), 86–87
Bird Songs (Franco), 91
Cheep! Cheep! (Stiegemeyer), 178
City Lullaby (Singer), 170–171
Cock-a-Doodle Quack! Quack! (Baddiel), 51
Dinosnores (DiPuccio), 74–75
Great Blue House, The (Banks), 52
Grump Groan Growl (hooks), 104
Jabberwocky (Myers), 141
Kikiriki/Quiquiririqui (De Anda), 72–73
Little Rabbit Who Liked to Say Moo, The (Allen) 47
Mung-Mung (Park), 148
Ohio Thunder (Mortensen), 138
Rain Stomper, The (Boswell), 59
Smash! Crash! (Scieszka), 166
Squeaky Door, The (MacDonald), 126–127
Train Goes Clickety-Clack, A (London), 126
Uh-Oh! (Isadora), 108
What's the Magic Word? (DiPucchio), 75
Whooo's There? (Serfozo), 167–168

Space

If You Decide to Go to the Moon (McNulty), 135

Sports

St. Patrick's Day

States

Sticks

Stores

Summer

Sun

Superheroes/Comic Characters

Teeth

Thanksgiving

Title Index

T

U

About the Author

Jennifer Bromann is the author of several books for Neal-Schuman, including *Storytime Action!*, *Booktalking That Works*, and *More Booktalking That Works* and articles for *School Library Journal*. She is currently the librarian at Lincoln-Way West High School in New Lenox, Illinois. In her spare time she teaches courses on college reading, multicultural children's literature, children's library services, reference, and information literacy at Joliet Junior College, Illinois State University, and Northern Illinois University. She is also pursuing a doctorate in literacy at Northern Illinois University. Contact Jennifer at bromannj@hotmail.com.